China and the American Dream

A

Philip E. Lilienthal [signature]

■　　　　■　　　　■

B　O　O　K

The Philip E. Lilienthal imprint honors
special books in commemoration of a
man whose work at the University of
California Press from 1954 to 1979 was
marked by dedication to young authors
and to high standards in the field of
Asian Studies. Friends, family, authors,
and foundations have together endowed
the Lilienthal Fund, which enables the
Press to publish under this imprint
selected books in a way that reflects the
taste and judgment of a great and
beloved editor.

China and the
American Dream

A Moral Inquiry

Richard Madsen

UNIVERSITY OF CALIFORNIA PRESS

Berkeley / Los Angeles / London

University of California Press
Berkeley and Los Angeles, California

University of California Press, Ltd.
London, England

Library of Congress Cataloging-in-Publication Data

Madsen, Richard, 1941–
    China and the American dream: A moral inquiry / Richard
Madsen.
        p.   cm.
    Includes bibliographical references.
    ISBN 0–520–08613–9 (alk. paper)
    1. United States — Relations — China. 2. China — Relations —
United States. 3. China — History — Tiananmen Square Incident,
1989. I. Title.
E185.8.C5M314 1995
303.48′251073 — dc20   93-45003

Printed in the United States of America

This book is a print-on-demand volume. It is manufactured
using toner in place of ink. Type and images may be less
sharp than the same material seen in traditionally printed
University of California Press editions.

To Judy and Susan

Contents

Preface

Some of the most dramatic public events of the second half of the twentieth century have centered around the United States' tempestuous relationship with China. In the 1950s, a bitter debate about "who lost China" was the breeding ground for McCarthyism. In the late 1950s and early 1960s, anxiety about the spread of Chinese communism — often portrayed at the time as a more virulent and evil version than its Soviet counterpart — clouded the atmosphere in which Americans made tragic decisions about going to war in Vietnam. In the 1970s, Richard Nixon's reestablishment of relationships with China was widely hailed as a triumph of statecraft and a beacon of hope for Americans immersed in the gloom of the Vietnam War.

By the 1980s, normalization of U.S.-China relations opened the doors to an explosively expanding exchange of ideas, people, and material goods. The scope of this two-way traffic quickly exceeded initial expectations on both sides and thereby generated new expectations too lofty to be fulfilled. For many Chinese the opening to the West in general, and the United States in particular, promised rapid growth in wealth and power and exhilarating new opportunities for personal expression. For many Americans the opening of China was a harbinger of the liberalization of the whole Communist world: finally, "they" were becoming like "us." These mutual expectations came to a tragic climax in the spring of 1989, as the excitement and joy of a vast Chinese student movement for "science and democracy" turned into the terror and anger of a brutal government crackdown. Undoubtedly, by the end of the 1990s, there will be new acts in this historical drama, and we may hope that they will have happier endings.

This book is specifically about the moral drama of the American relationship with China over the past quarter-century. It is not primarily about the purely political or economic dimensions of the relationship — although it tries to take them sufficiently into account — but rather about the way in which that relationship has become the stuff of public stories, on both the Chinese and American sides, about how each should understand its ideals in light of the other.

Dreams, Myths, and Master Narratives

As members of moral communities, we are the stuff that dreams are made of. We orient ourselves around common hopes and aspirations, expressed in stories about where we come from and where we are going. These are not the sober, analytic, prosaic accounts given by the social scientist but the visionary, poetic tales told by the dreamer, the mythmaker. The ever-evolving heritage of mythical stories — sometimes referred to in this book as "master narratives" — that convey American aspirations is known around the world as the "American Dream."

It is a dream about individualistic independence in a land of opportunity, a dream of not being constrained by the past or bound to community by rigid ties of convention. It is conveyed through stories about pilgrims and pioneers and declarers of independence. These contrast sharply with the stories many Chinese tell about themselves. After a sumptuous dinner in his office's private dining room, a Chinese general in Beijing tried to convince me of the validity of the PRC's claims to Taiwan by invoking a narrative of unbreakable connection. "Americans who support Taiwan's independence have no sense of history," he said. "The people on Taiwan speak Chinese, their culture is Chinese, their ancestors came from mainland China. Therefore they are Chinese, and Taiwan should be a part of China." To which my rejoinder is: "Although there may be good geopolitical reasons for considering Taiwan part of the PRC, your argument doesn't correspond to basic American understandings of moral value. If our founding fathers truly agreed with such an argument, we would still be part of England."

Societies need their dreams. Even though no two people in the

United States will define the content of the American Dream in exactly the same way, and even though everyone has different opinions about how this dream should be realized, the American Dream nevertheless provides a common reference point for an ongoing public conversation about what should be done to make American society into a good society. Without such a reference point, the public argument falls into confusion and incoherence. It is the same in China. As we shall see in Chapter 8, "Searching for a Dream" was the title of a segment of *Deathsong of the River,* a 1988 Chinese television series that provided the most provocative and creative intellectual response to the sense of confusion and cultural crisis then facing Chinese society.

A society's dreams remain alive only if they are constantly enriched to account for new realities. The American Dream of independence has to be revised to take into account the increasing interdependence of the modern world. Confrontation with China, a densely populated land with a distinctive ancient civilization, challenges the American Dream, even when—perhaps especially when—many Chinese seem to be eagerly embracing that dream by seeking to immigrate to the United States. And confrontation with the United States has stimulated and complicated the Chinese "search for a dream." Through this book, I hope to stimulate the mutual search among members of both societies for richer, more effective ways of dreaming their social selves in face of the realities of the other.

Sources and Methods

In recent years, other scholars have published excellent histories of the past several decades of U.S.-China relationships. Such publications—especially Harry Harding's *A Fragile Relationship: The United States and China since 1972,*[1] which does an extremely thorough job of synthesizing the monographic literature in both English and Chinese on the subject—have provided indispensable foundations for this book. Although built upon these histories, this book does not try to compete with them; it does not add more detail to the already rich accounts they provide. Indeed, it steps back from much of the detail in an attempt to see a big picture from a particular point of view, the perspective of someone trained in the sociology of culture and moral philosophy.

Besides the scholarly literature, major sources for my meditations have been direct interviews and observations. I have formally interviewed about 150 people, half in the United States, half in China (in Chinese), who have been actively involved, mostly at a "middle-management" level, in developing diplomatic, academic, economic, and religious contacts between the two countries. As indicated in footnotes at appropriate places in the book, I also participated in meetings, discussions, and delegations of several American academic, cultural, and religious organizations aimed at building relations with China. And in 1988–1989, a time when my Chinese colleagues were being especially frank about their hopes and frustrations, I worked for five months under the sponsorship of the Institute of American Studies in the Chinese Academy of Social Sciences in Beijing. These interviews and observations certainly did not provide a scientific random sample of the opinions of 250 million Americans and 1.2 billion Chinese, although I did take care to interview people who worked within a variety of institutional contexts and spanned a wide spectrum of opinion on major issues in U.S.-China relations. But the interviews and personal observations gave me a much richer sense than I could ever have gained from books of how members of those relatively small circles of Chinese and Americans who pay serious attention to U.S.-China relations talk to each other about the moral dilemmas inherent in those relationships and how this talk draws on widely shared assumptions from their cultures.

Finally, I have tried to reflect on my own life and commitments. I started my career in the late 1960s as a Maryknoll missionary to Taiwan; I subsequently became a sociologist and China scholar; and I am a member of various human rights organizations. I have drawn upon my own life experiences and tried to expose my own biases to many different critical perspectives.

Beyond Washington and Beijing

This study, then, is directed not to conventional political science or diplomatic history but to the sociology of culture and what my colleagues and I have called "public philosophy." My approach is distinguished by its focus on sociocultural processes rather than political elites and by its theoretical assumptions about how such processes can be studied.

Most studies of U.S.-China relations by political scientists or diplomatic historians characteristically focus on the calculations made by each
country's leading government officials as they formulated policies toward the other country's government. David Shambaugh's important
book *Beautiful Imperialist: China Perceives America, 1972–1990* moves
beyond the narrow circles of Chinese policymakers to study the professional "America watchers" who provide information and analysis.[2] But,
as is characteristic of studies by American political scientists, even this
book confines itself to "influential elites" close to the center of power.

A symptom of this focus on power centers is the way in which specialists on foreign affairs commonly use "Washington and Beijing" as
equivalents for "the United States and China." Of course, Washington
is not the same thing as the United States, nor is Beijing the same as
China. But to many specialists in foreign affairs, it makes sense to use
the name of the capital as a metonym for the whole society because the
public usually does not participate directly in the making of foreign policy. In China, indeed, the public is excluded by the very structure of the
political system, and in the United States the public largely excludes
itself by its legendary ignorance and apathy about foreign affairs that do
not directly and obviously affect domestic interests.

Yet underneath the deliberations of policymakers and the analyses of
influential experts is a cultural fabric of common understandings about
the goals and purposes of their work. What does it mean to be American
or Chinese in the modern world? What are the ideals and interests of
each society, and how should these interests and ideals be pursued? Often this fabric of understandings lies outside of the consciousness of
policymakers — they are too busy to reflect on it explicitly. Some of these
understandings are so thoroughly taken for granted that it is impossible
to reflect upon them critically.

But this underlying fabric is changeable. It is constantly, quietly being rewoven in response to sociological processes, especially those engendered by new patterns of global communication and commerce.
Sometimes major breaks in the fabric occur. Then policymakers and
their expert advisers find themselves confused, conflicted, bewildered,
uncertain. Sometimes, as a result, their policies become erratic, inconsistent, even incoherent. Such seems to have been happening in the past
several years, especially since the crackdown on Tiananmen Square, with
regard to Washington's policy toward Beijing and Beijing's policy
toward Washington.

Washington and Beijing are uncertain because changes have occurred in American and Chinese society and culture. In both the United States and China there is new, widespread questioning about what it means to be an American — for example, is there one American society or just a congeries of different ethnic communities competing for scarce resources on the same continent? — and what it means to be Chinese — is "real Chineseness" a political or a racial or a cultural matter? There also has been concomitant questioning about how Americans and Chinese ought to conceive of their relations with the outside world and what goals they ought to pursue across the globe. This questioning springs from a number of different sources, including changes in the global economy and the end of the cold war. In part it stems from sociocultural dilemmas faced by many members of Chinese and American society — ordinary citizens as well as influential elites — as their history drew them closer together during this past generation. This is what I want to explore in this book.

Theoretical Assumptions

This book extends my earlier studies of Chinese and American culture. My *Morality and Power in a Chinese Village*[3] explored the moral universe of Chinese peasants during the upheavals of the Maoist era. *Habits of the Heart* and *The Good Society,* coauthored with Robert Bellah, William Sullivan, Ann Swidler, and Steven Tipton,[4] explored the moral bases of social commitment in the United States and precipitated an extensive debate in American society about the meaning of its democratic traditions. I hope now to integrate and deepen these separate studies of Chinese and American culture by considering the interaction between the two.

Like my previous books, this one employs a theoretical perspective that denies the sharp distinction between subject and object characteristic of positive science. As social beings whose very identities and capacities for thought and action are constituted by the cultures within which we live, we can never completely study a culture from outside. If we learn deeply to understand another culture, we become changed; in some important sense, we become different persons than before our encounter. And our act of studying the culture, at least in some small way, changes the culture itself. For better or worse, the twenty-five years that I have spent studying China have made me a different person than

I would have been had I never studied it; I think differently, I have different sympathies and antipathies, and I have become engaged with the lives of a variety of Chinese friends. For better or for worse, too, my research and writing about China have changed the lives of at least a few Chinese and even influenced how some of them think about their own society. I think most of my American colleagues in China studies will acknowledge similar experiences.

The process of studying our native culture entails an even deeper blending of subject and object. It is impossible to remain indifferent to the language and institutions that shape our lives within our native culture. As intellectuals, I believe we can and should be responsibly critical about many aspects of our own culture. But in the very act of exposing unquestioned aspects of our culture to critical scrutiny, we change it. *Habits of the Heart* and *The Good Society* were animated by a deep concern about the future of American democracy; and for better or for worse, they have aroused public controversies that have changed the way that some Americans understand themselves.

If one acknowledges this intimate interplay between subject and object, which I believe is inevitable in any serious study of society, one does not have to resign oneself to a radical subjectivism. When we make statements about either our own culture or someone else's, we invite responses from other people who are also concerned about that culture. The ensuing dialogue leads to collective judgments about the validity of what we have written or said. The truth about complex social matters that emerges from this process is not as fixed, immutable, and universal as truth claimed by nineteenth-century physical scientists, but neither is it the arbitrary projection of our mind or will. Good social science invites and provides a coherent focus for widespread public discussion. Good social science fulfills its purpose not by demonstrating timeless truths but by helping a society understand itself through such public discussion.[5]

As advocated in *Habits of the Heart* and *The Good Society*, this piece of social science tries, then, to be a contribution to "public philosophy."[6] It is written not just for policymakers (though I hope that it can be read by them with profit) and not just for professional social scientists (though I hope they will find in it contributions to a theory of cultural change) but for general educated publics. In short, it attempts to speak not just to "Washington" or "Beijing" but to people enmeshed in the wide variety of institutions that constitute "America" and "China." It aims to help concerned citizens, especially in the United States but perhaps also in China, participate more actively and intelligently in giving purpose and direction to their societies' global relationships. A work that would speak to such publics must be normative as well as analytic. It must help members of a society deliberate about how to respond to the challenges facing it in light of the collectively shared (but inevitably differently interpreted) values that constitute the society's common good.

Moral Dilemmas and Troubled Dreams

I begin with an account of the moral dilemmas confronting American and Chinese societies in the present; then I trace a twenty-five-year historical path that led to our current dilemmas. In Chapter 1, I provide an interpretation of the Tiananmen massacre of 1989 and explicate the basic moral and political questions this incident poses for Americans and Chinese. This event, I argue, troubled Americans far out of proportion to its direct cost in human life and suffering. In recent years, things far more terrible and brutal than the Tiananmen massacre had happened in the world, but Americans were not troubled as deeply by them. The tragedy in China was so upsetting for many Americans because it contradicted widely cherished American understandings about the meanings of their democratic values — it challenged common interpretations of the American Dream.

In so doing, the Tiananmen massacre raised a host of new moral questions, especially about the relationship between American policies that foster capitalist economic development and those that promote democratic rights. Such questions cannot be answered within the spectrum of conventional American political discourse. To answer them, I believe, we must now reexamine the underlying assumptions of our culture. We must develop richer, more realistic interpretations of our common dreams. We must revise the myths, the master narratives, that help us understand our relationship to the rest of the world.

Usually, the myths that form the foundations of our social knowledge and action are too resilient to perish as a simple result of academic criticism. It takes widespread social change dramatized by scandalous historical events like the Tiananmen massacre to destroy a myth. Because myths insinuate themselves into our common sense, it paradoxically takes the destruction of a myth to make it fully visible to our critical scrutiny.

In my account, the Tiananmen massacre discredited an important American myth about China, but in the process it has brought that myth into critical awareness. That myth was, in my analysis, a liberal myth—a story about how American ideals of economic, intellectual, and political freedom would triumph over the world. After discussing the moral challenge of Tiananmen, I turn to the 1960s, when the myth slain by Tiananmen was born. That myth's creation, I argue in Chapter 2, involved the interplay of various kinds of public conversation—academic, political, and, importantly, religious—with public rituals during a time hot with controversy over the Vietnam War. In Chapter 3, I show how that myth came to dominate American public culture through the spectacle of Nixon's visit to China.

Chapter 4 shows how, in the mid-1970s, the liberal myth about China entered into the fabric of different American institutions, especially academic, religious, and civic institutions. An institution, in the sense in which I use the term here, is a moral enterprise, a set of sanctioned norms giving direction and shape to the way we live.[7] The liberal myth about China helped reinvigorate American institutions with a new, hopeful justification, seeming to provide a new validating purpose for their practices: new worlds to discover, new people to convert, new markets to open. Besides being moral enterprises, though, institutions are also systems of wealth and power. Accordingly, I show how the liberal myth about China stimulated competition within American institutions for control of their money and power.

Chapters 5 and 6 trace the development of the liberal myth about China through the controversies over normalization of U.S.-Chinese diplomatic relations in the late 1970s and into the rapidly expanding relationships of the 1980s. I show how the liberal China myth helped sustain an American sense of hopefulness about its own democratic identity, even in spite of anomalous dilemmas that should have contradicted that hopefulness.

Chapters 7 and 8 highlight those dilemmas by describing how Chinese viewed American society during the 1980s. It shows the confusion, dissatisfaction, and the unresolvable moral and political dilemmas that afflicted even those who most warmly embraced the good things American consumer culture promised to give. It shows how China, partly as an unintended consequence of doing what many Americans matter-offactly thought it should do, not only failed to become a liberal democratic society but fell into the tragedy of Tiananmen.

The conclusion summarizes the theoretical and substantive lessons of this moral history. It outlines a new global institutional and cultural environment in which old myths no longer provide either Americans or Chinese with a viable framework for fruitful moral deliberation about their place in the world, and it suggests some of the ways in which new frameworks might develop.

Although most of my research was done before 1990, I have of course continued to gather information both from readings and personal observations while writing this book. I took two short trips to China in 1992, and after finishing the final draft I spent two months in Tianjin in the fall of 1993, working on a different project. On the basis of my recent visits, I conclude that the China of early 1994 is much like the China of early 1989—only more so. There has been an intensification of both the positive and negative trends discussed in this book. Market-driven economic development, especially along the southern coast, has surged forward. Standards of material consumption have risen markedly, and urban young people in particular have become increasingly intoxicated with Western popular culture.

But feelings of insecurity and grievance have deepened among many urban workers. They are losing their jobs in state-run enterprises and seeing their incomes diminish under the onslaught of a 20 percent inflation rate. They are increasingly jealous because of the rising inequalities within Chinese society. Those who are middle-aged and older are worried about the declining morals of the youth. Almost all are bitter at the ever more blatant and cynical corruption of their officials. As one recently laid-off woman worker told me in Tianjin in 1993, "If you just follow the rules and work hard and do the right thing, you get nowhere. . . . Those who get rich are those who cheat and use their power and privilege."

The righteous anger and anguish felt by intellectuals in 1989 seem to have given way in many instances to numbness, which may cover over a deeply burning disappointment. Most of my friends from 1988 who have not emigrated have given up on intellectual pursuits. Unable to tolerate low salaries and political harassment, they have left their research institutes to go into business.

Meanwhile, the American press, awestruck over the pace of Chinese economic growth, expresses some concerns about persisting human rights violations but pays relatively little attention to the social tensions being generated by the economy.

The outlook at the beginning of 1994 is that the Chinese economy will continue to grow and that this trend will have increasingly important consequences for Americans. But this growth will be accompanied by periodic upheavals that will surprise many Americans who should have known better and will force continued rethinking of the global implications of the American Dream.

Acknowledgments

This project grew out of my fifteen years of collaboration with Robert Bellah, William Sullivan, Ann Swidler, and Steven Tipton. Over the years, their friendship, support, intellectual encouragement, and criticism have profoundly shaped how I think and feel about the world. Although they did not directly help me on this project, their influence pervades it.

In China, I was the first American scholar ever to be resident in the Institute of American Studies at the Chinese Academy of Social Sciences. The five months I and my family spent there were pleasant and extremely fruitful. My warmest thanks go to Zi Zhongyun, then the director of the institute, and He Di, who did an enormous amount of work arranging for my stay. Among colleagues too numerous to adequately acknowledge, I want to single out Zhang Yebai, Dong Leshan, Li Miao, Wang Jisi, and Yuan Ming. Finally, in Beijing I treasured the friendship and informal camaraderie of younger colleagues Wen Yang, Hou Ling, Gao Zhenya, and Zhang Yuehong—although none of my Chinese friends necessarily agrees with my views.

I began writing this book in 1989 during a semester-long fellowship at the Fairbank Center for East Asian Research at Harvard University. I am especially grateful to the then-director of the center, Roderick Mac-Farquhar, and to the late Patrick Maddox for their help in arranging my stay. While at Harvard, I profited immensely from ongoing discussions with Ezra Vogel, Benjamin Schwartz, Merle Goldman, James Watson, Rubie Watson, Kathleen Hartford, and Merry White.

While I was finishing the book at the University of California, San Diego, I was often inspired, stimulated, and challenged by my conversations with colleagues from several different departments, especially Michael Schudson, Bennett Berger, Gerald Doppelt, and Paul Pickowicz. Finally, Orville Schell, Michael Hunt, and Perry Link provided immensely helpful criticisms of an earlier draft of the manuscript. I am especially thankful to Perry Link for his encouragement and criticism not just during the last phases of revision but also during the days we spent together in Beijing in 1988, when I was learning about China and trying to pull together my conception of the book. Because I was unable to use all of the good advice of my friends and critics, I must, of course, take full responsibility for all of the inadequacies of this work.

Generous funding was provided by the Social Science Research Council's Foreign Policy Studies Program, the Committee on Scholarly Cooperation with China, and the Fairbank Center. In the early stages of the project I also received financial help from the Academic Senate and the Institute of Global Cooperation and Conflict of the University of California, San Diego.

My research assistants were Eva Maria Valle and Zhao Shuisheng. At the University of California Press, James Clark has been a treasured source of support, and Larry Borowsky made my writing much clearer and more concise.

And, as in everything else I have done, my wife, Judith Rosselli, and daughter, Susan, have provided the indispensable foundations of faith and love.

Note on Romanization

One of the changes over the past thirty years of U.S.-China relations has been in the system of romanization commonly used in the United States to render Chinese words. Before the normalization of U.S.-China relations, most books published in the United States used a form of romanization developed by missionaries in the nineteenth century. After normalization in 1979, American standard usage shifted to the "pinyin" form preferred by the People's Republic of China. Whereas books on contemporary China published before 1979 usually spelled Mao's name as "Mao Tse-tung," books after 1979 spelled it "Mao Zedong."

In this book, I will use the pinyin form except for a few names, such as Chiang Kai-shek, which are still currently romanized in the older manner. For the sake of consistency, I will use the pinyin for Chinese names even when I quote from books published before 1979. Thus, when I quote from Richard Nixon's memoirs, I will write "Mao Zedong," even though Nixon originally wrote "Mao Tse-tung." I will indicate in parentheses when I am making this change. However, when I cite authors and titles of books and articles in the footnotes, I will use the romanization employed in the original.

1

The Moral Challenge of Tiananmen

Shattering a Liberal Myth

In the late evening of June 3 and early morning of June 4, 1989, the Chinese People's Liberation Army shot its way through the streets of Beijing, crushing the mass movement of students and workers that had arisen that spring to protest government corruption and demand a more open society. Hundreds, possibly thousands, of protesters died that night in and around Tiananmen Square, while international news media recorded the carnage.[1] At the direction of Deng Xiaoping, the Chinese government arrested thousands of people who had helped to inspire, participated in, or simply been sympathetic to the protests. Some of those arrested were subsequently executed.[2] In China, "June 4" now stands for the whole movement of repression surrounding the Tiananmen massacre. It is remembered as a crucial, tragic day in the drama of that country's history.

It is also an important date in the drama of U.S. history. The Chinese, of course, must come to terms with the consequences of the June 4 massacre, but the burden is too great to be shouldered by China alone. The event is one of those whose reverberations have extended around the world, challenging the assumptions of many countries about how they should conduct foreign policy. It poses an especially deep challenge to Americans' common understandings about the purposes of their foreign policy and their place in world history.[3]

World leaders condemned the Chinese government's violent crackdown against its citizens. Within a few days after June 4, at least twenty governments, including those of the United States and most of Western

Europe, issued statements expressing outrage at the massacre. But the international public outcry was even more intense. Although many Southeast Asian governments were afraid to antagonize Beijing and refused to officially condemn the massacre, people throughout the region staged massive protests against the PRC crackdown, especially overseas Chinese resident in those countries. Anxious to consolidate the improved diplomatic ties achieved with China earlier in 1989, the Soviet Union declined to criticize the Chinese government—thus exposing Mikhail Gorbachev to withering criticism from Andrei Sakharov and other deputies in the newly established Soviet Congress.[4]

Outside of Hong Kong (where the crackdown galvanized a population already fearful about the prospect of reunification with the People's Republic in 1997), perhaps nowhere else in the world did the massacre engender more popular outrage, anguish, soul searching, and just plain fascination than in the United States. It was one of the most memorable and disturbing news stories of the 1980s. Most people interviewed in a *Los Angeles Times* poll published a week after the crackdown said they were paying "a lot" of attention to the turmoil in China. NBC News anchor Tom Brokaw said that not since the explosion of the space shuttle *Challenger* had a story "so penetrated the American consciousness. People everywhere I went were talking about it. I was doing a story about street gangs in Los Angeles, and one member of the Crips wanted to talk to me about what was going on in China."[5]

The more attention Americans paid, the less they liked what they saw. Of those interviewed, 78 percent expressed an unfavorable opinion of the People's Republic of China, only 16 percent a favorable opinion. This was virtually a reversal of a Gallup poll taken three months before, when 72 percent had expressed a favorable opinion and only 13 percent an unfavorable one.[6] Popular condemnation of China turned to confusion about U.S. foreign policy when President George Bush declined to level any severe economic or political sanctions against China and within a month of the massacre sent National Security Adviser Brent Scowcroft to visit the Chinese leadership. The Bush administration's effort to maintain cooperative relations with the Chinese government gave rise to a persistent, emotional debate within Congress, a debate that continues under the Clinton administration to cut across customary divisions among Democrats and Republicans. Advocates of sanctions included the conservative Republican senator Jesse Helms as well as liberal Democrats such as congresswoman Nancy Pelosi and former congressman Steven Solarz. Opponents of sanctions include both Republicans and Democrats. In the popular press as well as in specialized journals, a vigorous debate has continued among supporters of these various positions.[7]

Why did the events in China provoke such an intense reaction and such sharp debate around the world and especially in the United States? For one trusted Chinese friend of mine — a graduate student of political science at a distinguished American university — the outpouring of public concern about China in the United States seemed "irrational." On that fateful weekend of June 4, he noted, three other major events occurred. Iran's Ayatollah Khomeini died; Poland held its first free elections since the Communist Party had taken control of that country; and the Speaker of the House, Jim Wright, was forced to resign because of scandal. Each of these events, my Chinese friend observed, had potentially greater, more direct implications for the United States' self-interest than the China tragedy. Why then did Americans focus most of their attention on China?

One answer frequently given to such questions is that the events in China were made broadly accessible through television.[8] This explanation, to be sure, is partially correct. But during the 1980s international news media regularly brought even greater tragedies onto American television screens without capturing the attention of such a broad range of the public. Political violence in the Middle East and Central America caused far greater loss of life — and impinged more directly on U.S. economic and political interests — than did the violence in China, and television networks broadcast plenty of dramatic footage of these tragedies. But was this coverage enough to make even members of Los Angeles street gangs take notice? Most Americans usually pay little attention to international relations. At the height of the crisis in Central America in the mid-1980s, close to half of the American public was unable to describe which parties to the conflict were on the side of the United States and which were against, even though newspapers and television focused heavily on those issues.[9] Why did matters of such direct and immediate consequence for the United States fail to grip the American consciousness as firmly as the China crisis of June 4, 1989?

Perhaps the public had become numb to the protracted violence of the Middle East and Central America, so that one more outbreak of killing was simply taken for granted. But then why was the public shocked by the brutality in China? Compared with other episodes of violence, upheaval, and oppression in the history of the People's Republic of China, the June 4 massacre was relatively mild. The numbers of dead were modest in comparison with the hundreds of thousands of landlords (by conservative estimates) killed during the land reform of the early 1950s, the 20 million (by conservative estimates) who died during the 1959–1961 famine that followed the Great Leap Forward, and the hundreds of thousands who lost their lives during the Cultural Revolution of the late 1960s. And although something on the order of ten thousand people were imprisoned for their political activities in the wake of the June 4 crackdown, this hardly compares with the hundreds of thousands of intellectuals sentenced to labor camps during the antirightist campaign directed by Deng Xiaoping during the late 1950s.[10] Why did the Beijing crackdown inspire such anguish and soul searching outside of China? Why was it not simply discussed calmly, though bitterly, as another sad, reprehensible, but basically predictable calamity for an unfortunate people?

Tiananmen as Drama

The answer, I will argue throughout this book, is that the crackdown in China was for Americans a drama with an unexpected, incorrect ending. As such, it challenged the common meanings at the core of their major public institutions.

By "drama" here, I simply mean a moral story, a narrative in which the virtues and vices of the characters lead to a chain of actions culminating in a conclusion. A drama represents a moral vision, a set of concrete examples of good and bad conduct and a framework for illustrating the consequences of such conduct. In what we usually think of as a good drama, the relationships between virtue and vice are complicated, the ending ambiguous. But the ending is supposed to be consistent with the drama's distinctions between right and wrong. Vice is not supposed to be rewarded. A hero's demise is supposed to be due to a tragic flaw, not a virtue. In a satisfactory drama, the good guys may indeed suffer, but the bad guys shouldn't win. A good drama is not supposed to preach, but it most certainly is supposed to engage its audience. It is supposed to make members of its audience identify with its characters, to come to a deeper self-understanding in light of what happens to the drama's protagonists.

Most people want to see drama in history; they want to tell each other stories in which good or bad people impel themselves toward a fitting end. They want the type of history the Chinese used to write, wherein virtue or corruption leads to dynastic ascendancy or decline. Indeed, the kind of enlightened public that is the foundation of a democratic society *needs* to see history as drama. It is by debating the moral meaning of history that citizens in a democracy understand their responsibilities toward the future.[11]

Writers (particularly journalists) whose audience is the general public therefore usually represent history as drama, as a tale about good and evil told from the point of view of actors struggling to do the right or yielding to do the wrong thing.[12] People who write for religious communities — for example, theologians — are even more certain to depict history as a moral drama, as a part of "salvation history."

For Americans, there is a rich tradition of recounting the chronicle of U.S.-China relations within a dramatic context. In the first part of this century, American missionaries wrote extensively about China in such terms.[13] So did journalists.[14] Moreover, there developed in the twentieth century a substantial body of fiction set in China, of which the novels of Pearl Buck are the most famous. These writings created a tradition of dramatic discourse, a copious legacy that was interrupted by the rupture of U.S.-China relations in 1949 but was available to be revived when contacts were resumed in the 1970s. This legacy helped create and sustain an American habit of talking about China in dramatic terms — terms that are not so widely applied to societies that Americans know mainly through the research of professional social scientists.[15]

Although professionally trained to be dispassionate and analytical, American social scientists were by no means immune to taking a dramatic view of China. Many of the senior generation of scholars had gotten into China studies because they were children of missionary parents, and they tended to have absorbed some of the moralism of their families. (Before the development of modern language programs for the teaching of Chinese at the university level, which mainly took place after World War II, there was little opportunity for anyone to take up a purely academic study of China without having been exposed to Chinese language and society in some nonacademic capacity, the most common of which was being a member of a missionary family.)[16] An even more important factor was the influence of the cold war. U.S. political leaders cast Communist China in the most dramatic light possible: It was a threat to everything Americans held dear, the most menacing of evils in an epic battle between good and bad. American scholars did not have to fully accept this view to be deeply influenced by it; they had to engage themselves with it even if they disagreed with it. China could not be seen as a neutral object of investigation. If it did not represent a story of evil, then it had to be depicted as a story about good — or at least about an ongoing battle between the two. As I will argue more fully later in this book, this academic tradition of creating dramatic renditions of Chinese history has persisted down to the present day.

Thus, when the student demonstrations of the 1989 Beijing Spring began to occur, American writers of all kinds were accustomed to depicting such events in dramatic terms. The peculiar circumstances of early 1989 enhanced this tendency. Television news outlets had prepared to be in Beijing to cover the visit of Mikhail Gorbachev, so much of the unfolding student movement was captured live on television, a medium that thrives on dramatizing events. The student protesters, moreover, developed a very sophisticated sense of how to utilize the media to dramatize their case to the world. Because of the burgeoning of academic exchange programs with China, hundreds of American students and scholars were in Beijing, and each had a personal story to tell about how the events had touched him or her. Finally, tens of thousands of Chinese students had come to study in the United States, and they poured out their hopes and fears for China to American friends and colleagues — and, not infrequently, the news media. With the stage thus set, the events of the Beijing Spring were presented as a spectacular drama.

People can agree that an event is a drama — a story that signifies something — without agreeing on what exactly it means. In literature, what we usually think of as a good story is one that allows for a multiplicity of interpretations. Interpretations link the story portrayed in the drama with the interpreters' understanding of the basic values and purposes guiding their lives and their society.[17] A challenging drama inspires the audience not merely to reaffirm its basic values but also to see them as more complex or more contingent than imagined. For most Americans, perhaps, the 1989 drama of Tiananmen Square was a challenging one. It was hard to reconcile the outcome with the common understandings around which American institutions are oriented. Almost none of its possible interpretations were reassuring.

Freedom Complicated

The central common value for Americans is freedom. All major institutions of this society—economic, political, and cultural—aspire ideally to enhance the freedom of individuals. This very commitment to freedom means, of course, that all members ought to define freedom in their own way. Freedom is a common value that encourages a vast diversity of values.[18] American society perpetually simmers with controversy over the meanings and relative importance of its basic values, and Americans usually think such controversy is proof of the vitality of their freedom. Most of the controversies ultimately center around whether or how our major institutions can adequately protect or enhance the freedom of individuals. There is less discussion about the meaning of freedom itself. Freedom generally means independence: individual autonomy, privacy, the right to be left alone. It means being able to do whatever one wants, as long as one does not thereby restrict the ability of others to do whatever they want. Thus conceived, freedom is held to be a universal value, good for everybody at all times. China's recent history disturbs us because it challenges certain aspects of this conception of freedom. It forces us to think more deeply about what freedom really means and what its future will be.

Let us consider the main story line of the drama of Tiananmen Square, at least as presented by the major American news media. The heroes are Chinese students, who are calling for "democracy." What they are demanding is precisely what is most precious to us. Indeed, they seem to have learned about this value from us, mostly by reading the multitude of books on Western (especially American) philosophy and social science that have become available in China since its opening to the West under Deng Xiaoping in the late 1970s.[19] "Freedom," in the words of NSC 68, the 1950 State Department document that presented a comprehensive rationale for the cold war, "is the most contagious idea in history."[20] The movement for democracy in China is proof that the country's young people have been exposed to the idea and succumbed to its contagion. Arrayed against the students are some old, hard-line Communists who do not believe in freedom. This is the most compelling sort of historical drama, one that resonates richly with America's central myths.

If there were nothing more to the drama, it might have been intellectually satisfying even though it had an unhappy ending, even though the hard-liners' tanks rolled in and crushed the heroic students. The meaning would be that freedom must be heroically struggled for against implacable foes, that there will be tragic setbacks in the struggle, but that freedom will eventually triumph. However, there was more to the Tiananmen story, inconsistencies that have begun to render its meaning opaque.

First of all, the chief hard-line foe of the students was the person who, according to the American media, had made it possible for them to dream their dreams of freedom in the first place — China's formally retired but still "paramount" leader, Deng Xiaoping. Twice named "Man of the Year" by *Time* magazine, Deng had been credited with repudiating much of the legacy of Maoism, decollectivizing agriculture, encouraging experiments in instituting a market economy, and opening China's doors to foreign investment and academic exchange with the West.[21] Americans had been led to believe that Deng had caught the contagion of freedom. Why, then, was his heart not moved by the young people asking him to realize and act upon the full implications of the freedom he had introduced to China? Why did he turn out to be an enemy of freedom?

Why, for that matter, were the students so angry at Deng Xiaoping and his associates — even against some of those high officials who were identified as "reformers"? The students claimed that the reformers had become corrupt, had made vast profits by, among other things, being gatekeepers for trade with foreign companies.[22] How could reformers, who had brought a better life with the promise of increasing freedom to hundreds of millions of the Chinese people, become smothered in corruption and objects of hatred to the people? The path to freedom seemed more complicated than Americans liked to think it. Could it be, then, that the meaning of freedom was more complicated than most Americans wished to believe?

The Tiananmen massacre challenged several of the assumptions behind common American understandings of freedom. The first is the assumption that economic, political, and sociocultural freedom are so intimately interconnected as to imply and inevitably lead to one another. Deng Xiaoping had undoubtedly pushed China down the path to greater economic freedom. The predominant impression conveyed by the news media and, for that matter, most academic experts was that greater economic freedom would lead to greater political freedom and greater freedom for self-expression by artists and intellectuals.[23] There were, to be sure, academics and journalists who had reported on the dark side of Deng's China: the "spiritual pollution" campaigns against intellectuals, the imprisonment of political dissidents, the corruption of government officials.[24] But these reports did not make a deep impression on the American public. They were apparently not what most Americans wanted to hear, incongruent with the worldview that had developed among the 72 percent of the population holding a "favorable view" of China. Few experts on American public opinion would disagree with the sketch of that worldview outlined in an article in the *New York Times* published a few weeks after the massacre: "For some years this view of China has been emerging: that it was becoming a pro-Western semi-democracy, a place that almost inevitably with the passage of time, increase in contacts, and greater prosperity, has become more relaxed, open, and even free. The country had improved so much since the Maoist years."[25]

China had certainly changed vastly since the Maoist years. To say that the changes were an "improvement" is of course to place the changes in a moral narrative about historical progress, wherein the improvement was a matter not simply of fact but of common moral judgment. In this respect, some dimensions of the improvement were ambiguous. Least ambiguous were improvements in the economic realm: Rates of economic growth had risen dramatically, although they had begun to stagnate in the second half of the 1980s.[26] In most parts of China, the quantity and quality of consumer goods had risen remarkably: Televisions, cassette recorders, washing machines, a variety of colorful clothing, and a marked improvement in diet were widespread manifestations of a prosperity that benefited most Chinese. But these undeniable quantitative improvements had not necessarily led to a more satisfactory quality of life. They increased the sense of frustration among parts of the population—a frustration that had made at least some people unhappy enough to risk their lives in a desperate confrontation with the political system. Many of the Chinese people wanted and needed more than economic development. But they weren't going to get it, for now at least. How should the United States respond?

For a few days, the crackdown at Tiananmen united almost all sectors of the American public in a chorus of shock and revulsion. But there soon emerged significant differences in response, differences that can be explained in the light of tensions within and among major American institutions. The most basic of the tensions is one found within all institutional spheres: the tension between the commitment to freedom and the need for order.

When Americans debated how they should respond to the Tiananmen massacre, they divided into those preoccupied with punishing the hard-liners and those who balanced such urges with a concern for the stability of the Chinese social order. The uncompromising advocates of freedom demanded harsh economic and political sanctions against the Chinese regime. Calls for punitive action came from both the left and the right. Consider, for instance, the column that Pat Buchanan, widely read voice of the "new right," wrote in the *Washington Times* soon after the crackdown.

Neutrality, evenhandedness, calls for "restraint on both sides" are no longer enough. Now we must choose—between the people of China and their now naked enemy, the Stalinist regime of Deng Xiaoping. That choice has been forced upon us by the heroism of the Beijing students; President George Bush should not hesitate to confront it openly and forcibly.

The time for realpolitik is past; the love affair is over. . . . Mr. Deng and his comrades have declared war on the Chinese people; and America must stand with the people as allies against Mr. Deng.[27]

While Buchanan was publishing his column, a group of China scholars at Harvard's Fairbank Center for East Asian Research were drafting a statement that was remarkably similar in tone to Buchanan's, even though most of the signatories would have placed themselves in the middle or slightly on the left of the American political spectrum: "The events surrounding the Tiananmen massacre have aroused a storm of international condemnation and moral outrage. The perpetrators of this massacre will go down in Chinese history as evil men and as belonging to the list of those who have defied human rights and human dignity. We urge you not to forget the brave martyrs of Tiananmen . . . or to give succor to the perpetrators of the massacre."

In first drafts of this document, the scholars called for "complete non-cooperation in PRC state-sponsored cultural, scientific and educational exchanges. As these exchanges represent official expressions of support for the state apparatus that primarily organizes, supports and profits from them . . . we wish to do nothing to give credence to the current regime's hegemony over cultural exchange while it denies responsibility for the intellectual, social, political and physical suppression of its own people." The Harvard scholars also called for an end to any tourism sponsored through the state-owned China International Travel Service and for a continuation of the freeze imposed by President Bush on military sales to the People's Liberation Army "until the leadership responsible for the massacre—Deng Xiaoping, Li Peng, and Yang Shangkun—are removed and the officers who carried out the massacre are arrested and tried in a court of law." Finally, they advocated a package of economic sanctions: rejection of China's proposed entry into the General Agreement on Tariffs and Trade (GATT), a suspension of loans, a temporary freeze on China's status as a "most favored nation," harsh duties on all textile imports, and an end to all grain sales to the PRC "except for emergency relief and famine conditions."[28]

Both Buchanan and the Harvard scholars were giving obstreperous voice to a central value uniting both ends of the American political spectrum: respect for the human rights and human dignity of all people, a respect that finds fulfillment in each individual's freedom of self-expression. During the height of the cold war, right-wingers like Buchanan urged a crusade to destroy communism so that this vision of freedom might be spread around the world. Those in the center or left-center, like the scholars at Harvard, argued that the idea of freedom might best be implanted through peaceful trade and cultural exchange with Communist countries. But both affirmed that the energetic spread of freedom around the world was the proper goal of the U.S. government. Now the scholars were admitting that the hope of implanting freedom through trade and cultural exchange had been misplaced, and Buchanan was saying, in effect, "I told you so." All agreed that the promotion of freedom, American style, was the central goal of the American polity, one that ought to take precedence over everything else.

In the United States, an effective framework of laws and mores generally enables the pursuit of freedom to be consistent with a high degree of political order. Suppose, though, that the pursuit of freedom threatens to lead to disorder, to anarchy, in a culture that does not have such a framework of laws and mores. This scenario would be bad not only for international business but also for U.S. national security. Such was the concern of the American who had made the great breakthrough in undertaking a rapprochement between the United States and the People's Republic of China—Richard Nixon. He wrote:

In view of the cruelty and stupidity that led the Chinese government to resort to repression, lashing back with punitive policy would be politically popular and emotionally satisfying for the great majority of the American people. . . .

President Bush will be pressured to take harsher action by a strange coalition of China-bashers. Those on the far right who oppose any relations with China will demand economic and diplomatic sanctions. So will the human rights lobby, which calls for punishing every regime that does not live up to our standards, regardless of our interests or the millions living under those regimes whom sanctions would hurt the most. The Bush administration should continue to ignore these extremist voices and stay the prudent course it has already set.

The main reason for maintaining this prudent stance, Nixon argued, was "so that the United States can help maintain the balance among China, Japan and the Soviet Union." From his perspective, the preservation of order took precedence over the promotion of individual freedom.[29]

Henry Kissinger, Nixon's collaborator in the historic diplomatic breakthrough with China, even managed to express a note of sympathy for the predicament of China's leaders. In his op-ed pieces written around the time of the crackdown, he observed the events in China "with the pain of a spectator watching the disintegration of a family to whom one has a special attachment. . . ." Kissinger went out of his way to say kind words about Deng Xiaoping: "A sense of proportion requires us to remember that had Deng retired a year ago, history would record him as one of China's great reformers." He even skirted close to expressing sympathy with Deng:

To Deng Xiaoping the demonstrations recall the Cultural Revolution, when throngs of students sought to purify Communist ideology by means that led to loss of his liberty, made his son a paraplegic and disrupted the lives of tens of millions. In the end the Cultural Revolution produced so many diverse factions that China was at the edge of chaos. And chaos is the nightmare of a leadership that grew out of the civil wars and still remembers colonialism and Japanese domination, which it believes was facilitated by China's internal weakness. Hence Deng thought the new groups [created through modernization] should be satisfied with economic progress and be willing to forgo political change, at least until the economy was further along.[30]

For Kissinger, the U.S. national interest required not only a China friendly to the United States but also a stable China. Kissinger was sympathetic to rulers who merely did what it took to maintain stability. "No government in the world," he wrote in another op-ed piece, "would have tolerated having the main square of its capital occupied for eight weeks by tens of thousands of demonstrators who blocked the authorities from approaching the area in front of the main government building. [What would Nixon or Kissinger have done in the early 1970s if a mob of antiwar protesters had surrounded the White House for two

months and erected a big statue of Ho Chi Minh in Layfayette Park?]
A crackdown was therefore inevitable. But its brutality was shocking."[31]

Many American business leaders and their advisers were similarly
cautious about disrupting the forces of order in China. In the fall 1989
edition of its newsletter, *China Business: Current Regulation and Practice,*
the law firm of Thelen, Marrin, Johnson and Bridges, which helps corporations negotiate contracts in China, argued against basing economic
sanctions on moral outrage.

Although the writers [of this newsletter] agree on the appropriateness of expressing foreign reactions to features of domestic Chinese policies that are re-
pugnant, and on the desirability of supporting domestic economic and political
reform in China, we note also what seems to escape some of the strongest critics
of the Chinese government: the power of foreign governments to influence
events in China is limited, and moralizing does not constitute a policy.

Our concerns are all the stronger because the problems presented by the
sudden setback to reform are not likely to be limited to China. Reform of
centrally-planned economies and totalitarian political systems is sweeping the
Communist world. Yet the goals of reform are not well-defined and the processes of reform are agonizing and uncertain. The interactions among Communist political and economic institutions and the societies on which they have
been imposed are sure to be complex, and will not be explainable by easy for-
mulas. For example, although reforming Communist societies may become relatively more open and pluralistic, there is no reason to assume that they will
become Western-type democracies. For these reasons, Western judgments on
developments in China, the Soviet Union and Eastern Europe, even while criticizing political repression, could also benefit from restraint.[32]

This is an articulate example of the kind of thinking common among
corporations doing business with China: It's all right ("appropriate")
to express our dislike for the way the Chinese government is repressing
its critics; but there's nothing we can really do about it, and we shouldn't
hurt ourselves by cutting off profitable business relations. This stance is
consistent with the practical policy of most American corporations in
the Third World.

According to the evidence presented by many comparative political
sociologists over the past generation, authoritarian governments do not
necessarily hinder economic growth. On the contrary, they often help
developing countries achieve high growth rates through a market economy, at least during the early stages of development, by ensuring stability. The introduction of market relations produces insecurities, resent-
ments, uncertainties, hatreds — in short, a threat to public order. Most

of the newly industrializing countries of East Asia have strong, authoritarian governments that coercively establish the order needed to provide a safe climate for foreign investment. In some places (for instance, Taiwan and South Korea), an emerging middle class — engendered through economic growth made possible by decades of authoritarian rule — has begun to successfully push for democratic reforms (although the governments of these countries are still far more authoritarian than most Americans would tolerate). But the most optimistic view this evidence can sustain is that, in a poor country, economic development driven by the dictates of the global market economy may lead to democracy only after several generations of coercive politics.[33]

In 1980, South Korean paratroopers massacred between one and two thousand demonstrators in the city of Kwangju and imprisoned democratic leaders such as Kim Dae Jung.[34] Some scholars have even speculated that the Chinese leaders were consciously following the "Kwangju model" when they suppressed the 1989 demonstrations. Perhaps they calculated that foreign reaction to their crackdown would be as indifferent as it had been to the earlier crackdown in Korea. For most of those (relatively few) Americans who paid attention to it, the Kwangju massacre was tragic and unfortunate but not a cause for shaking the foundations of the U.S.–South Korean relationship and certainly no reason to impose economic sanctions. Today, foreigners who praise the South Korean economic miracle and applaud its recent steps toward democratization do not think much about Kwangju.

One of the main differences between the Beijing and Kwangju massacres, though, was that television cameras were present at the former and helped make it into a powerful drama with a worldwide audience. The drama focused attention on moral dilemmas that had usually been presented in abstract theoretical terms. Implicit in the institutions of a market economy is a vision of individual autonomy in which everyone is free to pursue his or her own self-interest. But in an interdependent modern economy, economic freedom must submit to the demands of large-scale organization. To flourish, a modern corporation requires social order and stability. Deng Xiaoping justified the Tiananmen crackdown by contending that the popular protest movements were leading to chaos, which would undo the great progress toward economic development that China had made during the 1980s. He may have been right. Since the crackdown, the Chinese economy has grown very rapidly (in 1992 and 1993, its growth rate was about 13 percent, among the highest in Asia). American corporations maintaining factories to produce export goods (toys, apparel, footwear, and electronics) in China have made healthy profits.

Most of the growth has come from enterprises allowed to operate outside the state sector — and therefore freer to "break the iron rice bowl" of job security and health and welfare benefits for employees. Worker docility is guaranteed by a government that will not allow the formation of any independent labor unions and will swiftly punish anything that looks like political protest. Post-Tiananmen China is a triumphant combination of market economics and authoritarian politics. This successful pairing challenges the common American view that market freedom and democratic political freedom are so closely intertwined as to be virtually one and the same thing.

The drama of Tiananmen, then, challenged common understandings of freedom that lay at the center of American political and economic institutions. It pressed home the moral point that a modern government and a modern economy must balance freedom with social order. Capitalist economic development, especially in societies whose major resource is cheap, semiskilled labor, does not necessarily imply democracy, because it requires a kind of large-scale organization and social control that can be inconsistent with the desire for individual freedom. And modern governments must do more than enhance the freedom of their citizens; they must regulate the activities of millions of people in an efficient, predictable way. If citizens are divided by mistrust and lack traditions of voluntary self-discipline, an insistence on democracy may be inconsistent with the need for administrative order.

The United States itself is having a difficult enough time realizing the promise of freedom, as the initiative of citizens is increasingly smothered by the bureaucracies of huge corporations and the administrative state. But the United States retains enough traditions of self-government, cushioned by a general economic abundance (at least compared with much of the rest of the world), to enable a celebration of independence to coexist with a reasonable degree of social order. China has no such traditions of self-governance, and in spite of its recent economic development its per capita income is still low by world standards.[35] In such a country the requirements of freedom and order are going to produce much more tension than in the United States. The Tiananmen tragedy dramatizes this tension and has forced many Chinese to make a choice between freedom and order that most Americans do not have to confront—and would prefer not to contemplate.

After the June 4 crackdown, the Chinese government claimed that the "counterrevolutionary rebellion" it had been forced to suppress was the result of an infiltration of "spiritually polluting" ideas of "bourgeois liberalism" from abroad, especially from the United States — all of which was part of an imperialist plot to bring about a "peaceful evolution" away from socialism.[36] On one level, the accusation sounds absurd to most American ears. As used by the Chinese propaganda apparatus, the term "bourgeois liberalism" sounds like an ideology—a political theology such as Marxism-Leninism — with a written canon of doctrines and a corps of authoritative interpreters. Most Americans think of themselves as having no ideology—only the freedom to believe whatever they wish.

However, if by "ideology" one means a widely shared system of norms and values enforced not by government authority but by entrenched customs and widespread peer pressure (in such a way as to sustain powerful economic and political interests), then Americans do have ideologies. Americans often take pride in exporting particular values around the world. As a U.S. official who was involved during 1988 in negotiating a presence for the Peace Corps in China told me, "I wouldn't mind causing a little spiritual pollution. That after all is what the Peace Corps is for—to open minds." This American, cosmopolitan and well read in the latest anthropological theories of cultural relativism as well as in Chinese history, would by no means want to say that Peace Corps volunteers should be agents of an official American ideology. But he assumed that it would be good for Chinese to be challenged, even in ways their government leaders might find dangerous, by the freely expressed ideas of Peace Corps volunteers. These ideas would not constitute a rigid orthodoxy—they would probably be diverse and in many ways contradictory—but they would discredit official Chinese political dogma and lead to a liberalization of Chinese culture, which in the long run would make China better by making it more similar to the United States.

Most Americans would probably spontaneously agree with this sentiment. They would regard the openness of mind, the absence of dogmatism, the tolerance of diverse opinions as self-evidently good. Their belief in the self-evident goodness of such traits, they would say, is not an ideology but rather a protest against all state-enforced ideology. But from the point of view of Communist Party officials, it does indeed look like an ideology.

The Meaning of Freedom

The further we deepen our scrutiny of the Tiananmen drama, the more basic the challenges to our self-understanding. The U.S. Constitution is based on a Lockean political philosophy that presumes the existence of certain universal political rights, good for all people everywhere. As Tom Paine put it, "the Independence of America was accompanied by a Revolution in the principles and practice of Governments. . . . Government founded on a moral theory . . . on the indefeasible hereditary Rights of Man, is now revolving from west to east."[37] From the surface, it looks as though the "democracy movement" in China confirms the universal validity of American understandings of freedom. But the events at Tiananmen really call that assumption of universal validity into question.

Consider the relation between the American media's dramatic rendering of Tiananmen and what is now known about the episode. In the widely disseminated version of the events cited above, the heroes of Tiananmen were mainly students, the best and brightest of China's youth. They had developed a hunger for democracy by reading about the moral theory at the basis of Western liberal democracies, risked their lives for democratic ideals, and been martyred by a reactionary Communist old guard. A careful look at eyewitness accounts of the Tiananmen massacre, however, turns up important details ignored by the standard American coverage.

A common response of American TV viewers to questions about the goals of the Chinese protesters was, in the words of a woman polled in New York, "They want just what we have."[38] It now seems clear, however, that they did not want just what we have. Indeed, many of them were not at all clear about what they wanted. As Orville Schell noted, on the basis of firsthand observations, "Although the students tried to make their demands specific by calling, for instance, for dialogue with government leaders . . . when pressed to be more precise about their vision of reform or their notions of how democracy might work in China, they tended to become vague and even flustered. . . . As one student only half-facetiously said, 'I don't know exactly what we want, but we want more of it.'"[39]

If the content of the students' demands was vague, the form in which they expressed those demands suggested commitment to values inconsistent with common American understandings of democracy. As Sarah

Lubman wrote in a *Washington Post* article, "In the May 4 issue of Beijing University's independent student newspaper, one student wrote, 'The tide of democracy allows no obstruction; all must comply with this trend. If not, they will be condemned by history.' One word has been changed, but the rhetoric is the same as that of Marxist arguments for the historical inevitability of socialism. Propaganda leaflets used similar language."[40]

The students' behavior as well as their language expressed undemocratic values. As described by Lubman:

Left to their own devices, the students created an overly bureaucratic, highly policed system which, like the old, operated on personal credentials, or *guanxi*. . . . What began as an efficient and necessary security system degenerated into a petty abuse of authority. Security guards, originally posted to protect the hunger strikers from infiltrators as well as the hordes of foreign press in town for Soviet leader Mikhail Gorbachev's visit, multiplied and became increasingly aggressive. . . . One security guard . . . , asked who his superior was, replied in the manner familiar to anyone who has had the frustrating experience of dealing with the Chinese bureaucracy, "I don't know. I'm only responsible for this step."

The students' makeshift society resembled the communist state in structure as well as operation. The Self-Governing Association had a standing committee, liaison offices with provincial students' organizations and the foreign press, and a tireless propaganda department. The movement undoubtedly needed organization, but the form that it took grew as bureaucratic as the adversary itself.[41]

Lubman's article was one of the very few in the mainstream press that suggested that the students might not really want "just what we have." One reason Lubman arrived at this conclusion may have been that she was not a seasoned, well-known journalist. She was a University of California graduate student taking part in that institution's Education Abroad program in Beijing; when the crisis broke out, she got a part-time job helping the main *Washington Post* correspondent in the capital. The best-known American reporters from the most prestigious newspapers and television networks were eagerly sought out by Chinese student leaders. They all recognized Dan Rather and flocked to be interviewed by him when they saw him on Tiananmen Square. Thus, a prominent reporter might not have had to endure the quasibureaucratic officiousness of student leaders, as Sarah Lubman did. But junior reporters with experiences such as hers didn't get to contribute many articles to the mainstream press.

Another cause for the media's reticence about the motives of the protesters, though, was the pressure of having to create a vivid story centered around an easily understandable conflict between good people and bad people. According to media critic Mark Hertsgaard, "I watched dozens of hours of broadcast coverage and read every article published about the events in China in the *New York Times*, the *Washington Post*, the *Wall Street Journal*, *Time*, and *Newsweek* without finding a single story about the ideology and political goals of the protest movement. It was as if journalists had become so enthralled by what the protestors were *against* — an authoritarian regime that called itself communist — that it didn't matter what they were for."[42] To American reporters, expending a lot of effort trying to understand what the protesters were *for* would only detract from a very good story. Better to spend one's time on things that amplified rather than dampened that dramatic story.[43]

It doesn't — or shouldn't — detract from the justice of the students' cause to say that many of them wanted something different from our kind of democracy. But if we admit that they did want something different, we may have to think more deeply about what we mean by freedom and democracy. Embedded in all of our major institutions is a notion that freedom is a universal value, as desirable to all rational people everywhere as it is in the United States. Inspected closely, the 1989 protest movement in China does not deny the universality of freedom, but it does force middle-class Americans to think of freedom in more of an ecumenical fashion. It forces us to consider that freedom must be taken in context, that different understandings of freedom are possible in different cultures, and that we might profitably learn something from them.

A still closer scrutiny of the Tiananmen event forces yet another revision to the original dramatic American interpretation and further deepens the challenge to our common assumptions about the universality of our values. The victims of the crackdown were not mainly students peacefully seeking political freedom but workers boisterously seeking economic security.

The first newspaper and television reports of the massacre, usually based on eyewitness accounts by foreign reporters, spoke of "scores" of people having been killed as the army indiscriminately fired into crowds blocking its way along the roads that lead toward Tiananmen Square. Within the next several days, however, newspapers such as the *Washington Post* and *New York Times* were reporting the accounts of unnamed witnesses describing thousands of deaths. About three hundred students were said to have been shot, bayoneted, beaten, and trampled to death when they tried to escape at the Monument to the People's

Heroes in the center of Tiananmen Square. The reports spoke of students being crushed by tanks and bodies of protesters being burned in Tiananmen Square. "Immortality will give us democracy," one of these students supposedly said to a witness before being killed. "We're not afraid to give our young blood for the future of the republic."[44] The Chinese Red Cross was quoted as saying that at least 2,600 people were dead.[45]

Within two days, the Chinese government was issuing a very different story. In a televised news conference, Yuan Mu, chief spokesperson for the Chinese government, declared that there had been a "counterrevolutionary rebellion" incited by a handful of "thugs and hooligans."[46] These hoodlums threatened to throw Beijing into chaos. Soldiers bravely confronted them to reestablish order and protect the people. The insurgents used a variety of deadly weapons, including Molotov cocktails, to burn military vehicles and kill soldiers. The soldiers fought back in self-defense. Inevitably, some innocent bystanders were killed. When the soldiers got to Tiananmen Square before the dawn of June 4, they called on the protesting students to leave the square. This the students did. With a bit of a nervous laugh, Yuan Mu said flatly that no students were killed in Tiananmen Square. About three hundred people were killed in Beijing during the operation, he said, about twenty-three of them students. Yuan Mu strongly suggested that about half of the rest were soldiers.

Chinese television broadcast a report illustrating these points. Citizens were shown immobilizing military vehicles, pelting their occupants with rocks, and setting the vehicles on fire — in some cases with the occupants still inside. There was grisly footage of soldiers who had been strangled, burned, and mutilated. A long line of students was shown peacefully, under military supervision, leaving Tiananmen Square.

Later in the week, Yuan Mu, the government spokesman, repeated this version of events in an interview with Tom Brokaw of NBC News. None of the students in Tiananmen Square had been killed, he said. American television networks had tampered with videotapes to make it appear that there had been murders. Brokaw's demeanor upon being told this story doubtlessly reflected the sentiments of most Americans who viewed the interview. As Orville Schell described it, "I thought Tom was going to leap from his chair and eat this guy from the feet up. He was clearly incensed by what this man was saying. . . ."[47] For American viewers, the interview was a visual representation of democracy against dictatorship, of Truth against the Big Lie.

Evidence gathered and analyzed by a variety of independent foreign observers in the weeks and months following the massacre, however, corroborates some of Yuan Mu's account. Nicholas Kristof, in the June 21 edition of the *New York Times,* noted, "There are many witness accounts of a mass killing around the Monument to the People's Heroes at the center of [Tiananmen] square. But most of these accounts began to appear after several days had passed, rather than immediately, and they directly contradict the accounts of other Chinese and foreigners who were on the square all night."[48] Based on information such as that cited by Kristof, most foreign China experts now think the majority of the students did vacate Tiananmen Square and that few if any killings took place in the central part of the square, around the Monument to the People's Heroes. In this sense Yuan Mu was right.

In the same article, Kristof wrote that "based on the evidence that is now available, it seems plausible that about a dozen policemen and soldiers were killed, along with 400 to 800 civilians."[49] The low end of this estimate is not far from Yuan Mu's estimate of three hundred deaths, although, unlike Yuan Mu, it suggests that many more civilians than soldiers were killed.

Thus, the Chinese government's official account may not be factually correct, but neither were the most widely publicized accounts of the major American news organizations in the immediate aftermath of the massacre. But what about moral correctness? In the American media's dramatic depiction of Tiananmen, innocent, idealistic students were gunned down at the command of cynical, corrupt old Communists. In the Chinese government's version, a rebellious rabble was held in check by guardians of essential social order. I have talked to some trusted Chinese intellectual friends, strong advocates of political and economic reform who have suffered in various ways because of their support of the protesters. To my initial astonishment, these individuals agreed with much of the Chinese government's official story. They dispute that version in that they believe the Chinese government acted irresponsibly in refusing to enter into any dialogue with the students, thus laying the groundwork for a violent confrontation. But they feel the students also were "irresponsible" — that, although many of their complaints were valid, the students should have backed off before precipitating the threat of chaos that invited the military crackdown. And they think many American reporters and academic commentators also acted irresponsibly in giving excessive credence to the most extreme voices in the protest movement.

There do not exist, of course, any public opinion polls on Chinese reaction to the crackdown. But in the minds of the many Chinese I have talked with about this event, there is much more of a worry about the kind of disorder that might have been unleashed by the protests than is found in popular, dramatic American accounts. "Despite seeing all the footage of the Beijing massacre on Hong Kong television," says a resident of Chen Village in Guangdong province, "the older men in the village argued that the demonstrators had gone too far, and that they deserved what they got."[50] The response of the members of the older generation in Chen Village — which is near the border with Hong Kong, more prosperous and more open to the outside world than most communities in China's interior — suggests that many more people in China than in the United States are afraid of the anarchy that can result from the overthrow of established authority.

If we look more closely at what happened on June 4 and further revise the dramatic story initially told by the American media, we will notice good reasons for many Chinese citizens to have feared anarchy. As we have seen, most of the student demonstrators left the square peacefully. Relatively few students died. It turns out that the bloody confrontations of June 4 were not primarily between disciplined, peacefully protesting students and a fanatical army (the soldiers of which were injected with amphetamines before being sent out to kill the students, according to some published but unconfirmed news reports).[51] The confrontations were mainly between the army and masses of enraged Beijing residents, mostly workers but also some unemployed members of the "floating population" of peasants that flooded into the city illegally with the relaxation of political controls in the late 1980s. Most of the killing took place on access roads leading toward Tiananmen Square. Some was the result of pitched battles between soldiers and citizens armed with Molotov cocktails. The forces of order were confronted with a vast insurrection of the urban working class.[52]

This version of the Beijing massacre does not justify the government's use of lethal force. It still seems clear that the military suppression was crude, indiscriminate, and brutal. Many eyewitnesses testify that Beijing citizens used violent means only after the soldiers themselves had begun to use deadly force. There are also plenty of firsthand reports by foreign journalists of soldiers firing not in self-defense but randomly at citizens, even as the latter were fleeing.[53] Nor does this revised account absolve the government of responsibility for the obtuse arrogance that precipitated the crisis in the first place. But it does make Chinese fears about anarchy seem more rational and less paranoid than in the dramatic account narrated by most of the mainstream American media.

It also casts further doubt on the idea that the Chinese protesters "want just what we have." The insurgent citizens were venting a generalized rage against the corruption, arbitrariness, and unfairness of the Chinese system, not voicing a positive desire for democracy, at least not American-style democracy. The Chinese workers, who sustained most of the casualties of June 4, seem to have been much more concerned about issues of practical livelihood than freedom of expression. Henry Rosemont nicely summarized the differences between students' and workers' aspirations:

The workers were no less unhappy than the students in the Square, but the two groups were unhappy about different things. In addition to wages proportional to their services (i.e., higher than worker's wages) young Chinese intellectuals wanted freedom to live and work where they chose, and freedom from the endless papers, permits, and interference in their private affairs insisted upon by petty bureaucrats. Workers on the other hand wanted freedom from a murderous inflation, and from the increasing threats to their job security stemming from the search for profits under the "individual responsibility" system that underlies the economic reforms.[54]

The insurgent workers wanted the wealth that some American capitalists have, but they did not want the insecurity many American workers now face. They were protesting inflation and loss of job security, which were by-products of the introduction of a market economy. By mismanaging the economy, the government may have exacerbated these dislocations, but market reforms would have eroded the salaries of workers and threatened their job security no matter what the government did. The market reforms were only partial, and most American economists urged the Chinese government to move more rapidly toward full marketization. If anything, though, more rapid change would likely have increased the dislocations of workers in the short term and probably intensified their anger, although if Western economists are to be believed, complete market reform might eventually lead to better living standards for all.

But the Beijing workers' reaction to the insecurities and inequalities of an incipient market economy threatens common American understandings about the intimate link, indeed the virtual equivalence, between a market economy and democratic forms of government and about the universal appeal of both. Insofar as the Beijing uprising was worker- rather than student-driven, it may have been not a social movement in favor of democracy but a rebellion against the market, a demand for some form of protection from the insecurities of a market economy rather than simply an appeal for a quicker transition to it.

If we take all of these new considerations into account, the revised Tiananmen drama becomes more challenging than ever. It continues to be about the forces of freedom versus the forces of reaction, but it becomes less clear that what the Chinese protesters meant by freedom is what most Americans mean by it. It also becomes less clear whose side we are on, because the Chinese no longer appear as a great mass of freedom fighters pitted against a small but entrenched old guard. It turns out that there are many different kinds of Chinese divided along many different lines. In this chapter I have focused on one of the most obvious and important divisions in Beijing during the June 4 movement, that between workers and intellectuals, but I could have refined my analysis by considering other rifts, such as those defined by urban versus rural residence or by region, dialect, and generation. It seems that freedom means different things to Chinese in different situations in a rapidly changing society.

These differences challenge us to think of differences among ourselves. Whose side are we on in China? Are we on the side of those who would disrupt social order for increased personal freedom of expression? Are we on the side of those who wish to maintain enough order and stability to allow the flourishing of export-oriented industries producing commodities with cheap labor for the world market? To answer these questions, we need to think more carefully about who "we" are. If we are businesspeople engaged in trade with China we might think differently about the meaning of freedom in China than if we are human rights activists. Tiananmen forces us to see ourselves as a divided "we" interacting with a multiplex "they."

Tiananmen also makes us feel some of the tensions among the meanings of freedom embodied in American economic, political, and cultural institutions. Is the economic freedom of the market really compatible under all circumstances with the political freedom of the democratic polity? And is the responsible pursuit of political freedom really compatible with the hedonistic self-absorption encouraged in the name of freedom by an advanced consumer society?

The travails of China further show that the way we manage these tensions in our own society may not be possible in another society. The United States, like China or, for that matter, any large, complex, modern society, is intricately divided. But our divisions are not as stark as those in China. We generally speak a common language. We are a middle-class society, where members of the lower classes still have a more realistic hope of moving into the upper classes than almost anywhere else in the world and where all except the underclass enjoy what is by global norms a comfortable standard of living. Increasingly we are an administered society dominated by huge bureaucratic organizations, but leaders and subordinates within these organizations are united by bonds of trust that, though eroding, are nowhere nearly as attenuated as those in China. Lacking most of these social goods — which we far too easily take for granted in the United States — Chinese society is inevitably going to experience pain and tragedy as it adapts to a world dominated by a triumphant market economy and new globe-spanning networks of communication. If we are to be committed to the forces of freedom in China, we have to listen more carefully to Chinese views about what freedom would mean in that nation's social context; and to do this we have to reflect more subtly on what freedom can and should mean for us in an interdependent modern society. China challenges us to know ourselves more deeply. Unsettling as it can be, such deepened self-knowledge is a vital necessity in a world bound together by modern mass media.

The final challenge presented to our common understandings by the drama of June 4 is our growing awareness that the story told by the media was not the full story, not the only story, but simply a story framed in terms of American cultural conventions. Yet the technology of the modern media disturbs those conventions and forces us beyond them.

To an unprecedented degree, modern technology — especially television, with its instantaneous satellite transmission and its versatile, portable cameras — made people around the world participate vicariously in the events of Tiananmen. The media provided something never before achieved in the history of the West's relationship with China: a wrenching experiential connection to China's sufferings, not only the agony experienced in the terror of June 4 but also the indignities implicit in everyday life. Some of the most memorable moments in the media's coverage of the China crisis were those that engaged foreigners in a collective experience of culture shock. For instance, after the imposition of martial law in May, an officious bureaucrat entered CNN's office in Beijing and demanded that the network cease broadcasting. When CNN's directors protested that they had a contract allowing them to broadcast, the bureaucrat got out a piece of paper and wrote an "official" announcement that the contract was terminated. All of this took place live on CNN; after the official scribbled out his order, the broadcast abruptly ended. This incident made such an impact on the American viewing public — and was so good for CNN's ratings — that several days later CBS tried to arrange a live television broadcast during its nightly news program, hoping it would be similarly cut off in mid-broadcast by the Chinese authorities. (To the network's disappointment, it was not.)[55]

Practically any American who has worked for any significant amount of time in China has faced similar arbitrary frustrations from officious bureaucrats. After a while veteran "China hands" get used to this and, like most Chinese citizens, devise ways to work partially around it. But the termination of the CNN broadcast enabled millions of Americans to feel for themselves what it is like to experience such bureaucratic harassment. The media powerfully conveyed what it is like to be powerless in China.

Vicarious participation is not the same thing as understanding. The public that participated in the Tiananmen events through the media was all too often a poorly informed, confused public rather than an enlightened, reflective one. As we have seen, the story of Tiananmen was framed in a way that confirmed rather than challenged common assumptions. Nonetheless, the vicarious experience was rich enough and powerful enough to push beyond the boundaries of conventional thinking.

The public may resist the push, may fail to respond. But it cannot escape the challenge. Knowledge of China is not "optional" for Americans in the age of global telecommunication and commerce. We will increasingly be forced to make important decisions about how our economic, political, and cultural institutions should relate to China. But if we do not understand the meaning of the relationships, we will be at their mercy.

Situated Freedom

Such an understanding of China — which implies a deeper understanding of ourselves — must be situated in history. It must constantly change in response to new challenges, and it is inevitably both limited and strengthened by the heritage of attempts at mutual understanding that have preceded it. To understand the challenges posed by the drama of Tiananmen, I will in the following chapters retrace the paths that led to it.

Throughout, I will pay special attention to the challenges each society has posed to the other's understanding of freedom. By the end of the cold war, many people in China, especially intellectuals, had developed a strong taste for freedom. This arose mainly from indigenous roots: their disgust at the incompetence and brutality of a tyrannical and corrupt government. But it was also stimulated in part through their new ability to participate in international economic, political, and cultural institutions centered in the United States. At the same time, many Americans have learned from their experience with people in China that freedom is a complex ideal. Pure, unfettered individual autonomy is an impossibility. Freedom is always situated: it can flourish only if it is balanced by norms, rules, social constraints—even though these constituents of social institutions always threaten to smother the spark of freedom.[56]

Freedom has become a universal aspiration—everybody wants it, and truly having it implies respecting the freedom of everybody else. Thus, the moral relativism that acquiesces in the Chinese government's brutal suppression of the brave quest for freedom on the part of China's dissidents is unacceptable to one committed to the universal idea of freedom. But no society is perfectly free. No configuration of institutions limits and protects freedom in the same way. Our ways of becoming free are not the same as Chinese ways. Our debates about what freedom means are going to be different from those carried out in China. Americans committed to the cause of liberty should staunchly—in my view much more staunchly than most of our political and business leaders have done—support those Chinese counterparts who bravely seek such liberties. But we will deceive and harm both ourselves and our Chinese friends if we try uncritically to impose our variety of situated freedom on them. We can help each other best if we each comprehend more profoundly the challenges facing ourselves. And we can only do that if we expand our horizons to understand more fully the travails facing the other. By examining how we have or have not achieved such understanding in the past, the following chapters will help us to face the future.

2

America's China

Creation of a Liberal Myth

The massacre at Tiananmen fundamentally called into question the mythical master narrative — what I will call the liberal China myth — that for a quarter-century had guided Americans' relationship to China. Before Tiananmen, Americans could generally agree upon the basic plot of that story, though we might disagree on its implications for concrete policy toward the People's Republic. Like all the stories we use to understand our national identity and purpose, the central American story about China did more than simply reflect empirically verifiable facts — it also imposed a socially constructed vision upon the ambiguities of historical experience.[1] It was as much about America as about China; it construed American relations with China in terms of common understandings of the core values of American society. In this chapter I will describe that myth, show how it was reborn (for it has antecedents earlier in this century) in the 1960s, and discuss how it was embodied in social organizations.

The liberal China myth portrayed China as a troubled modernizer. Collectivist Chinese Communists appeared to threaten the liberal American Dream — individual advance in a competitive market economy — both ideologically and politically. But this dream was not under any serious threat; it was, after all, the inevitable expression of modernity itself. As Communist China modernized, its leaders and citizens would learn to follow this dream. In the meantime, Americans should help the process of modernization along by becoming actively engaged with China economically, politically, and culturally.

Three decades ago, however, the liberal myth of China as troubled modernizer had to contend with two other powerful impulses within American public opinion. The first was a story about China as Red menace. This story was vividly evoked for me by a memorable conversation I had in 1967 with an unemployed worker named Wesley as we sat together during a hot summer night on a stoop in Harlem. "The people I'm most scared of in all the world," said Wesley, "are the Chinese. They're crazy! Like in the Korean War, when they would fight you, nothing would stop them. They would just come at you, wave after wave. They didn't care 'cause they were all hopped up with that opium shit." Different versions of the same story were widespread among the middle class. When he was in high school, recalls Kenneth Prewitt, who later became head of the Social Science Research Council, China was part of a "map with a big red blob, representing the expansion of communism." As Red menace, China could not be edged toward the path of modernization but had to be fought in a protracted cold war.

The other challenger to the troubled modernizer myth was the myth of China as revolutionary redeemer. This story was told mostly by the kinds of middle-class university students who decorated their apartments with posters of heroic workers and peasants and big pictures of Mao Zedong. In it, China—especially the Maoist China of the Cultural Revolution—represented a noble experiment that gave hope to all people in the world. For Americans reveling in defiant alienation, China provided hope for escape from the nightmare that the American Dream had become for them.

During the turbulent 1960s, these three master narratives contended for hegemony in American public opinion. By the early 1970s, the troubled modernizer story had won. How was that story created, and how did it eventually gain a central place in public discussion of China?

Religious Foundations

Proponents of the troubled modernizer story would say that its public acceptance was simply a triumph of social scientific reason over the irrational forces of ignorance and illusion. But the matter is not so simple. As with all central master narratives, a strong nonrational component of belief and ritual went into its construction. In fact, an important force in its creation was religious.

This may come as a surprise, because in more recent years American public conversation about China has largely become secularized. The churches are only marginally involved in public discussion of U.S. foreign policy in East Asia. National debates about China today stress calculations of U.S. self-interest and perhaps promotion of "democratic values." Why was religion more central to the debate on China in the 1960s?

Part of the answer lies in the history of missionary activity by American Protestant churches in China. During the first half of the twentieth century, China had been a major focus of missionary work by the American churches, at a time when they were more central to public life than they are now. Some of the United States' most powerful elite families, including the Rockefellers and the Luces, were deeply involved in the missionary effort. This effort was not devoted exclusively to religious faith; much of it aimed to cultivate in the Chinese an appreciation of the liberal values of science and democracy through the establishment of modern universities and hospitals. Many of the key diplomats who played roles in U.S.-China relations during the fateful decades preceding the establishment of the PRC (such as Leighton Stuart and John Service) were from missionary backgrounds, as were many of the journalists and scholars (Pearl Buck, Henry Luce, A. Doak Barnett, John Lindbeck) who played prominent roles in interpreting the Chinese experience for the American public.[2]

This history of missionary activity did not decisively influence views about what policies the United States should take toward China. The missionary legacy was one of profound ambivalence. The daily prayer book used by the Catholic Foreign Mission Society of America (the Maryknoll Fathers) in the early 1960s included prayers that suggested the Chinese people were "sitting in darkness and the shadow of death" but also prayers casting China as a "field ripe for the harvest." In the late nineteenth and early twentieth centuries, the missionary movement had alternated between rosy predictions that China would before long "become like us" and bouts of angry damnation against a society that rejected Western beliefs. The liberal myth of China as troubled modernizer and the myth of China as Red menace were secularized versions of these optimistic and pessimistic missionary views.

People associated with the missionary cause could thus be found on all sides of the policy debate. On the right, one could find figures such as Walter Judd, the congressman from Minnesota who had started his career as a medical missionary and was the key figure in the "Committee of One Million" devoted to keeping Red China out of the United Nations. In the middle were figures such as Leighton Stuart, the former president of Yanjing University (the famous missionary institution in Beijing) and subsequently the U.S. ambassador to China during the Chinese civil war, who had championed a role for the noncommunist, non-nationalist middle class of liberals in China. Somewhat to the left were people such as John Stewart Service, foreign service officer and son of China missionaries, who, for his honest assessments of Communists' popularity in China in the 1940s, was denounced as a traitor by the McCarthyites during the 1950s.

A missionary background by no means led all people to similar conclusions, but it did impart a particular tone to the debate. It made the debate about China more emotional and more charged with moral concern than, say, the debate over political conflicts in Indonesia, where few American missionaries had served.[3] Key participants in the discussion viewed China as a familiar place, where their fathers and mothers had invested enormous personal effort, where they themselves had grown up, where they had personal friends. Now China was led by people who had expelled the foreign missionaries and often cruelly persecuted many of those who had worked with them. Missionary organizations published books with titles such as *Calvary in China*.[4]

Such perspectives were shared by Americans not directly involved in the missionary effort. Their churches had taught them to *care* about China; it was not simply a place that had strategic significance. The debate about China was infused with sadness, anger, and dread. American effort seemed to have been wasted, American ideals rejected. Because of the legacy of religious contact, it was difficult for many Americans to argue dispassionately about China.

In fact, because of the legacy of the McCarthy era, it was difficult for them to argue publicly at all. Key targets of the McCarthy witch-hunts had been China experts, both in the State Department and in academic life. Brandishing the slogan "Who lost China?" McCarthy's followers destroyed the careers of diplomats such as Service and John Patton Davies and academicians such as historian Owen Lattimore. They harassed many other distinguished "China hands," notably John K. Fairbank, the Harvard historian who perhaps more than any other single individual shaped the field of academic China studies. Such people, it was alleged, had been sympathetic to Chinese communism and had used their influence to make the Communist victory possible.[5]

The effects of the McCarthy era lingered long after McCarthy's demise. The Committee of One Million Against Admission of Red China into the United Nations, a powerful, well-funded (partially with money from Chiang Kai-shek's Nationalist government on Taiwan), and very effectively organized lobbying group, threatened the political lives of congressmen who opposed it and intimidated nonofficeholders by orchestrating a barrage of negative publicity against them. Any American who publicly struck anything even resembling an accommodating attitude toward the PRC risked his or her career.[6]

It was possible to advocate a more flexible policy toward China if one were an academic with tenure and did not aspire to having any influence on public policy. But for economic, political, and cultural elites to talk about China in a public forum with any hope of influencing U.S. foreign policy, a vehicle for collective action was needed. Someone who was respected yet did not have a lot to lose would have to take the lead in forming a broad-based coalition of citizens wishing to talk openly about U.S.-China policy. A group representing diverse interests would have to be united around broad moral concerns. The mainline churches were ideally suited for the role of establishing such a group.

Yet because of their missionary ties with China, many of the churches themselves were caught up in the partisan passions of the China debate. One religious body that was not so afflicted, however, was the Quakers. They had not been involved in seeking converts in China. They were centrally committed to promoting world peace and dedicated to reforming political systems. They were by and large accepted by the American establishment. Their small, quiet voice urging an end to conflict might not be heeded, but they were respected for making that voice heard. Though not *of* the establishment, like the Episcopalian or Presbyterian churches, they were hardly regarded as a sect on the fringes of American life. They were part of the mainstream — to an important extent *in* the establishment.[7]

Through their social action organization, the American Friends Service Committee (AFSC), the Quakers became the catalyst for a new national dialogue on U.S.-China relations. As recounted in an unpublished history written by Robert Mang, a Quaker closely connected to the events, "In the spring of 1964, the American Friends Service Committee, through its national and regional Peace Committees, sought to establish a new set of program priorities for the coming two or three years. From these discussions and communications came two programs related to China. The national AFSC in Philadelphia convened a Working Party in September 1964 to analyze U.S.-China policy and recommend a set of proposals."[8]

Around the same time, the Friends Committee on National Legislation invited Eugene Boardman, a China scholar from the University of Wisconsin, to come to Washington, D.C., to "stimulate interest in China and U.S. policy among members of Congress."[9] And the San Francisco AFSC asked Cecil Thomas, the associate peace secretary there, to develop a regional conference on China.

Academic Articulations

Entitled "An Institute on China Today," the one-day conference was held in December 1964 in Sproul Hall at the University of California at Berkeley. It was jointly sponsored by the American Friends Service Committee, the World Affairs Council, and the UC Berkeley political science department. Speakers ranged from the fervently pro-PRC British journalist Felix Greene to Clare Booth Luce and Henry Luce, hostile critics of the People's Republic. A thousand people filled the hall to capacity, and another five hundred had to be turned away. Two northern California public television stations broadcast the conference, and the proceedings were widely reported in the press. The first large public dialogue on U.S. policy toward China was a huge success.[10] Thus began a citizens movement to rethink that policy. Even though the conference took place in Berkeley, reported the London *Economist*, "its movers were not the 'Vietniks' for which that university is notorious. Almost all were middle-class and middle-aged."[11]

The chief organizers of the conference were a study in contrast. The instigator of the event was Cecil Thomas, the associate peace secretary of the AFSC and director of the Berkeley YMCA. The person who set the conference's intellectual agenda was Robert Scalapino, a professor in the UC Berkeley political science department. An energetic, sophisticated scholar of East Asian politics, Scalapino played the worldly realist to Thomas's idealist. "Cecil," Scalapino told me, "was one of those persons who loved to go around doing good. If I have a soft spot in my heart, it was for Cecil. . . . Over the years Cecil would call me about doing good for something and I would usually respond." He continued, "Cecil and I really had very little in common. But I had general sympathy with people who have no ax to grind yet who are involved in trying to make the world better. Cecil and I had very little in common other than the desire to do good."

The contrast between the two men, though, was a matter not only of personalities but also of institutional contexts. Scalapino was a professor of political science at a leading research university, one that was rapidly expanding into a prototype of the modern technocratically oriented "multiversity," a supplier of specialized information and expertise to industry and government. As the director of the Berkeley YMCA, Thomas was ministering to the moral and social needs of people connected with the university, needs the university itself no longer pretended to fulfill. The university provided knowledge; the surrounding community, through its families, churches, and voluntary associations, was somehow to take care of goodness. The kinds of people most successful in such a university were going to be different from those most successful in the YMCA and the AFSC.[12]

Yet the connection between the two kinds of institutions was closer in the mid-1960s than it is today. The connection was made not through any formal articulation of institutions but through personal affinities — affinities grounded in common moral understandings among those who were "middle-class and middle-aged." Three decades ago in the social science departments of leading research universities there were perhaps more professors like Scalapino who combined a broad general knowledge with a deep engagement in public affairs. Now, though such people are still found in universities, leading social science departments tend to privilege those swift in formulating theoretically elegant papers rather than those engaged in current public issues. (More hospitable environments for the latter are to be found in professional schools of public policy or in independent think tanks.)

At the same time, it is perhaps less common for individuals such as Cecil Thomas involved in "campus ministries" to productively collaborate with leading social science professors. Representatives of religious institutions tend either to be wholly concerned with the moral issues surrounding private life or, when concerned with public affairs, to take highly partisan approaches to them.[13]

Buoyed by the success of the Berkeley conference, Thomas and Scalapino undertook to organize a similar conference in Washington, D.C. Now on leave from his YMCA job and supported full-time by the AFSC, Thomas did most of the practical organizing for the event. According to Robert Mang, "Aided by numerous letters and telephone introductions to China scholars at various other universities and by an old friend and China hand, Harry Kingman, Thomas set out for the East Coast in January 1965. Funded now by the national office of the AFSC, he travelled up and down the Atlantic seaboard, from Washington to New York to Boston to Philadelphia, meeting with scholars, potential sponsors, always willing advisors, and well-wishers, for a solid three months."[14]

The result of all this effort was more than an academic conference, more than an exchange of information and a debate among theories. It was a political ritual. In the words of Mang, it "was truly a political demonstration of the first order; yet no one took to the streets for longer than it took to walk from a cab to the front door of the Washington International Inn, where the National Conference on United States and China was held on April 28, 29, and 30, 1965."[15]

A ritual symbolically expresses and reaffirms an ideal pattern of social relations and helps impart a moral gravity to such relations. What was important about the 1965 National Conference on China was not so much what the participants said about Chinese politics as what American political values they expressed and reaffirmed by the very act of participating.

As ritual, the conference was decidedly "high church." Most of the other great political rituals of the time — the demonstrations of the civil rights movement, the "love-ins" of the hippie movement, or the angry marches of the antiwar movement — were "low church," condemning hierarchy, celebrating spontaneity, drawing sharp boundaries between themselves and a society rejected as corrupt. The National Conference on China, conversely, was a grand affirmation of the hierarchies of American life. In a letter written at the time to Edgar Snow, Cecil Thomas named some of the groups he tried to involve in the conference, including "the United Nations Association in New York City, the Council on Foreign Relations, members of the State Department, business leaders in the East, Dr. Andrew Cordier, Dean of the School of International Affairs at Columbia University and former executive assistant to Trygive Lie and Dag Hammarskjöld, Professor Roger Hilsman at Columbia and former head of the Far Eastern Affairs Office at the State Department. . . ."[16]

Thomas secured a long list of participating organizations associated with business, labor, academia, and, not least, religion (including the Protestant National Council of Churches, the Catholic Association of International Peace, and the Union of American Hebrew Congregations). He established an advisory council that included prestigious leaders from each of these kinds of organizations: for instance, Jack Gomperts, president of the San Francisco World Trade Association; Victor Reuther, president of the United Auto Workers; Rabbi Hirsch of the Union of American Hebrew Congregations. These advisory committee members were important as much for who they were as for what they could substantively contribute. As Mang put it, "Some of the advisory committee members . . . were quite active in the Conference planning; others such as Victor Reuther helped by allowing use of their names."[17] The official sponsors of the conference were the American Friends Service Committee, Georgetown University, and American University's School of International Service. Cecil Thomas called the representation of Georgetown "very significant because Georgetown is a very well-known Catholic University and considered very respectable, and some would even say conservative."[18] Like an Episcopalian conference of bishops, the National Conference on China represented a corporate social world consisting of interlocking social orders organically connected at the top by duly ordained elites.

Thomas and his advisory committee took pains to assure that the diversity of the American public would be represented. Observes Mang:

The program brought together an extensive and wide range of expertise and viewpoints. Senators George McGovern and Peter H. Dominick, opposites in Party affiliation and political stance on China, co-signed a letter of invitation to the Conference to their ninety-eight other colleagues in the U.S. Senate. The two Senators also shared a luncheon platform at the conference where they debated their disagreement about U.S.-China policy. China scholars from Harvard, U.C. Berkeley, the University of South Carolina, Cornell University and from the sponsoring universities, spoke from a variety of perspectives and opinions. The State Department sent Assistant Secretary of State, Harlan Cleveland, to participate in a colloquy on China and the U.N. with the Ambassador from the Republic of China on Taiwan. Any difference in their views was imperceptible. Deputy Assistant Secretary of State for Far Eastern Affairs, Robert W. Barnett, joined in a discussion on travel and cultural exchanges with Mainland China. Several U.S. businessmen explored trade with Mainland China on a panel with Canadian businessmen who had firsthand experience.[19]

What this gathering represented was a commitment to the principle of diversity itself, a belief in a free marketplace of ideas. Unlike the McCarthyites, the conference participants affirmed that diversity was safe, not something that threatened to fragment the liberal republic. It was safe because it was rational, comprising nothing more than the different opinions of professional experts; because it was deferential to the prestigious elites who had lent their names to the gathering; and because it was blessed by an assemblage of religious and civic bodies whose patriotism had been demonstrated for a long period of time. It was safe, in short, because it was not really too diverse. It was an affirmation of the social commitments of its generation's middle-class and middle-aged.

Unlike the more unruly, Dionysian political rituals of the counterculture during the 1960s, the National Conference on China enjoyed the mass media's blessing. The media were not just spectators of the event but concelebrants with it, helping to determine the nature of the event itself. Cecil Thomas made a major effort to ensure that the conference would attract wide press coverage. One ultimately unsuccessful strategy was to get the journalist Edgar Snow to address the conference. In his invitation to Snow, Thomas was very explicit about his objectives: "Our experts here tell us that if the kind of meeting can be held which makes a good story in the *New York Times* or the *Washington Post* then it is read by the members of Congress, their assistants, and by the leaders in the Administration. . . . [T]he combination of Edgar Snow and a variety of academic and business leaders from Canada and the United States makes for a total program that the press and other mass media will not ignore."[20]

The attempt to get Snow revealed one of the tensions implicit in the process of initiating a public dialogue about China. Snow would have been important to have at the conference because he was attractive to the media. He was one of the few Americans who had actually been to the People's Republic of China, and he had firsthand knowledge of its leaders. But in the later part of his life, Edgar Snow had adopted a rather uncritical view of support for the Communist regime in China.[21] Cecil Thomas seems generally to have agreed with many of Snow's views. "It has not been my pleasure to meet you yet," he wrote, "but I feel that I almost know you since we have sold many of your books over the years in California at our American Friends Service Committee (AFSC) conferences. Many times we wished you could be with us to be able to directly answer many of the misstatements we hear from the platform about the People's Republic of China." Yet academics who, like Robert Scalapino, considered themselves "centrist" were critical of Snow's perspective. Scalapino and Thomas wanted a "balanced" conference — which meant one that would balance out to the centrist position. Scalapino's self-described centrist speech was the last event of the conference. But the organizers also wanted a conference that would catch media attention, and that called for a keynote speaker like Edgar Snow with strong opinions and fascinating personal experiences in China. Such a person might tilt the balance.

In the end, Snow was unable to attend (though he sent a written statement, mainly criticizing U.S. involvement in Vietnam rather than discussing U.S.-China relations). Even without him, the conference was widely reported on all over the nation. "The conference's objective," reported the *New Republic*, "was to stimulate attention on the problem, rather than to promote any particular viewpoint."[22] In this, it was indeed successful. *The Nation* reported that "the two days belonged to individuals and groups advocating some accommodation with Communist China" and closed its article by quoting from the mimeographed statement that Edgar Snow had sent from Switzerland.[23] However, most newspapers emphasized that the conference presented both sides of the argument about China, and several quoted Scalapino's centrist closing remarks:

Containment by isolation has not been successful and never can be successful. It only serves the cause of fanaticism in China. We ought to complicate decision making for the Chinese Communist leaders, as it would be complicated if they had multiple contacts with the international community.

It is time for us to say, "We will exchange scholars with you, we are interested in trade, we will accept you in the United Nations under certain circumstances."[24]

Another theme in the newspaper reports was that the conference demonstrated "the need for far greater knowledge of the basic facts about China and all its ramifications."[25] Some papers bolstered this contention by reporting on a survey that had been taken, with AFSC support, the previous winter. The survey found that 28 percent of Americans did not know that mainland China was ruled by Communists.[26]

The stated purposes of the national conference had been achieved: "to focus nationwide attention upon the problem of U.S.A.-China relations . . . to provide information on the subject and to stimulate thought so as to prepare the public for a more intelligent grasp of the problems that divide the two nations."[27] The conference had indeed started a public dialogue. Now, as Robert Mang put it, "China was an issue to be addressed out loud, not whispered with a glance over the shoulder."[28]

In a letter to Edgar Snow, Cecil Thomas pointed out the enormous importance of initiating such a dialogue:

[I]f we do not have hearings to open up this dialogue we simply will keep on having more than 350 members of Congress signing these ridiculous Committee of One Million statements opposing the admission of China to the UN and opposing opening up any kind of relationship with China. We have talked to many of the Congressmen who have signed these statements and they say that until there is some public demonstration of real concern about re-examining and perhaps changing our relationships with China, it is political suicide for many of them not to let their names be used by the Committee of One Million. Obviously then, they feel that they cannot afford to do the more visible thing of making a major speech on U.S.-China relationships.[29]

Constitution of a Liberal Center

The last sentence of Thomas's letter gives some sense of who the important parties were to the dialogue. They were not the 28 percent who did not know that China was ruled by Communists, nor were they "Vietniks." They were well-established, responsible leaders of major American institutions, "an assorted group of scholars, bureaucrats, ministers, Congressmen, newsmen, ladies and old China hands," as *The Nation* described the conference participants.[30] They were people who strove for orderly, balanced discussions based on reason and on the facts; who gave great deference to professional experts but could be a little swept away by celebrities, too; who respected religious convictions as long as they were not fanatical; and who were used to having their convictions make some difference in the world of public affairs. They represented the cultural center of American society.

It was a center constituted not so much by common economic and political interests as by common moral values, common conceptions of the good life. Although the material self-interests of the business leaders, labor leaders, academics, clergy, and government bureaucrats attending the conference might have differed, all shared an interest in maintaining a particular kind of life based upon the multidimensional value of freedom—freedom of enterprise, of conscience, of speech. This is the syndrome of values that constitutes liberalism, which I define broadly, in the words of William Sullivan, as "the philosophy of government that has dominated political discourse in modern America" and the "general cast of mind found throughout the society and typical of much of American culture." Shared not only by most "liberal" Democrats but also by most self-styled "conservative" Republicans, liberalism so defined is a way of thinking that sees the American Dream as individual success and personal self-expression within a competitive economy.[31] This central way of life was now under assault, perhaps even in danger of crumbling. And one occasion for the assaults was what had happened in faraway China—Communist China, as nearly everyone called it in those days.

The United States was locked in a cold war to defend the "free world" against communism. There was extremely broad consensus within the United States that this cold war was necessary because communism was a mortal enemy of freedom. Almost all of the "middle-class and middle-aged" Americans who attended the Institute on China Today and the National Conference on China would have agreed with that proposition. But they were concerned about some of the means being used to combat communism.

Their chief concern sprang from the domestic terrors of the McCarthy era. Did the fight against communism in the name of freedom require the destruction of freedom in the United States? Would fear of communism engender a collective paranoia that would lead to witch-hunts against innocent people? Would that not endanger the freedom of self-expression that American elites had claimed was central to their way of life? The common goal of the diverse people who organized and participated in the National Conference on China and similar dialogues in the 1960s was not to accept the validity of Chinese communism but to contain and ultimately defeat it. However, they wanted to do so in ways that were better rooted in the American commitment to freedom, as they saw it.

Their hopes of defeating communism in a way consistent with the liberties of an open society were threatened not only by the dying embers of McCarthyism but by the rising flames of controversy about the Vietnam War. The new dialogue on China included many people, like Robert Scalapino, who recommended an escalation of U.S. military involvement in Vietnam after the Gulf of Tonkin incident in August 1964. For much that they believed in, that involvement was starting to turn into a disaster—not in the jungles of Indochina but in the streets of the United States. Domestic controversy over Vietnam was starting to destroy the foundations of civil discourse. The opportunity for a new dialogue on China gave them a glimmer of hope that rational, factually based discussion about Asian affairs among responsible, self-disciplined people could still overcome the confusion created by bitter polarization.

Perhaps this hope explains the tremendous response from individuals across the country to the opportunity to talk about China. In the words of Robert Mang, "the sparks from the 800 people who attended the National Conference continued to show up here and there across the nation even after the press died down, and these sparks grew into campfire-size discussions needing more information and speakers."[32] The League of Women Voters and the American Association of University Women produced reading lists for their study projects on modern China. A series of conferences was held in the Midwest. Many requests for help in setting up local conferences came to Cecil Thomas, who had returned to his work with the AFSC in San Francisco.

This intellectual effervescence popularized the story of China as troubled modernizer. Of course, the speakers who lectured at the various conferences and wrote the books and articles that ended up on the burgeoning reading lists differed widely in their views. But their presentations generally fell within a common narrative framework, a framework nicely laid out by leading academic experts on Chinese affairs in testimony before the Senate Committee on Foreign Relations, chaired by Senator J. William Fulbright, in 1966.[33]

In that story line, China was a complicated society driven by several different impulses. First of all, it was a revolutionary society—this indeed was what was wrong with it. As a revolutionary society, it featured a totalitarian social order led by radical ideologues who practiced unremitting class warfare, favored equality over efficiency in economic matters, wanted to impose a uniform set of revolutionary values on the population through propaganda, pursued grandiose but eventually futile social experiments such as the Great Leap Forward, and dreamt of exporting their brand of revolution around the world.

But viewing China solely as a Red menace that threatened the free world was too simplistic. China was basically a modernizing society, and successful modernization eventually would mean the abandonment of revolutionary values. Robert Scalapino testified before the Fulbright Committee that "there is a growing struggle which in its essence poses the primitivism implicit in Maoist political-military doctrines against the professionalism that is implicit in the whole modernization program."[34] If China were not excessively forced on the defensive by outside pressure, this moderate, pragmatic element would come to the fore. Chinese society would then become more orderly, predictable, and humane than it was at present.

Another set of impulses came from Chinese cultural traditions. China was accustomed to seeing itself as the Middle Kingdom, cultural center of Asia and indeed of the world. Its pride had been grievously injured by the aggression of imperialist powers in the nineteenth and early twentieth centuries, and this wounded pride, combined with a traditional sense of cultural superiority, had produced a potent nationalism. It was in China's national interest to protect itself from external threats and to trumpet the glories of its way of life around the world. But it was not in its national interest to engage in military adventures far from its borders. China's traditional culture, moreover, gave it a repertoire of behavioral styles that differed from those of the West and were easy for the West to misunderstand. For instance, Lin Biao's talk about spreading "people's war" around the world did not mean the same thing it would mean if uttered by a Westerner. As John Fairbank put it in his testimony, "in the Chinese cultural scene, there is a different function performed by words"; words such as Lin Biao's were more like a ritual expression of doctrine than a real predictor of future conduct.[35]

In such a rendition, the China story was not simply about the rise of a mighty enemy that challenged the United States in the Pacific but also about a nation with many contradictory impulses trying to find its way to a better future. The Chinese Communists represented these diverse popular impulses, a mixture of good and bad. The revolution had not simply been an unrelieved disaster for the Chinese people; it had produced some genuine benefits along with human tragedies (the balance between the two was, of course, a matter of great debate). If the United States opened economic, cultural, and even diplomatic relationships with China, some of the better impulses would come to the fore. The United States had to contain Chinese communism by the threat of military force, but such pressure might have the self-defeating effect of inflaming some of the most fanatical, nationalistic passions among the Chinese people. If Americans balanced military containment with renewed communication, the better angels of Chinese nature might prevail.

If China were to become integrated through diplomacy, trade, and cultural exchange with the world system, testified Doak Barnett, the "technical bureaucrats" would be strengthened.[36] The process would also, as John Fairbank put it, be "therapeutic" for the Chinese leadership:

How to get the Peking leadership into the international order, instead of their trying to destroy it according to their revolutionary vision, is primarily a psychological problem. Therapy for Peking's present, almost paranoid, state of mind must follow the usual lines of therapy: it must lead the rulers of China gradually into different channels of experience until by degrees they reshape their picture of the world and their place in it.

The remolding of Chairman Mao, the greatest remolder of others in history, is not something I would advocate as feasible. But I think it is high time we got ourselves ready to deal with his successors and their successors in years ahead.

In practice this means getting Peking into a multitude of activities abroad. China should be included in all international conferences, as on disarmament, and in international associations, both professional and functional, in international sports, not just ping-pong, and in trade with everyone, including ourselves, except for strategic goods. One thinks naturally of the U.N. agencies and participation in the Security Council as well as the Assembly. Yet all this can come only step by step, with altercation all the way—not an easy process but a lot more constructive than warfare.[37]

What would a better future for a place like China be? What would be a happy ending to the emerging new China story? China would become a society governed by "technical bureaucrats" who acted "pragmatically" rather than "ideologically." Ideology told them that salvation lay in "continuous revolution" and in confrontation with the power of American imperialism. Pragmatism was founded in reason rather than belief; it simply entailed facing facts. There were laws of economic development and political survival to which every society had to conform if it was to prosper. These laws required accepting the rules of a market economy and cooperating with the structures of power established by the United States. As long as the Chinese leaders someday faced facts, their political economy would become like ours, only a little poorer. China's culture, however, would remain distinctively Chinese.

Such is a sketchy but I think basically accurate overview of the testimony of Barnett, Fairbank, Scalapino, Benjamin I. Schwartz, John M. H. Lindbeck, and Alexander Eckstein before the Fulbright Committee. The views of these scholars were central to the new national public dialogue that had been sparked by the work of Scalapino and Cecil Thomas. At the Fulbright hearings, however, there were several other prominent figures—Walter Judd and George Taylor among them—who represented the Red menace view of China, which these mainstream liberal scholars were trying to supplant. Taylor ridiculed Fairbank's notion that the Chinese leadership might be changed by the "therapy" of induction into a world community. According to Taylor, there was

no world community . . . into which we can induce the Chinese to enter. Unfortunately we live in a world in which there are at least two violently opposed concepts of international relations, of political and social organization, and of

world order. The dialog between them is still minimal. . . . The agrarian reformers of the forties are now the aging paranoids of the sixties, to be handled, it
would seem, by group therapy. If they were really nationalists masquerading as
Communists, then Chinese tradition as well as the humiliations of nineteenth-
century imperialism would be relevant to their mood, but in my view the Communists represent a complete break with the past. Their world view is not condi-
tioned by the imperial past, although they are willing to exploit it. . . . There is
nothing about Chinese nationalism that calls for the hate campaign of the Chinese Communists against the United States, for the militarization of a quarter
of the people of the earth, for the racial invective that pervades so much of their
propaganda . . . or for the support of revolutionary movements in southeast
Asia, Africa, and Latin America.[38]

For Judd, the worst thing about the Chinese Communists was their
attempt to destroy the "civilized" character of the Chinese people:

[I] have a great respect and affection for the Chinese people because they are a
highly civilized people. They have good manners, they are mature, and have a
rich mellow culture. They have been trained that way for centuries. But you
know . . . that people are what they are taught to be, and the Communists are
perfectly sure that, given time, they can change these qualities of the Chinese. . . . So my concern about the Chinese is primarily for our own country. If
the Chinese are free and friendly, as they would be if they were free, there is no
insoluble problem in Asia.[39]

By the early 1970s, the views of people such as Taylor and Judd,
definitely a minority position in the 1966 Senate hearings, were destined to fall to the margins of influential public discourse. But in the
wake of the 1989 Tiananmen massacre, it has again become fashionable
to argue that Taylor and Judd were in fact correct and that the views of
the liberal center were tragically misguided. As Miriam London put it
in an article written after the Tiananmen massacre, the China portrayed
by the center was a fantasy created mainly by credulous, opportunistic
scholars:

The fictional land created by these China experts cannot be blamed on insufficient information at the time. The so-called bamboo curtain made information
about the real China difficult but not at all impossible to obtain. For all their
bristling academic credentials, the fact is that the China experts did not wish to
know—but to believe. Like some Soviet experts before them, on whom they
cast no backward glance, they were practicioners of the intellectual pseudo-faith
of the century, dreaming up the City of Perfect Justice on earth. The bamboo
curtain was indeed essential to the believing Sinologists, freeing them to elaborate their fantasies (in their esoteric way, with footnotes) unconcerned by the
intrusion of messy reality or the possibility of verification on the scene.[40]

Are London and critics like her correct? I agree that the story told over the past quarter-century by those she calls the "China experts" was a fiction. But every story about any complex society is to some degree a fiction. Our knowledge of history is gathered *within* history. In the human sciences, we can never attain the total objectivity claimed by natural scientists because we can never completely stand apart either from our own society or the world we are studying. The stories told by Judd, Taylor, and Miriam London and her colleagues are fictions, too. But some fictions are truer than others. In the context of the late 1960s, the stories told by the leading China experts who appeared before the Fulbright Committee were truer than those of their rivals.

The story told by what I have called the liberal center was truer because it led American society to a better self-understanding, a better grasp of the moral dilemmas implicit in its relationship toward China. Scholars of the liberal center were not just sitting in ivory towers and absorbing as much information as possible about China. They were engaged in debate with fellow Americans who portrayed the brutalities of Chinese communism to increase American self-righteousness and paranoia in the cold war. The right wing exaggerated the unity of the Chinese Communist leaders and the gulf between the Communist Party and society. In correcting these exaggerations, the liberal center was pushed into exaggerations of its own. In its rhetoric, it underemphasized the tragic depths of cruelty the Chinese revolution had brought upon the Chinese people, and it overestimated the potential of technical reason to bring peace and prosperity to China.

Still, the story told by the liberal center paved the way for a more constructive relationship between the United States and China than that advocated by the right wing — a relationship based not purely on hostility and fear but also on a modicum of cooperation and mutual understanding. Yet precisely because of its success in allowing the United States to achieve a more relaxed, less bellicose, and more mutually beneficial relationship with China, the story about China told by the liberal center took on a life of its own. It failed to change in accordance with a changing reality. After a quarter-century it has become a hindrance rather than a help in achieving a deeper understanding of China and a deeper understanding of ourselves.

The liberal center's China story did not grow out of the credulity or opportunism of individual China scholars, as Miriam London would have it. It grew out of the commitment of certain scholars, journalists, policymakers, and concerned citizens to maintain the peculiar mix of liberty and order that constituted their major institutions. One can discern their vision of the United States and the nature of their commitment not only in the books and articles they wrote and the speeches they gave but also in the organizations they created to disseminate and implement their views. By the late 1960s and early 1970s there had formed three major national organizations aimed at preparing the way for economic, cultural, and political ties with China: the National Committee on U.S.-China Relations; the Committee on Scholarly Communication with Mainland China (later renamed the Committee on Scholarly Communication with the People's Republic of China); and the National Council on U.S.-China Trade. Each of these had a somewhat different mission and emphasized different interests, but all justified their work on the basis of the story of China as troubled modernizer. Let us take for example the National Committee on U.S.-China Relations.

The National Committee on U.S.-China Relations

To continue the momentum begun by the National Conference on China, to provide resource materials for continuing conferences, and to keep the China issue before the press, there was a need for an ongoing organization. The San Francisco regional office of the AFSC gave Cecil Thomas a mandate to develop such an organization, which came to be called the National Committee on U.S.-China Relations. Once again, Thomas called upon Scalapino to help him. Scalapino recruited old friends Doak Barnett and Lucien Pye, both of whom had spent their youth in China in missionary families and become political scientists specializing in China. Thomas lined up several supporters from the San Francisco business establishment, such as the president of the San Francisco Trade Association and the chairman of Levi Strauss.

A national committee on an issue as important as U.S.-China relations would have to be in close touch with the centers of culture, wealth, and power in the United States — which at that time meant it had to have close ties with the elites of the East Coast. Thomas went east looking for such support and found it in people such as Joseph E. Johnson, president of the Carnegie Endowment for International Peace and chairman of the National Policy Panel of the United Nations Association; Everett Case, president of the Sloan Foundation; Benjamin But-

tenweiser, limited partner of Kuhn, Loeb and Co.; David Hunter, deputy general secretary of the National Council of Churches; Robert
Gilmore, a Quaker who was president of the Center for War/Peace
Studies; Eustace Seligman, partner of Sullivan and Cromwell; and Carl
Stover—all representatives of "substantial business, foundation and organizational communities on the Atlantic Seaboard."[41] There was
sufficient support from this eastern establishment to justify locating the
headquarters of the proposed national committee not in San Francisco
but in New York.

Together with a steering committee and considerable help from Scalapino, Thomas drafted a statement of purpose for the committee and a
list of persons to be invited to founding membership. The statement
went through multiple revisions before attaining its final form:

> The National Committee on United States China Relations believes that we
> urgently need a public discussion of our current China policy: the basic issues,
> present problems, and possible alternatives. Such a discussion is essential in
> terms of our national interest and the peace and security of the world. . . .
>
> The Committee—representing a wide variety of Americans in public life
> from business, labor, religious, academic and nongovernmental organizations—
> exists to encourage and facilitate a nationwide educational program on United
> States China relations. The Committee where proper and feasible will assist con-
> cerned organizations and individuals in such an educational effort.
>
> We do not intend to advocate any policy proposals, but are hopeful that out
> of a national dialogue on the subject there will emerge a consensus as to whether
> any modifications in our existing policies are desirable.
>
> We urge all Americans, who share our belief that public discussion and in-
> creased knowledge and understanding of U.S. China [sic] relations are needed,
> to join with us in this effort.[42]

The response to the letter of invitation came more quickly than expected. By June 1966, sixty people from the list of about a hundred
invitees had accepted. On June 9, the inaugural membership meeting
of the national committee took place in the directors' room of the Sloan
Foundation in Manhattan. Scalapino was appointed chairman, David
Hunter of the National Council of Churches was named vice chairman,
and Cecil Thomas became executive director. That afternoon, at an international press conference, the founders announced the formation of
the National Committee on U.S.-China Relations to the world.

In the rules through which it chose its members and conducted its
business, the National Committee embodied a liberal vision of the
American polity. Only one class of Americans was formally excluded:
officials of the federal government. They were barred, it was explained,

so that the committee could "function as a completely private institution." Yet in its initial statement of purpose, the committee described itself as "representing a wide variety of Americans in public life." It was a "completely private" institution insofar as it did not represent the interests of political officeholders, but it was public in that it represented the voices of independent citizens. It was the embodiment of an ideal liberal image of the American polity: a diverse, democratic society in which citizens governed themselves by deliberating about public affairs and making their views known to the state.

Even as it represented itself as inclusive, though, the National Committee was set up as an exclusive organization. Membership was at first limited to only about sixty people. The size was kept small to facilitate the active participation of members. According to an early brochure, this small body of participants, consisting of a "group of prominent Americans, representative of industry, the academic world, the professions, labor, the churches, and of the nation's major geographic areas," was supposed to represent the United States as a whole. These categories manifested the multidimensional nature of American pluralism. The United States was portrayed as divided into functional sectors (industry, education, religion), social classes (the professions, management, and labor), and geographic regions. There could, of course, have been other ways of cataloging the diversity of American society—for instance, according to ethnic divisions. The committee might have explicitly said that it was going to include prominent Americans representing the Asian-American community as well as whites, blacks, and Hispanics. In internal memos among the committee's leaders at various times, there was some concern that Chinese-American members be included. (The original list of members included one: Professor Tsou Tang of the University of Chicago.) The general stance suggested by the committee's public characterization of itself, however, was that such racial divisions did not represent the United States, or for that matter the world.

The committee also characterized itself as strictly nonpartisan. It was not to be a lobbying group advocating one particular point of view but rather a forum for the expression of a full range of views. "Nonpartisan" did not simply mean "bipartisan." (I once referred to the committee as "bipartisan" to a member of its staff and was quickly corrected.) "Nonpartisan" meant being above politics, above the struggles and unprincipled compromises of organized interest groups. Instead, the National Committee was to reach for a general consensus about national purpose.[43]

How could such a small group of unelected persons formulate an expression of the national interest? The process of active deliberation among well-informed, prestigious citizens representing a full spectrum of views was supposed to lead to an objective understanding of a controversial issue, which would commend itself on its own merits to opinion makers and decisionmakers for the society as a whole. As Robert Mang put it: "The Committee's major, if not only claim to legitimacy, as a new organization in a highly controversial field, was the respectability and the widely representative nature of its membership list. Without a roster that included a credible political spectrum, the Committee's claims to neutrality were open to challenge; without a position of non-advocacy, such a spectrum was unlikely to be obtained."[44]

The National Committee, then, was officially constituted in such a way as to represent the American body politic. It was to be a community of diverse individuals who came together to seek an objective understanding of the facts about China through open discussion in a neutral forum. In reality, though, this formally inclusive polity of rational, free, diverse individuals was made possible because of informal rules for limiting diversity and constraining uninhibited free expression. Mang's history of the National Committee was candid about this point.

It should be noted that "broad political spectrum" was never meant to include those on the extreme right or left. (As can be imagined, some interesting discussions took place on where one draws the line.) This was dictated by the conclusion that neither the Committee's proposed audience of opinion and policy makers, nor its proposed list of prestigious members, would be comfortable with members of either political extreme. It was felt that to ask people who were jealous of their reputations to stand out on a controversial issue was the limit of what could be asked successfully. The fact that membership was invitational provided control.[45]

A society of free people, by this admission, is coherent and effective only if it does not contain people who are immoderate, who are too bound up with moral ("emotional," in the parlance of the academics connected with the National Committee) considerations to carry out reasonable discussions on the basis of the facts. This commitment to moderation, however, is a commitment to particular social circles, particular kinds of friends sharing a particular lifestyle. It entails an ability to discern through "interesting discussions" who fits and who does not.

In this centrist understanding of American society, the open discussion of public issues upon which a democratic government is supposed to be based also depends on a commitment not to speak about everything, to bracket issues upon which agreement cannot be reached. In the early period of the National Committee, such an issue was Vietnam. Wrote Robert Mang:

Perhaps because the staff [i.e., the Mangs and Cecil Thomas] and Scalapino were, from before their Committee association, on opposite sides of the Vietnam issue, it was clear from early on that a "gentleman's agreement" not to use China to argue about Vietnam was essential. This also led to the exclusion from potential membership of any non-specialist who had become too publically tied to a strong position on Vietnam (Dr. Spock being one example).

The importance here was not the issue of Vietnam — it could have been Republican Spain or the Nuclear Test Ban Treaty, depending on the era — but that it was seen as essential to steer as clear as possible of any extraneous controversial issues that could cloud the focus and cause disharmony within the Committee ranks. The organizers agreed to this unanimously, and successfully maintained the discipline of it throughout.[46]

"Discipline" was an important theme in Robert Mang's history of the early days of the National Committee. Discipline was needed not only to keep the committee from getting sucked into the swirling passions of the Vietnam debate but also to steer it clear of the destructive remnants of the McCarthy era. "It must not be forgotten," Mang wrote,

that for all the men and women who signed the committee roster, but particularly for those in the China field, the blight of the McCarthy years was a vivid memory. Though rarely, if ever, mentioned openly, it is difficult to believe that some thought of what such a list would have meant to their careers fifteen years before did not cross their minds as they each made their decision to join. If, at times, a certain paranoia seemed to creep into the evaluation and re-evaluation of every name proposed for membership, of every statement and publication going out in the Committee's name, it was understandable in light of this unhappy heritage. On the positive side, however, this extra caution, which might otherwise not have existed to such a degree, was an important daily discipline for maintaining an unassailably neutral posture.[47]

Where did this discipline come from? It was not based on a simple consensus on values. Key members of the organizing group differed sharply on important national issues and in their professional commitments and religious affiliations. What they shared were character traits common among the "middle-class and middle-aged" of the time: self-discipline, a preference for rational argument rather than emotional confrontation, a desire to improve the world through moderate reform rather than radical upheaval.

These shared character traits were necessary but not sufficient for the effective cooperation of the founders of the National Committee. Also important were the trust and mutual understanding built up by the organizers through years of personal acquaintanceship. By the time they had established the National Committee, they had already been working together for several years on the China question. As Robert Mang put it, "There was a basis of trust based on the kind of judgment each had displayed to the other over the years. . . . Until the Committee took on a publically defined shape, a mutual confidence and trust among organizing members and staff that each knew what needed to be done and how to do it, was almost essential."[48]

At its inception, then, the National Committee was grounded in a particular set of unspoken moral assumptions and practices, which in turn facilitated and were enhanced by bonds of trust among the group of friends who founded it. These particular assumptions contradicted the committee's public assertions of absolute neutrality, total inclusiveness, and openness to all points of view. There were definite limits (though unwritten and often unspoken) on who could become a member of the National Committee and who could participate in its forums.

The existence of limits did not appear to the founders of the National Committee as hypocritical. It was simply a commonsensical, realistic condition for carrying out a dialogue on China free of "emotionalism," the horizon of taken-for-granted, nonrational faith that typically encloses American assertions about the power of reason. This open-ended commitment to rational discussion was consistent with the committee founders' own particular convictions about what the truth actually was. Although the formal purpose of the committee was to discuss different viewpoints about China, observed Mang, "the founding staff members, without exception, and most of the original organizing group, favored a change in policy leading to a 'normalization' of relations with the People's Republic of China." They believed that "the truth will out, if only the truth can be exposed and heard."[49]

This analysis of the structure and operating practices of the National Committee suggests that the story it told was as much about the United States as about China.[50] The idea that China was a complicated society full of diverse individuals fit the centrist perception of *American* society, in contrast to the right-wing perception that there was a conflict between a large mass of red-blooded, patriotic citizens and a small but dangerous minority of crypto-Communists. The idea that China would make progress if it followed the laws of economic and political development corresponded to the idea that the United States had advanced by following just such laws under the guidance of reasonable, scientifically trained experts.

Corresponding to the values of most of those near the top of major American institutions — universities, mainline churches, major corporations, government bureaucracies — this liberal master story about China had a powerful chance of dominating American discourse about China, as long as Chinese society acted in a way that would seem to corroborate it. But in the late 1960s, China was in the throes of the Cultural Revolution, which seemed to contradict everything the liberal center wanted to believe. Revolutionary Redness, not reformist expertise, was the order of the day in China. This contradiction between the story the American liberal center wanted to tell and the realities of China helped make the liberal center vulnerable to a new attack, this time from the left.

China as Revolutionary Redeemer

The story that developed in the late 1960s on the left was that China was, as one advocate recalls, "the redeemer revolution. There was a profound impulse to idealize it, to say that everything about it was progressive and perfect." This revolutionary redeemer nation was the leader in the struggles of the world's poor and oppressed against U.S. imperialism and monopoly capitalism. The Cultural Revolution was a grand experiment in creating a more just society, one that eliminated inequality and achieved authentic participatory democracy, a society in which the aspirations of masses and leaders were unified under the charismatic leadership of Mao Zedong, a society that overcame divisions between mental and manual labor, between moral Redness and technical expertise. This was a China that was rewriting the laws of economic and political development and showing the United States and the West the way toward a more humane future.

Today, no Americans believe this story except small political sects — the Revolutionary Spartacus League, perhaps. But in the late 1960s and early 1970s, this view was widespread among university-educated Americans who identified themselves with "progressive causes," especially with the anti–Vietnam War movement. Like the story about China told by the liberal center, the left's story about China was also a story about America, and it gained its popularity from its resonance with widespread concerns with the moral dilemmas of American institutions.

The most visible new national organization advocating a radical re-thinking of East Asian policy was the Committee of Concerned Asian Scholars (CCAS), founded in 1968. Most of its core members were graduate students in East Asian studies who were also caught up in the antiwar movement.

"CCAS was post–Port Huron, post-SDS," says Marilyn Young, who was an early active member of the organization and eventually an editor of its bulletin. "SDS [Students for a Democratic Society] was basically focused on American domestic issues; CCAS was concerned with anti-imperialism." Like the National Committee on U.S.-China Relations, the CCAS had its origins in a conference — in this case, a "Vietnam cau-cus" held during the 1968 annual convention of the Association of Asian Studies in Philadelphia. The immediate purpose of the Vietnam caucus was to provide a forum for Asian scholars to speak out en masse against the war, but it ended up launching an evaluation of the profes-sional "conscience" of Asian scholars. The CCAS was formed as a ve-hicle for this purpose.

Its primary stated objective, like the National Committee's, was edu-cational: "The CCAS seeks to develop a humane and knowledgeable understanding of Asian societies and their efforts to maintain cultural integrity and to confront such problems as poverty, oppression, and im-perialism. We realize that to be students of other peoples, we must first understand our relations to them."[51] However, the form of education the CCAS espoused was different from that attempted by the National Committee. In many respects, its ways of envisioning public education, China, and U.S. foreign policy were the exact opposite of the National Committee's. As with the National Committee, the CCAS's visions of U.S.-Asian relationships were expressed in the very form of the organi-zation.

The National Committee was avowedly elitist, a group of prominent Americans chosen by invitation. By contrast, membership in the CCAS was open to everyone willing to pay the $5 annual dues ("$10 for those with greater resources") and to agree to the statement of purpose. Pro-spective members did not have to be professional Asian scholars (al-though unless they had some commitment to teaching and writing about East Asia, they would not have subscribed to its purposes). Most of the founding members were graduate students or junior faculty mem-bers at major research universities such as Harvard, Columbia, Michi-gan, Berkeley, and Stanford; but many later members were "indepen-dent scholars" who had dropped out of graduate school or failed to get tenure. The most important qualification for membership was not a socially conferred distinction but a voluntary commitment to a common statement of purpose.

Unlike the National Committee, the CCAS thus made no pretension at all of political neutrality. By its own description, it was a "scholarly/political organization." Its statement of purpose began: "We first came together in opposition to the brutal aggression of the United States in Vietnam and to the complicity or silence of our profession with regard to that policy. We are concerned about the present unwillingness of specialists to speak out against the implications of an Asian policy committed to ensuring American domination of much of Asia. We reject the legitimacy of this aim, and attempt to change this policy."[52]

Whereas the National Committee made an effort to isolate discussion of U.S.-China policy from discussion of Vietnam, the whole purpose of the CCAS was predicated on a conviction that U.S. relations with East Asia had to be seen as a whole, of which the most morally illuminating part was U.S. policy toward Vietnam. The National Committee sought to carry out an objective debate based on expert knowledge and thus "devoid of emotionalism"; the CCAS embraced moral passion, the passion of young people who faced the real possibility of being sent to fight in a war they did not believe in.

Whereas the National Committee attempted to represent all major segments of American society, the CCAS claimed to speak for only one segment: the victims of poverty and oppression. "Like so many white groups in the anti-war movement," wrote Jim Peck, one of the most articulate voices in the organization, "we came to political awareness on the backs of the Vietnamese and the blacks. Without their success in beginning our liberation, CCAS would have little prospect of being anything else than an intellectual ornament, a gadfly and a way station for those on their way to fulfilling more important 'professional' obligations."[53] The National Committee described itself as national, but the CCAS described itself as *inter*national. It aimed to bring together Americans involved in anti-imperialist struggle with those oppressed by imperialism around the world.

The National Committee claimed to be "completely private" and above politics because it included no officeholders in its membership and received no money from the government. Conversely, the CCAS boasted of being engaged in politics despite including no officeholders and receiving no government money. The "Statement of Directions" published in the first issue of the *CCAS Newsletter* (later called the *CCAS*

Bulletin) declared: "Politically, we submit that Asian scholars are, in fact, involved in politics, that we acknowledge this, and that we address ourselves to the issue of how we are going to be political."[54]

The liberal ideals enshrined in the National Committee's constitutive documents rested on unspoken moral understandings, which set practical limits on the realization of those ideals. The same was true for the CCAS. However, these unspoken understandings worked in opposite directions in the two cases. The National Committee stressed pluralism but in fact limited the diversity of its members; the CCAS stressed commitment to a common objective, but its membership was in fact more diverse than the organization's statement of purpose might have indicated. Although most students of contemporary Asian studies at the nation's major campuses joined, they varied in how thoroughly they believed in the part of the statement of purpose that read: "We recognize that the present structure of the profession has often perverted scholarship and alienated many people in the field."[55] Many of them in fact would eventually go into established positions in that profession.

As time went on, there were sharp debates within the CCAS on many issues, including how to evaluate the Chinese revolution and what kind of policy toward China to advocate. As with most leftist organizations during the 1960s, these debates were much harsher, more emotional, and more overtly moralistic than those carried out in associations such as the National Committee. Yet the CCAS did not break apart.

What held it together was a kind of bonding resembling that found in the National Committee: bonds of trust and understanding built up through close interaction among people of a common social class and generation. However, whereas the National Committee was mainly an organization of the "middle-class and middle-aged," the CCAS was mainly an organization of the middle-class and the young. Remembers Marilyn Young, "We talked about how old people were, the music they listened to, whether they smoked dope or not."

The main experience they shared was a sense of alienation from their faculty mentors. Part of this was due to graduate students' dependence on their mentors throughout the American academic system. In the field of contemporary Asian studies in the 1960s, that dependency was even greater than it is now. The field of contemporary Chinese studies was relatively new; it had only recently begun to expand rapidly because of funding from the Ford Foundation and the National Defense Education Act (which provided scholarships for study of languages, such as Chinese and Vietnamese, that were considered important for American national security).[56] Most of the research money was funneled through a handful of senior professors, including John Fairbank at Harvard, Doak Barnett of Columbia, and Robert Scalapino at Berkeley, all of whom knew each other and cooperated closely. If a certain mentor had a low opinion of a particular student, word would travel quickly among the small circle of senior figures, and the student might have a hard time getting a job. (In its early years the National Committee maintained a speakers' bureau on Chinese affairs. In connection with this purpose, it created a central file of almost all China scholars, including graduate students, who might be potential speakers. The entries for graduate students and junior scholars included comments by their senior mentors on their academic promise and political judiciousness.) Experiences of dependency are usually powerful incubators for the seeds of resentment.

To this resentment must be added the general anger felt by 1960s youth against their elders, intensified especially by the fear that the youth were being asked to die in a war the elders had started. The specific dependency of graduate school resonated with a more general feeling of being dependent on a dangerous political system created by the earlier generation. The revolt against such dependency was carried out in the name of the freedom that America was supposedly all about.

The notion that China was a revolutionary redeemer seemed to make sense in terms of the moral experience of young Americans in this situation. It helped them give voice to some of the contradictions they perceived in their country. American institutions promised freedom but demanded discipline, and the rules of discipline worked to the advantage of those at the top of the hierarchies rather than those at the bottom. In the Cultural Revolution, China seemed to be promising liberation from such oppressive institutional constraints. It seemed to give American youth something to hope for.

From what we now know about life in China during the Cultural Revolution, it is clear that the China story told by the American new left in the 1960s was a fiction, even further removed from reality than the stories told by the right and the liberal center. In the late 1960s and early 1970s, though, the left's story could seem very plausible to intelligent, serious young people who prided themselves on being well informed and critically rational, subjecting what they wanted to believe to tests of the facts. Information coming out of China was very meager and hard to interpret. If one read the available documents, one would receive a huge dose of propaganda about the Cultural Revolution. To get an inkling of what was happening to ordinary people in China, one had to search out tiny scraps of information buried within the propaganda, a task requiring cultural and linguistic skills beyond the reach of the vast majority of Western scholars. Even when it was within their reach, any conclusions drawn from such shards were bound to be speculative and tentative. In the anti-authoritarian climate of the 1960s, younger scholars mistrusted senior scholars who might have been able to extract such information. Indeed, the polarization of the era sometimes pushed them to believe just the opposite of what their mentors told them. The young scholars ingested huge quantities of propaganda, which they wanted to believe anyway and against which they were defenseless. They accused more experienced China experts of building out of extremely ambiguous evidence a speculative picture of the possibilities of China's modernization while ignoring vivid tales of revolutionary aspiration staring them in the face.

Social Fictions and the Limits of Understanding

By the end of the 1960s, then, Americans were faced with three main competing master narratives about the direction of Chinese history, stories grounded in different understandings Americans had about the crisis within their own institutions.

For all their differences, though, the stories shared certain common limitations grounded in the structure of American society itself. They all postulated that both China and the United States, as different as they were, could fit into a universal model of the good society. Right-wing spokesmen such as Walter Judd assumed that most Chinese were "free and friendly people," presumably like Americans, and that they would manifest these virtues once they were liberated from the wicked Communists. Left-wing utopians like those associated with the early days of the CCAS believed that the Chinese had developed a universal model for revolution that was applicable to all countries, even one as different from China as the United States. And the liberal center assumed that there were universal laws of economic and political development that China would have to follow eventually.

These were the assumptions of a superpower culture, of a society that aspired to unite the whole world under its leadership and saw itself locked in deadly competition with a Communist rival that claimed to do the same. As U.S. hegemony has waned in the past generation, these axioms are starting to be questioned. Now that nobody believes that Leninist communism is a path to the good society, perhaps we can entertain the idea that American-style liberalism isn't for everybody, either. Perhaps there are different paths to a good society.

The three stories of China also took for granted a high degree of national unity, not only for China but also for the United States. They assumed that the same political culture could be found everywhere in China. Politics were defined in terms of clashes between some unitary traditional Chinese culture and Communist ideology, between revolutionary rebels and capitalist roaders,[57] or between ideologues and pragmatists. They did not imagine China in terms of clashes between ethnic groups or even between regions, reflecting a tendency to view American culture as all of a piece. None of the three main stories of China considered the perspective of Chinese-Americans relevant to the debate about China, which was dominated by the white middle class. By the 1980s, these assumptions, too, would begin to be challenged, especially by the ascendancy of Asian Americans but also by the general interpenetration of economies and cultures in the Pacific Rim. There would arise a need for new public stories about how the United States — or different parts of a multifaceted United States — could relate to a multifaceted China.

The three major stories about China that shared the public forum in the late 1960s were all fictions, all socially constructed. They all accounted for enough observable facts about China that each could be considered plausible by reasonable people. But the story told by the liberal center was destined to gain hegemony in American public discourse. As we shall see in the next two chapters, it did so partly because it better stood the test of the facts as they increasingly became available in the 1970s. But it was also because, for a time at least, it fulfilled the moral aspirations of at least one of its rivals — the left — better than that rival's own story could.

3

Nixon's China

Propagation of a Liberal Myth

In the late 1960s, the liberal China myth began to take root among small circles of influential Americans. In the 1970s, it spread beyond these circles and gained political power by stimulating the imaginations of millions of ordinary Americans. This sequence of events was propagated by a spectacular, larger-than-life event, what one might call a "mythical fact" — Richard Nixon's 1972 journey to China.

Facts and Myths

To dominate public discourse, a master narrative about a society's place in the world has to accord with that society's dominant values — or at least with the dominant values of a hegemonic social group. But I do not intend to advocate a completely relativistic view of knowledge. To maintain its dominance, such a story must in some sense accord not only with social values but also with the facts.

But what is a "fact"? Contemporary Western philosophy is rife with debate about this.[1] I will define "facts" in terms of practices. In human affairs, a fact is an external response to some action, a response that determines whether the action succeeds or fails. If we try to accomplish something in China, our initiatives may or may not evoke a cooperative response from our Chinese counterparts. To be able to act consistently, we need to know the facts relevant to our intentions: that is, whether or not we can regularly expect a hostile or a cooperative response.

But, as we have also seen, the "facts" about a complex society such as China are almost always ambiguous: They are generalizations derived from a variety of specific initiatives, and they have different levels of meaning. When we try to reach out to any such society, whether intellectually, economically, or politically, we encounter many different responses at different times, and we combine these responses into overall conclusions about what we can expect in certain circumstances. Moreover, because individual actions are usually part of some larger project, we can describe them in terms of either immediate goals or broader intentions. When describing our actions in terms of broader intentions, we tend to broaden our language as well: For instance, instead of saying, "I negotiated successfully with this Chinese official," we say, "Our two governments negotiated an agreement" or, even more grandly, "Our two nations reached a mutual understanding."

To give coherent direction to our action, we create the kinds of overarching stories I have described. These master narratives — dramatic, emotion-laden — are based upon "mythical facts" — facts involving large, morally ordered collectivities: nations, peoples, societies. Mythical facts are built upon smaller, more pedestrian facts — the actions of particular individuals under particular circumstances. Once a master narrative becomes established, it takes more than a few contradictory pedestrian facts to discredit it. When, in the wake of an event such as the Tiananmen tragedy, a major shift takes place in our understanding of a society, we can always point to small facts that have been widely known for years and that in hindsight confirm our new perspective. But at the time these pedestrian facts first became known, they were not seen as discrediting our basic story line about China. The master narrative can be changed only by a collectively experienced, emotionally and morally charged triumph or frustration — what I have called a mythical fact.[2]

In 1972, the American public experienced such a mythical fact — Richard Nixon's triumphant journey to China. Nixon and Henry Kissinger seemed to have demonstrated that China would respond cooperatively to initiatives that represented the vital national interests of all Americans. Through the power of the mass media, they gave millions of Americans a feeling of vicarious participation in these successful events. Transformed into a mythical fact, Nixon's China initiative helped establish the credibility of the liberal center's story about China, much to the delight of the middle-class and middle-aged scholars, journalists, businesspersons, and bureaucrats who were its principal supporters.

Nixon in China was a complicated, multilayered fact, the top layer being the mythical one. At the most basic level, Nixon and his assistant Henry Kissinger met with Zhou Enlai and Mao Zedong and got them to cooperate on the basis of a mutual interest in checking the power of the Soviet Union. This we might call the geopolitical level of Nixon in China. At another level — which we might call the "spectacular" level — Americans experienced and participated in Nixon's and Kissinger's excitement over this deed. Finally, at what I have called the mythical level, American national interests were reconciled at least partially with China's national interests.

The Geopolitical Revolution

In the wake of the Tiananmen massacre, Nixon wrote: "China has a limitless capacity to fascinate. But it is not Disneyland. It is, as it has been since 1949, a communist dictatorship held together by brute force. . . . Those who insist on romanticizing relations between nations will always be disappointed when the realities of national self-interest and survival inevitably intrude."[3] Thus spoke Nixon, the master of geopolitics — one of the many, often contradictory Nixons that inhabited this extraordinarily complex man. China policy was the greatest of triumphs for the geopolitician Nixon. But it was also, as we shall see, a triumph for one of the other Nixons — Nixon the romantic, the Nixon that Henry Kissinger portrayed as brooding alone, late at night, "sitting solitary and withdrawn, deep in his brown stuffed chair with his legs on a settee in front of him, a small reading light breaking the darkness, and a wood fire throwing shadows on the wall of the room. The loudspeakers would be playing romantic classical music, probably Tchaikovsky. He was talking to me, but he was really addressing himself."[4] Nixon's diplomatic breakthrough with China had a powerful impact on Americans' understandings of their place in the world precisely because it was not pure geopolitics — it was romantic adventure as well, Disneyland and realpolitik. To see how this combination came into being, let us examine its separate elements, starting with the geopolitics.

Within three months after taking office in 1969, Nixon and Kissinger, his national security adviser, had taken their first, extremely tentative steps toward changing U.S. policy toward the People's Republic. In order to disquiet the Soviets, Nixon wanted to create the impression that the United States was exploring moves toward China. Accordingly, Kissinger initiated an interagency study of China policy. In March, border clashes between Soviet and Chinese troops on the frozen Ussuri River turned Sino-Soviet hostility into an international crisis. Under these circumstances, the mere hint that the U.S. might be changing its attitude toward China sparked expressions of anxiety from the Soviet leadership. Slowly, Nixon and Kissinger worked to exploit that anxiety.[5]

By July, when Nixon visited foreign capitals around the world, he was "leaving visiting cards for the Chinese at every stop."[6] In October the Chinese leadership seemed to pick up one of those calling cards. The president of Pakistan, Yahya Khan, passed a general message to the Chinese leaders about U.S. willingness to improve relations. The Chinese requested that he ask U.S. leaders to be more specific. Wrote Henry Kissinger, "Thus began an intricate minuet between us and the Chinese so delicately arranged that both sides could always maintain that they were not in contact, so stylized that neither side needed to bear the onus of an initiative, so elliptical that existing relationships on both sides were not jeopardized." By the end of 1969 it had become apparent, to Nixon and Kissinger at least, that "China, too, had made a strategic decision to seek rapprochement with us."[7]

Within the U.S. government, however, there were widely differing views about what should be the basis for this rapprochement and how it should be pursued. According to the State Department's China experts, for example, the key to ending hostility between the two countries lay in resolving bilateral issues between them. Progress in Sino-American relations would be "identified with a renunciation of force in the Taiwan Strait, participation in arms control negotiations, or assurances of peaceful conduct in Asia—none of which Beijing (Peking) would even consider except in a wider context."[8] For most State Department experts, the key issue dividing the United States and China was the status of Taiwan—and that issue was in the short term unresolvable, for obvious reasons. The PRC had long and vehemently insisted that the fundamental precondition for any reduction of its hostility toward the United States was the latter's renunciation of its 1955 defense treaty with the government of the Republic of China on Taiwan.

In the United States there was little mainstream political support for an abrogation of that treaty. A multitude of commercial and cultural ties connected the United States and Taiwan. The Republic of China had been an old and faithful ally, and it was represented by an extraordinarily well-connected and well-financed lobby in the United States. Support for Chiang Kai-shek's regime was a central, sacred, passionately held principle of the conservatives who provided Nixon with key political support. And although there was sometimes sharp debate within the liberal center on what conditions should be accepted for an improvement of relations with China, most favored some version of a "two China" policy that would allow the United States to maintain good relations with both Taiwan and the People's Republic.

Thanks to the dialogue that had been established by groups such as the National Committee on U.S.-China Relations, few Americans were willing to accept Chiang Kai-shek's contention that the PRC government was fundamentally illegitimate and that the United States should aid him in retaking the Chinese mainland. However, if it was a sacred principle for both Mao Zedong's government and Chiang Kai-shek's government that Taiwan was an inalienable part of the Chinese nation, it was also a sacred principle for the United States that defense treaties were to be faithfully honored. The United States was fighting a terribly costly war in Vietnam because, its leaders said, it had made treaty commitments to South Vietnam. It was precisely through its array of defense treaties that the United States assured the allegiance of small states around the world.[9] This network of alliances constituted the sinews of American empire, the basis for its ability to maintain order in the world. An important reason the United States fought in Vietnam was to assure its various treaty partners that it was a reliable ally. As Dean Rusk put it twenty years later in his memoirs, "When an American president makes a commitment, what he says must be believed. If those opposing us think that the word of the United States is not worth very much, then those treaties lose their deterrent effect and the structure of peace dissolves rapidly."[10]

Such moral considerations precluded U.S. acceptance of the PRC's principal demands about Taiwan. For the State Department's China experts, there could be no dramatic improvement in U.S.-China relations, at least until the passing of the old-guard leaders of the Republic of China and the PRC. For Kissinger and Nixon, however, the possibility of a U.S.-China relationship rested on a fundamentally different basis, a common interest in checking the power of the Soviet Union. As they saw it, this common interest was more important than all the other factors that had divided the two countries.

The truth of this assertion was by no means obvious, though. In 1970, Chinese propagandists continued fiercely to condemn American imperialism and to denounce "U.S. occupation of China's sacred territory Taiwan by armed forces." Kissinger often had to dig far beneath the surface of Chinese official communications to discern hints of some interest in a changing relationship with the United States. The examples given in his memoirs of reinterpretations of Chinese documents seem labored, even far-fetched.[11] In any case, at the time they did not seem plausible to many China experts at the State Department. It seems that for Kissinger and Nixon, the theory and practice of geopolitics, at least with regard to China, did not derive inductively from indisputable facts; the facts appeared only in the light of theory and practice. The theory and practice in a sense *created* the facts; they helped to bring into being, in both the United States and China, interests that neither side was initially aware of, at least not clearly.

A major breakthrough in the U.S.-China relationship came a few minutes after 6:00 P.M. on December 8, 1970, when Ambassador Agha Hilaly of Pakistan delivered a handwritten note to Henry Kissinger from the Pakistani president, Yahya Khan. It contained a personal message to Richard Nixon from the Chinese premier, Zhou Enlai. China, the message said, "has always been willing and has tried to negotiate by peaceful means. . . . In order to discuss the subject of the vacation of Chinese territories called Taiwan, a special envoy of President Nixon's will be most welcome in Beijing."[12] Kissinger characteristically found a deeper meaning beneath the surface of this message.

To be sure, the purpose of the meeting was said to be "the vacation of Chinese territories called Taiwan." But I considered this a standard formula, perhaps to ensure against leaks or bad faith in Washington; it was less a breach of ideological purity to couch the invitation to the archenemy in such terms. Mao, Lin Biao (Lin Piao), and Zhou Enlai (Chou En-lai) would not associate themselves with any invitation patently incapable of fulfillment. To be eager for the visit of an American emissary they had to be driven by some deeper imperative than the future of one of China's provinces; it had to involve the security of China itself.[13]

The reply drafted by Nixon and Kissinger was sent to Zhou Enlai via the Pakistani president, unsigned and typed on plain white paper without a letterhead or a United States government watermark. The State Department was not informed. The reply indicated a willingness to engage in high-level discussions in Beijing "on the broad range of issues which lie between the People's Republic of China and the United States, including the issue of Taiwan."[14] Thus began a complex process of secret diplomacy extending through the first half of 1971.

Though conducted in secret, this process was not without public manifestations. The most spectacular public event was the "Ping-Pong diplomacy": In April 1971, at the World Table Tennis Championships being held in Japan, the Chinese team (acting, it appears, under the instructions of Mao Zedong himself) invited the U.S. team to visit China.[15] As Kissinger puts it, "Like all Chinese moves, [this invitation] had so many layers of meaning that the brilliantly painted surface was the least significant part."[16] The American Table Tennis Association reciprocated by inviting the Chinese team the following year to the United States, and the National Committee on U.S.-China Relations, to the immense excitement of its directors and members, was selected to manage the visit.

The secret diplomacy reached a climax on July 9, 1971, with a clandestine trip by Kissinger to Beijing. The two-day meeting — codenamed "Polo" by its U.S. planners — concluded successfully, leading to the following surprise public announcement of July 15:

Premier Zhou Enlai and Dr. Henry Kissinger, President Nixon's Assistant for National Security Affairs, held talks in Beijing from July 9 to 11, 1971. Knowing of President Nixon's expressed desire to visit the People's Republic of China, Premier Zhou Enlai, on behalf of the Government of the People's Republic of China, has extended an invitation to President Nixon to visit China at an appropriate date before May, 1972. President Nixon has accepted the invitation with pleasure.[17]

It was, as Kissinger put it, "the announcement that shook the world." It was a revolution in diplomacy — a geopolitical revolution.[18]

"Geopolitics" was a new term in public discourse, representing a new approach toward foreign policy introduced by Kissinger and Nixon. "[A]n essentially geopolitical point of view," Kissinger lamented, "found no understanding among those who conducted the public discourse of foreign policy in our country. There is in America an idealistic tradition that sees foreign policy as a contest between good and evil. There is a pragmatic tradition that seeks to solve 'problems' as they arise. There is a legalistic tradition that treats international issues as juridical cases. There is no geopolitical tradition."[19] For Kissinger and Nixon, the success of their China initiative proved that there should be such a tradition. What exactly does geopolitics mean?

Geopolitics is balance-of-power politics, carried out consistently and globally. Geopoliticians see the world as a Hobbesian arena filled with competing states, each striving to maximize its power. A stable world is one in which these competing states reach an equilibrium. It is the task of a geopolitician to make accurate assessments of where his or her state stands in relation to the global balance of power and to carry out policies aimed solely at maximizing that state's power position. Most competent diplomats throughout history have been guided by such balance-of-power considerations. In the 1930s, in his classic book *Moral Man and Immoral Society,* the American Protestant theologian Reinhold Niebuhr quoted with approval a German author who declared, "No state has ever entered a treaty for any other reason than self interest," and who added, "A statesman who has any other motive would deserve to be hung."[20]

What distinguishes "realists" such as Niebuhr from geopoliticians such as Nixon and Kissinger? The difference lies in the single-mindedness with which each claims to pursue the balance of power. In the words of Kissinger, the chief requirement of geopolitics was to "purge our foreign policy of all sentimentality."[21] He applies the term "sentimentality" very widely, referring to many people who surely saw themselves as hardheaded rationalists. Labeled as sentimental were not just ill-informed demagogues but also meticulous China experts who undoubtedly knew more about China's history and politics than Kissinger did and bureaucrats who thought the United States should honor its treaty commitments to Taiwan. Any intellectual position influenced by one's peers within a bureaucratic office tends to be called "sentimental," as is any position based on legal or moral grounds rather than pure expedience. Sentimentality in this universe of discourse is a large nebula of concepts including everything from impulsive emotionalism to entrenched habit to carefully considered moral commitment. It is set against the shining star of single-minded calculation of strategic self-interest. Geopolitics represents a move away from a Lockean vision of a social order dependent on legally enforced contracts legitimized by voluntary agreements between self-interested parties to a Hobbesian view emphasizing only stalemates in a "war of all against all."

In his Chinese counterparts, especially Zhou Enlai, Kissinger found what he called "natural geopoliticians." In long discussions, he and they arrived at a mutual understanding of common geopolitical interests — chiefly the need to check the power of the Soviet Union — which constituted the basis for a productive cooperative relationship. The quality of this relationship, as Kissinger described it, fit the requirements of geopolitics perfectly: "There were no reciprocal commitments, not even an attempt to develop coordinated action. A strange sort of partnership developed, all the more effectual for never being formalized. . . . Two great nations sought cooperation not through formal compacts but by harmonizing their respective understanding of international issues and their interests in relation to them. Cooperation thus became a psychological, not merely a legal, necessity."[22]

Of all governments on earth, the Chinese state in the early 1970s was perhaps the ideal partner in such a pursuit of geopolitics. The Chinese leaders ruled absolutely, above any law, unconstrained by any public opinion. Having severed almost all diplomatic relations during the Cultural Revolution, they were unencumbered by treaties, alliances, and other international commitments. They were shorn of all the distracting responsibilities that Kissinger called "sentimental."

Because the Chinese were so secretive, Kissinger and Nixon could begin a dialogue with them outside the view of all people with "sentimental" attachments. Only a handful of close aides knew anything about the plans for Kissinger's secret flight to Beijing. Away from any public scrutiny, a framework for Sino-American cooperation could be built from scratch with no considerations other than the leaders' perceptions of their mutual interests.

Kissinger marveled at how the "subtle" Zhou Enlai carried no cumbersome briefing books to their discussions, only a sheet of paper with some handwritten notes scribbled on it.[23] Zhou could do this because, for the time being at least, he did not have to answer to any constituency except Chairman Mao. Although the Chinese negotiators were bemused by Kissinger's massive pile of briefing papers, they found their task simplified by the way the Americans had organized the initiative. As one of them, Zhang Wenjin, put it to me, "We on the Chinese side didn't understand much about American society. Even now it is difficult to understand [how institutions such as Congress influence foreign affairs]. With us, it was much simpler. If Zhou Enlai and Chairman Mao approved, it would be done. But we figured that since Nixon was anticommunist, if he was in favor of this initiative, it would pass."

Through the process of secret, unencumbered, one-on-one negotiations, the top officials of the Chinese and U.S. governments could find a basis for cooperation based on a "psychological" perception of mutual interests. They could even bring to the foreground common interests that had long been subordinated to other considerations. According to a member of that first Chinese negotiating party, Kissinger "wanted us to help solve the problem of Vietnam. We wanted to talk about Taiwan."

Although "very capable and very sincere," Kissinger was "also very pushy. We found him hard to take. But Premier Zhou told us that we should have patience with him." Having exercised such patience and achieved a degree of mutual forbearance, the two sides were able to focus on their common desire to check the power of the Soviet Union. On this basis they were able to build a framework for cooperation. That was the "fact" established through the practice of this rarefied, pure form of geopolitics.

But whose interests were being expressed? Kissinger assumed they were the interests of "two great nations." But how did he know that his interests, articulated in secret without consultation with the separate branches of the U.S. government or even his own foreign affairs bureaucracy and without a survey of public opinion, were the same as the interests of the United States or for that matter of the Chinese nation? He assumed that the interests of the state were the same as the interests of the nation — a problematic assumption, especially vis-à-vis a Chinese state profoundly estranged from its people in the aftermath of the Cultural Revolution. He also equated the interests of a few top officials of the state with the interests of the state itself — another problematic assumption, especially for an American state that constrains its officials by bonds of legality and democratic accountability.

For this undisputedly successful stroke of geopolitics to receive public support in the United States, it would have to be made into a different level of fact, a more ambiguous level constituted by an aura of public feelings and interpretations rather than by discrete, verifiable actions. A successful geopolitical gambit between top government officials would have to become a successful encounter between two great nations — two hitherto estranged peoples with distinct values and interests but seeking common ground. Nixon seems to have sensed this need better than Kissinger. Once Kissinger had engineered the geopolitical breakthrough, Nixon turned to assistants such as H. R. Haldeman, John Ehrlichman, and Ron Ziegler (who had begun his career as a public relations officer for Disneyland) to transform secret geopolitics into public spectacle through the media.

To the initial chagrin of both Kissinger and the Chinese, Nixon's advisers quickly concocted elaborate proposals to make the trip, as one aide put it, into "one of most exciting events in TV history."[24] The Chinese were astonished by the size and the technical ambitions of the advance party for the trip — one plan would have preempted every telephone line in Beijing. Kissinger was at times dismayed that some of

Nixon's attempts to dramatize the event endangered the conditions for effective geopolitical diplomacy. For instance, Nixon initially wanted Kissinger to hold his secret meeting with Zhou Enlai somewhere outside of China, so that Nixon would be the first U.S. official to set foot on the soil of the People's Republic. Kissinger simply ignored Nixon's request.[25]

Nixon's Adventures in China: A Televised Spectacle

For the American public, Nixon's trip to China was a spectacular fact that riveted their attention in a new way on China. Mediated through television, the journey became a collectively experienced triumph, a successful national encounter with an exotic country. It could be experienced as a triumph because it was a romantic fact, drenched in sentiment, as well as a geopolitical one. It was the romantic dimension of Nixon's journey to China that enabled it to grab the American imagination and to convince most Americans that their interests were being served through Nixon's and Kissinger's geopolitical machinations.

The romance was not just a product of television coverage. It was also part of the experience of the officials who went to China, of the antisentimental Kissinger as well as Nixon. In both Kissinger's and Nixon's memoirs, the most lyrical passages are those dealing with the journey to Beijing. Consider Kissinger's description of the beginning of the "Polo" trip:

It is not often that one can recapture as an adult the quality that in one's youth made time seem to stand still; that gave every event the mystery of novelty; that enabled each experience to be relished because of its singularity. As we grow older we comfort ourselves with the familiar for which we have developed rote responses. In the same measure, as the world becomes more routine time seems to speed up; life becomes a kaleidoscope of seemingly interchangeable experiences. Only some truly extraordinary event, both novel and moving, both unusual and overwhelming, restores the innocence of the years when each day was a precious adventure in the meaning of life. This is how it was for me as the aircraft crossed the snow-capped Himalayas, thrusting toward the heavens in the roseate glow of a rising sun.[26]

A "precious adventure in the meaning of life"—this trip was more than just a clever piece of diplomatic business! As an act of geopolitical diplomacy it was indeed masterly and of great importance for the strategic position of the United States. But from the perspective of America's dominant values, there was something sordid about this dance with China's dictators, people who, as Nixon described them in 1989, held their country together by brute force. Kissinger and Nixon were in effect ratifying the defeat of two decades of U.S. efforts in Asia. The United States had backed the losing side in the Chinese civil war. Then for twenty years it had spent hundreds of billions of dollars and sacrificed tens of thousands of lives to contain and perhaps to "roll back" communism in Asia. Nixon had built his political career by condemning fellow Americans who had allegedly been insufficiently committed to this task. Now it was time to change course.

"We were in a period of painful adjustment to a profound transformation of global politics," wrote Kissinger;

we were being forced to come to grips with the tension between our history and our new necessities. . . . I was convinced that the deepest cause of our national unease was the realization — as yet dimly perceived — that we were becoming like other nations in the need to recognize that our power, while vast, had limits. Our resources were no longer infinite in relation to our problems; instead, we had to set priorities, both intellectual and material. In the Fifties and Sixties, we had attempted ultimate solutions to specific problems; now our challenge was to shape a world and an American role to which we were permanently committed, which could no longer be sustained by the illusion that our exertions had a terminal point.[27]

Geopolitics amounted to what Kissinger called "diplomatic judo," enabling the U.S. government to maintain its dominance in a world it could no longer control by overwhelming force. Americans may have rightly felt a satisfying sense of relief in lowering their expectations from the days when journalists like Henry Luce could proclaim that they had entered the "American Century." But this wasn't exactly a triumph.

Nixon, however, clearly viewed it as a triumph. When, on the night of June 2, 1971, Kissinger handed him the letter from Zhou Enlai inviting the president to meet with the Chinese leaders in Beijing, Nixon — as he recounted it in his memoirs — said,

"Henry, I know that, like me, you never have anything to drink after dinner, and it is very late, but I think this is one of those occasions when we should make an exception. Wait here just a minute." . . . I found an unopened bottle of very old Courvoisier brandy that someone had given us for Christmas. I tucked it under my arm and took two large snifters from the glass cupboard. As we raised our glasses, I said, "Henry, we are drinking a toast not to ourselves personally or to our success, or to our administration's policies which have made this message and made tonight possible. Let us drink to generations to come who may have a better chance to live in peace because of what we have done."

As I write them now, my words sound rather formal, but the moment was one not just of high personal elation, but of a profound mutual understanding that this truly was a moment of historical significance.[28]

What about the China initiative evoked such sentiment in Nixon? What made it into a "precious adventure in the meaning of life" for Kissinger? Precisely, I think, its quality of adventure: Nixon and Kissinger as Marco Polos. It was this quality of adventure, the China initiative as an "errand into the wilderness," that captured the public imagination of Americans. The hero of Kissinger, the geopolitician, was Metternich. But Metternich does not commonly inspire the American imagination. Americans do not make movies and TV miniseries about him. They do about Marco Polo.

Webster's Dictionary defines "adventure" as "an undertaking involving risk." In the language of Western literature, however, adventures are defined in terms of risks that pay off. Stories about risks that don't are usually called tragedies. Adventures are voluntarily undertaken trials in which the hero grows by courageously challenging fate.

The China initiative possessed many elements of this adventure motif. It was risky. The safeguards of normal diplomatic procedure were abandoned. It required boldness. And it was successful. Most Americans like to think of themselves as having undertaken adventures, even when they have minimized most risks — for instance, by taking a package tour of an exotic foreign country. Adventures magnify the self. Often in their imaginations people amplify the adventurous aspects of pedestrian things they have done.

Both Kissinger and Nixon seem to have done so in their accounts of the China initiative — especially Nixon. Consider his rendition of the advice given to him by André Malraux, the great French writer and friend of China's top leaders. A few days before leaving for China, he invited Malraux to the White House.

Malraux had known Mao Zedong and Zhou Enlai during the 1930s and had kept up intermittent contact with them through the years. His description of the Chinese leaders in his *Anti-Memoirs* was among the most valuable and fascinating reading I had done in preparation for my trip.

. . . I asked Malraux for his impressions of Mao. . . . Malraux rushed on with a torrent of words and ideas.

"You will be dealing with a colossus," he said, "but a colossus facing death.

The last time I saw him he told me, 'We do not have a successor.' Do you know what Mao will think when he sees you for the first time," he asked. "He will think, 'He is so much younger than I!'"

That evening at a dinner in his honor in the Residence, Malraux advised me on how to approach my conversation with Mao.

"Mr. President, you will meet a man who has had a fantastic destiny and who believes that he is acting out the last act of his lifetime. You may think he is talking to you, but he will in truth be addressing Death. . . . It's worth the trip!"

I asked him again what came after Mao. Malraux replied, "It is exactly as Mao said, he has no successor. What did he mean by it? He meant that in his view the great leaders — Churchill, Gandhi, de Gaulle — were created by the kind of traumatic historical events that will not occur in the world anymore. In that sense he feels that he has no successors. I once asked him if he did not think of himself as the heir to the last great Chinese emperors of the sixteenth century. Mao said, 'But of course I am their heir.' Mr. President, you operate within a rational framework, but Mao does not. There is something of the sorcerer in him. He is a man inhabited by a vision, possessed by it."

. . . Later, over coffee, Malraux told me, "You are about to attempt one of the most important things of our century. I think of the sixteenth-century explorers, who set out for a specific objective but often arrived at an entirely different discovery. What you are going to do, Mr. President, might well have a totally different outcome from whatever is anticipated."[29]

Kissinger characteristically offered a less breathless version of the Malraux conversation, noting for example that although many of Malraux's judgments proved "remarkably incisive," he was unfortunately "grossly out of date about China. And his predictions of China's immediate purposes were outrageously wrong."[30] Yet Nixon's imagination characteristically focused on Malraux's description of his journey as a grand adventure, "one of the most important things of our century," worthy of "the sixteenth-century explorers." For someone who grew up modestly in Yorba Linda, California, and sometimes "was awakened by the whistle of a train, and then I dreamed of the far off places I wanted to visit someday,"[31] the trip to exotic Beijing to see a colossus acting out the last act of a fantastic lifetime must indeed have seemed like one of the greatest adventures of the century. There was enough that was novel, exotic, perhaps even dangerous about it to make it appear adventurous to people who really wanted to see it that way.

This was a case where Nixon's sensibility resonated with that of a broad cross-section of the American public. Millions of ordinary Americans, who must have had their own childhood fantasies of visiting far-off places, were perhaps starved for excitement in a world that by the early 1970s seemed to be closing in on them, a world where many foreigners no longer welcomed them, a world where they had been humiliated by a determined enemy in Vietnam. Millions of Americans wanted to believe that the China initiative was a grand adventure. And through television, they were able to feel part of it.

The Nixon visit to Beijing was the first major diplomatic event of the age of global telecommunications — the first event since the development of communications satellites enabled live broadcasts from around the world. The Nixon administration, hostile to print journalists but somewhat more confident of its ability to manipulate television journalists, invited a preponderance of the latter to Beijing. "The television spectacular built around a diplomatic spectacular did not just happen," according to columnist Don Oberdorfer. "The White House and the major TV networks have been working hand-in-glove for many months to bring it about." [32] In one of the first major examples of the new era in Sino-American relations, Chinese officials, too, worked hand-in-glove with the White House and the American media. From the moment that Nixon and his wife descended the steps of Air Force One to shake the hand of Zhou Enlai (Nixon had ordered his entourage to stay inside the plane so that at that moment the television spotlight would be solely on the couple),[33] the Chinese officials complied with Nixon's public relations ambitions by staging a series of spectacular events for the American party — lavish banquets with strangely delectable foods served in magnificent halls, visits to the Forbidden City, the Great Wall, the misty lakes of Hangzhou, and other imposing and exotic monuments to an ancient past.

The television news coverage invited the American public imagination to soar. Middle America could travel along with the poor boy from Yorba Linda on a great voyage of discovery to a strange new land, to break down walls of fear and ignorance, to negotiate a new structure of peace with the representatives of a great people who had through unfortunate misunderstandings recently become estranged, and to open up new opportunities for security and prosperity for future generations of people throughout the Pacific. Television coverage was not really necessary to create the impression that Nixon was leading the nation on an adventure in diplomacy across the Pacific; even if there had been only newspaper coverage, I believe, the public, along with Nixon, would have understood the journey to Beijing to be a great adventure. But television made this adventure into a powerful collective experience, a spectacular fact that for a whole generation shaped the story Americans told themselves about their relationship with China.

Television coverage framed the event as a daring enterprise in which all risks paid off. All of the equipment for satellite transmission had to be brought into Beijing. Its use was under the control of Chinese officials. Completely unfamiliar with conditions in Beijing, reporters and technicians moved along paths carefully laid out by the government. "We created a kind of Potemkin village for the American press," laughed one of the Chinese officials who had planned that visit twenty years later. "There was the possibility of a kind of social discipline that is not possible now. So when Nixon went to the Great Wall, he was surrounded by friendly crowds. We had swept the road to the Great Wall clean. Everything was orderly. It wouldn't be possible to do that now." What the American public saw was what top officials in both China and the United States wanted them to perceive: a spectacular, ritual-laden encounter between two teams of leaders representing fully the interests and sentiments of two great nations embarking on a new era of mutual understanding.

The rapprochement with China became a complex, spectacular fact that combined geopolitical practices with romantic gestures. Thus, what amounted to a series of political defeats for the United States could be experienced as a moral victory. The new relationship with China was possible and necessary because the United States was no longer as strong as it had been in the 1950s. Its empire was in decline. Through what Kissinger called "diplomatic judo,"[34] the U.S. government coped with this loss of power by establishing a new relationship with China. But the American public did not see this as merely making the best of a bad situation.

In the end, the China initiative was a collectively experienced triumph not because it was a strategic retreat, an adjustment to a new balance of world power, but because it was a journey toward a new frontier. This, in Kissinger's acute analysis, is what gave meaning to the pursuit of power that was the geopolitical goal of the initiative: "The fundamental objective of both sides was not territorial but geopolitical. Each had concluded that it needed the other for maintaining the balance of power. China's need was somewhat greater from the point of view of security, ours from the point of view of psychology."[35] And what were these psychological needs? "The drama of ending estrangement with this great people, in human terms and for what it meant to the global prospects of peace, would be a breath of fresh air, a reminder of what America could accomplish as a world leader. To do so in the midst of a divisive war would prove to ourselves and others that we remained a major factor in world affairs, able to act with boldness and skill to advance our goals and the well-being of all who relied upon us." [36]

By Kissinger's admission, then, in forging a new relationship with the Chinese government, he and Nixon had to act not simply as geopoliticians, soberly calculating balances of power, but also as psychologists and dramatists, forging a romantic bond between their individual efforts and the feelings of an adventure-hungry American public.

Political power, whether domestic or international, is not something that can be measured and calibrated in scientific fashion; it is a psychological and moral state, a sense of accomplishing common goals in a way that makes the members of a society better people. But the strategic, therapeutic, and histrionic dimensions of politics do not easily mesh; indeed, they often work at cross-purposes. (Unfortunately, modern political theory by and large lacks a conceptual framework for understanding the interaction among these different dimensions.) In the case of Nixon's China initiative, these dimensions happened to complement one another nicely. In the case of some of his other political adventures, as we shall see, they did not, leading to Nixon's downfall.

From a purely geopolitical point of view, it would have made good strategic sense to carry out a rapprochement with China even if Nixon — and the American public — had admitted that the Chinese leaders were brutal dictators with the blood of millions on their hands. To have admitted this, however, would not have satisfied American psychological needs and moral purposes. And if the China initiative had not been psychologically and morally satisfying, it would have aroused deep dissension that would have weakened Nixon's geopolitical hand. Therefore, Nixon and Kissinger were strongly motivated to pay attention to the more positive qualities of their Chinese counterparts.

Nixon described Mao Zedong in much more favorable terms in his memoirs than he did from the hindsight of 1989. Central to Nixon's account in his memoirs was the idea that he was testing his own and his country's mettle by entering into conversation with an awesome giant of history. He did more than solve a troublesome foreign policy problem by developing a working relationship with this giant; he achieved a kind of mythical glory simply through his association.

Just when many Chinese had begun to feel profoundly disillusioned by the cult of Chairman Mao, Nixon seems to have fallen under its spell. Consider Nixon's description of his meeting with Mao:

We all sat in overstuffed armchairs set in a semicircle at the end of the long room. While the photographers continued to bustle around, we exchanged bantering small talk. Kissinger remarked that he had assigned Mao's writings to his classes at Harvard. Indulging in characteristic self-deprecation, Mao said, "These writings of mine aren't anything. There is nothing instructive in what I wrote." I said, "The Chairman's writings moved a nation and have changed the world." Mao, however, replied, "I haven't been able to change it. I've only been able to change a few places in the vicinity of Beijing."

As Nixon's meeting with Mao drew near its conclusion, Nixon offered this bouquet of sentiment to the chairman:

"I would like to say, as we finish, Mr. Chairman, that we know you and the Prime Minister have taken great risks in inviting us here. For us also it was a difficult decision. But having read some of your statements, I know that you are one who sees when an opportunity comes, and then knows that you must seize the hour and seize the day."

Mao's face beamed when the translator came to these words from his own poem.

Nixon concluded the session with Mao with this final statement:

"Mr. Chairman," I said, "your life is well known to all of us. You came from a very poor family to the top of the most populous nation in the world, a great nation.

"My background is not so well known. I also came from a very poor family, and to the top of a very great nation. History has brought us together. The question is whether we, with different philosophies, but both with feet on the ground, and having come from the people, can make a breakthrough that will serve not just China and America, but the whole world in the years ahead. And that is why we are here."[37]

Nixon seems to have convinced himself that for all their differences in ideology he and Mao were kindred spirits sharing one of the most fundamentally American of traits — upward mobility. In Nixon's view, they had both started out poor and made themselves great, and because of that each had a special claim to representing his people. Yet one senses in Nixon's remarks a note of envious awe. Born into a working-class family, he had become president of the United States. But Mao had been born into a peasant family and had become a colossus! One gets a similar sense of deferential identification in Henry Kissinger's remarks about his opposite number, Zhou Enlai. Kissinger described Zhao as "born of a middle class family . . . a brilliant student" with a cosmopolitan education, who eventually became one of the subtlest geopolitical thinkers Kissinger had ever met. Kissinger made Zhou's career sound very much like his own; if anything, Zhou's looked even better. Kissinger thought him "one of the two or three most impressive men I have ever met. Urbane, infinitely patient, extraordinarily intelligent, subtle, he moved through our discussions with an easy grace that penetrated to the essence of our new relationship as if there were no sensible alternative."[38]

In fact, neither Mao's nor Zhou's background was parallel to that of his American counterpart. The Mao family's large, rich peasant household in Shaoshan, Hunan province, lived a fundamentally different lifestyle and, for its time, enjoyed a considerably higher social status than did the Nixon family in Yorba Linda. Zhou Enlai had come not from China's middle class but from a rich gentry family. Moreover, for all of their politeness, the Chinese leaders may not have thought Nixon and Kissinger equal to them. What Nixon called Mao's "self-deprecating" remarks about his writings may have been a kind of condescension. In Chinese culture, old men often affect such patronizing politeness toward younger people whom they perceive to be beneath them. Nixon, after all, like tribute bearers of old, was making the journey to the Middle Kingdom to visit China's supreme ruler — who lived now in Zhongnanhai, a part of the old imperial palace.

From Spectacular Fact to Mythical Fact

In Nixon's and Kissinger's idealized understandings of their opposite numbers lay the beginnings of a new sentimental mythology of China that dominated American thinking about that country for two decades. In this mythological construal of what Nixon called "the week that changed the world," the People's Republic was not just a piece in a complicated geopolitical chess game; it was a great nation with a natural affinity for Americans. In some respects its leaders and its people were even better — smarter, grander, more disciplined, more subtle — than most Americans. Interacting with them could spur U.S. leaders to bring out the best in themselves and inspire the United States to bring out the best in itself.[39]

If this was a fiction, it was not the product of Nixon's and Kissinger's mendacity. I believe that they were quite sincere in their assessments of the Chinese leaders — if they deceived the American public, this time at least they had the courtesy to deceive themselves first. This mythical understanding was a product of Americans' credulity. Most wanted to believe the good news about China that Nixon and Kissinger proclaimed with all their public relations skills. Given the horizons of American self-understanding, a basically positive view of China was indeed necessary if Americans were to have a psychologically and morally satisfactory relationship with it.

Central to this self-understanding is the idea that the United States is founded on certain universal human values. It is a "new nation," a nation of immigrants. To be an American is not simply to share a certain ethnicity or a common history but rather to subscribe to certain ideals. Thomas Pangle described well the special kind of patriotism that such a national identity evokes:

America is not a traditional society, and therefore its patriotism must be of an untraditional kind. To a perhaps unparalleled degree, this nation is founded on the contention that patriotism must express more than simply loyalty to one's own, that it must express loyalty to what is good, and some truly self-conscious awareness of the possible tension between what is one's own and the good. . . . The Declaration by which Americans made themselves independent marked the birth of the first nation in history explicitly grounded not on tradition, but on appeal to abstract and universal principles of political right.[40]

If the United States was to have more than just a geopolitically useful agreement with China, Americans would have to believe that the Chinese also embraced these universal principles, at least in some primitive and obscure way — or that they would embrace them once they learned about them.

"One result of this trip, we hope," said Nixon to American television reporters interviewing him on his visit to the Great Wall, "may be that walls erected — whether physical like this wall, or whether they are other walls, ideological or philosophical — will not divide the people of the world."[41] What captured the American public imagination was just this aspect of the China initiative. But if there were no ideological or philosophical walls, didn't that mean that in the long run there should be one reigning ideology? And, given American self-understandings, wouldn't that ideology eventually have to be basically . . . American?

In their accounts of their China initiative, Nixon and Kissinger often noted that they were dealing with Communists with fundamentally different ideological views. Nonetheless, there is the sense that the top Chinese leaders were reasonable people who were not just using the Americans for their own purposes but were in some way open to American values. They seemed to share with Americans common sensibilities, common aspirations and experiences. The leaders were not aristocrats but ordinary people who made good. They represented the aspirations of millions of people wanting to become modern and to have a better life. In a world without walls, wouldn't such people, or their successors, adopt the same ideas about progress or liberty that Americans cherish?

All of these assumptions were based more on American moral needs than on accurate information about Chinese society. We now know that there was extraordinary estrangement between the Chinese rulers and their society. In the 1980s, village studies, urban histories, and personal memoirs alike showed that after enduring the brutal traumas of the Cultural Revolution most ordinary citizens were sullen, fearful, and cynical about their government. (Some of the reporters who so helpfully showed the American press corps around the "new China" had in fact been released from exile in the countryside just for that purpose.) Meanwhile, the top levels of the Party and army were consumed with overt and covert factional intrigue much more like the court politics of a decaying imperial dynasty than anything in the political experience of the modern West.[42]

Information about all of this was publicly available, at least in a general sense, at the time Nixon journeyed to China. (For instance, the *China News Analysis,* published biweekly by Laszlo Ladany, the Hungarian Jesuit China watcher in Hong Kong, provided what in retrospect appears to be generally very accurate information about such problems.)[43] But Nixon, Kissinger, most American China scholars, and the American media did not focus their attention on it at the time of Nixon's visit. Those who did, primarily the right wing and the Taiwan-sponsored China lobby, were seen as having a political ax to grind — as wanting to stop the rapprochement with China. Even that fact confirms my argument. For the American public, it was not enough to say that there were good geopolitical reasons for undertaking a cooperative relationship with the Chinese government, even though that government was led by a gang of thugs. If one was to play geopolitics with it, one had to think of it as a basically good — or at least reformable — government that represented the general interests of its people.

Mainstream, middle-class Americans wanted to believe that the People's Republic of China was good because they needed to believe that their own values were good and effective. They wanted to believe that their government represented their basic values. They wanted to believe that their president and his advisers were expressing basic shared values in dealing with foreign countries, not just engaging in geopolitical machinations to enhance the government's power. They wanted to believe that when their official representatives shook hands with and offered laudatory toasts to foreign leaders, those leaders were people that ordinary, decent Americans would be proud to have as friends. Americans wanted — needed — to believe that once their values received a fair hearing, they would win the hearts of all good people.

They needed, in short, to create a new mythical understanding of China to sustain their mythical understanding of themselves. Collectively held myths enable a society to understand the linkage of the individual pursuit of self-interest with pursuit of the common good. In the case of China, they enabled the public to see and feel a connection between Nixon's geopolitics and the values that should guide national purpose. In a *Washington Post* column written "en route to Beijing" with President Nixon in 1972, journalist Joseph Kraft chronicled the genesis of this mythology, noting that

all of us, from the President on down, are reaching, trying to connect up the unknown with the familiar. In the process, there is already emerging a new myth about China.

It is the myth of China as a great power, able to shoulder some of the security burden borne for so long by the United States in the Pacific. It is a myth that is going to be very hard to down, for solid reasons cause Americans to itch for self-deception on China.

The central fact about relations between this country and China is that we are not much mixed up in each other's affairs. American security does not depend, in any clear and present way, on what happens on the mainland of Asia. Neither does American economic, cultural, or moral well-being.

Precisely because we're not deeply engaged, China has been for American opinion a focus of narcissism, an occasion for striking self-adoring poses. The Chinese provide a stage for acting out, without having to pay for it, our own notions of American generosity and disinterest and concern for the underdog. . . .

The new myth, while not so easy to pin down, can be palpably felt in conversations with the White House staff and the press entourage accompanying the President to China. The immense achievements of the Chinese revolution seem to be accepted on faith. There is a strong disposition even to believe that there has been brought forward in China "a new Maoist man."

Between Mao's China and Nixon's America there are suddenly seen all sorts of harmonies.[44]

Ironically, the creation of this new myth was being undertaken in the name of liberation from myths. In the early 1970s, a common theme in public discourse about China was the need to overcome myths. As Hans

J. Morgenthau put it, in a foreword to Tsou Tang's *America's Failure in China,* "What most of us think about our relations with China partakes of the quality of myth, and it is indeed a pernicious myth. It meets our emotional needs but not the requirements of right judgment and correct action. . . . Only a small and almost inaudible minority have dared to look at the historic record with dispassionate objectivity."[45]

Once the veil of myth was pierced, this rhetoric suggested, China could be seen and dealt with in a rational manner. Clearheaded realists like Kissinger saw themselves as solving the problem of China by perceiving China precisely as it was, without illusions. It is part of America's mythology that its citizens can and must face the world *without* myths, armed only with the enlightened power of reason. The story I have told would suggest, to the contrary, that any nation, even the United States, is held together by stronger cultural cement than reason. What appears to be politically rational behavior is actually driven by common stories about the origins and destiny of the nation, about its place within the larger community of nations and within the process of history. These mythical master stories provide the nation with its fundamental conceptions of collective identity and therefore of its national interests. They represent the assumptions underlying rational political action and the ends toward which it is directed. They embody the moral force that impels citizens into politics and the goals that beckon them. In order to meet the demands of a constantly changing world, myths need to be revised through public debate and criticism. When Americans exhort one another to discard myths in favor of rational knowledge based on facts, they all too easily believe that they have discovered the "real" truth — and then ironically become prisoners of the new mythical world they have created.

As Joseph Kraft described them, the older myths Americans once held about China had proven dangerous, even disastrous:

The open door policy was the first example of the myth-making bent. It rested on the implicit charge that the wicked Europeans and Japanese were illegitimately carving out for themselves hunks of Chinese territory. We Americans, in high-minded contrast, pledged ourselves to maintain the "territorial integrity" of China.

But from the turn of the century through 1950, no regime in China could even begin to assure law and order. The true choice for foreigners was either intervention or abandonment of all interests. That fact the United States recognized in practice by repeatedly winking at various incursions — particularly by the Japanese.

But for our own self-esteem, we kept bright and burnished the legend of

China's "territorial integrity." In the name of "territorial integrity" Washington took many of the steps that led to Pearl Harbor. With the same thought in mind, this country, during the war years, heaped upon Chiang Kai-shek's China great-power attributes, including membership in the National Security Council, which now seem absurd.

With the collapse of Chiang's regime, another myth was served up—the myth of aggressive Communist China, sponsor of subversive wars in Asia and Africa and the forcer of the revolutionary pace on the Soviet Union. . . .

This country convinced itself that it was helping peace-loving smaller nations stand up to the Chinese bully. Our presence in Southeast Asia was thus invested with the powerful moral purpose that worked to drive the country so deep into Vietnam.[46]

Would the new myth be better? In the early 1970s, it was better than its alternatives. History has proven, I believe, that it was in the best interests of both the United States and China to enter into the working relationship established by the Nixon visit. Given the character of American self-understandings, that relationship entailed the construction of a new myth about China. But would the United States and China again become prisoners of this myth, or would they be able to construct better understandings of themselves and each other through this new relationship?

Myth and Misdemeanors

Myths are essential to human life. They focus our attention on common goals and enable us to hope. But attention focused on one goal is attention directed away from other, perhaps more important, goals. Worse, the hope that myths inspire may be unrealistic hope. So, essential as they are, our myths occasion the danger of tragedy.

Perhaps the first tragic victim of the new American myth about China was the man whose spectacular achievement did so much to help bring it into being—Richard Nixon. After his trip to China, Clare Booth Luce told him that every person in history can be summed up in a single sentence and that his would be "He went to China." But in an interview with *Time* magazine two decades later, Nixon noted that the sentence that summed him up now was "He resigned the office."[47] There was no direct connection between the China initiative and Watergate, of course. But the understanding of the United States' place in the world, and of the president's place in the United States, that was brought to life in the China myth was a dangerous understanding for a president to work within. It encouraged unrealistic expectations of the president, and it encouraged irresponsible behavior on the part of the president.

Consider the expectations generated by the most tangible result of the "week that changed the world," the diplomatic document known as the Shanghai Communique. Most of this document had been negotiated during Kissinger's preliminary visits to China, but its crucial sections on Taiwan remained to be worked out during long negotiating sessions between Kissinger and Zhou Enlai that were not concluded until hours before the signing of the document. An unusual document in the annals of diplomatic history, it was not a vague statement of areas of agreement but a frank listing of principled differences in how the two governments viewed the world. A final section described areas where the two countries' interests were congruent enough so that cooperation would be mutually beneficial. The key area of agreement was that neither side "should seek hegemony in the Asia-Pacific region and each is opposed to efforts by any other country or group of countries to establish such hegemony"—a reference to the interest of both sides in limiting Soviet expansion in the region. The most difficult area on which to reach agreement was the status of Taiwan. The formula that broke the impasse on this issue was the following:

The United States acknowledges that all Chinese on either side of the Taiwan Strait maintain that there is but one China and that Taiwan is part of China. The United States Government does not challenge that position. It reaffirms its interest in a peaceful settlement of the Taiwan question by the Chinese themselves. With this prospect in mind, it affirms the ultimate objective of the withdrawal of all U.S. forces and military installations from Taiwan. In the meantime, it will progressively reduce its forces and military installations on Taiwan as the tension in the area diminishes.[48]

In effect, the U.S. government affirmed the legal status of China as a sovereign nation-state and the attendant right to settle its conflicts with the province of Taiwan as an internal matter. This was a sacred principle for China. But at the same time, the United States was saying that international law was only of secondary importance in a world governed by geopolitics. As a practical matter, the national interests of powerful states were the deciding factors for action in such a world, and the United States had a national interest in keeping China from reannexing Taiwan by military force. The Chinese leaders accepted this because, in the near term at least, they needed the cooperation of the United States to contain the threat of Soviet power. Someday, perhaps, the logic of geopolitical power could be superseded by the logic of international legal principle. But once law has been systematically subordinated to the requirements of politics, it can be difficult for legal principle to gain precedence over power—as Nixon's second term would soon demonstrate.

The Shanghai Communique turned out to be the basis for a very effective working relationship with the government of the People's Republic of China. It demonstrated that good could be accomplished in international affairs by systematically working outside the law. Politicians representing democratic nations have always had to balance the demands of power with the requirements of law. Yet they have usually averred that, in principle at least, power and law should be reconciled. In both theory and practice, geopolitics denied this principle. What mattered was power, not "sentimentalities" like the law. The China initiative succeeded because the United States descended to China's own level. American propagandists had long branded China an "outlaw nation." But in international affairs, at least, the U.S. leaders seemed to agree with Chairman Mao's famous dictum that "political power grows out of the barrel of a gun." In this case, outlaw diplomacy seemed justified because it produced good results: a productive working relationship with China, which was welcomed by much of the American public.

The process of secret diplomacy that led up to the breakthrough with China also demonstrated how much good could be accomplished if statespersons could operate outside of their own government's framework of regulations. Bypassing official procedures, Nixon and Kissinger relied on foreign friends to pass secret documents written on plain paper, devoid even of a White House watermark. They systematically withheld knowledge of what they were doing not only from the American public but also from responsible officials in their own administrations and from the leaders of important allies. In an interview with Oriana Fallaci, Kissinger once described himself as a "cowboy who leads the wagon train by riding ahead alone on his horse."[49] In their China diplomacy, he and Nixon were indeed like the individualistic cowboy heroes of the old frontier, acting alone, standing outside of established institutions, righting wrongs by the sheer power and integrity of their characters. "Americans," Kissinger thought, "like that immensely."[50] He and Nixon may have ignored cumbersome bureaucratic regulations, but they did good: They affirmed central moral aspirations of the American Dream.

Their success, turned into a fact of mythical stature, seemed to demonstrate, if not a formal legal connection, at least a natural resonance between geopolitical interests and the interests of both the Chinese and American publics. Perhaps the dramatic success of the China trip encouraged Americans excessively to hope that all of their intractable international problems could be handled with similar brio. Perhaps this tempted Nixon to presume that geopolitical machinations and American public expectations would generally flow together as smoothly as they had with China.

Yielding to the temptation, he entered the slippery slope to tragedy. He had already begun his way down in the fall of 1971, only a few months after Kissinger's triumphant Polo trip to the Middle Kingdom. The eastern part of Pakistan seceded from the western part and became the nation of Bangladesh. By December 1971, a war was on between India and Pakistan. In both the American public and the U.S. government, there was considerable support for India, which though friendly with the Soviet Union (and hostile to China) was after all a reasonably well-governed democracy with many institutional ties to the United States. But Kissinger had relied on Yahya Khan, then the dictator of Pakistan (who in February 1971 had turned his army against east Pakistan, resulting in the massacre of at least 300,000 persons),[51] for help in arranging his secret trip to China. The same geopolitical calculations that had directed the China initiative now directed Kissinger and Nixon to back Pakistan (and China) against India (and the Soviet Union). This "tilt" toward Pakistan was so contrary to the U.S. government's expressed principles and commitments that Nixon and Kissinger wanted to keep the decision completely secret. However, some officials leaked it to columnist Jack Anderson. The resultant public outcry against the tilt toward Pakistan embarrassed the Nixon administration. Outraged by the leak and its consequences, Nixon stepped up the activity of his "plumbers," the extralegal team of investigators he had set up (in July 1971) to discover the sources of news leaks.[52] It was this team of plumbers who less than a year later committed the Watergate burglaries.[53]

Having seen how Nixon's adventure in China produced a new myth and a new collective hope, we can see in his subsequent misadventures a preview of the dangers that such a myth can entail if embraced too uncritically.

4

Hopes and Illusions

The Institutionalization of a Liberal Myth

Nixon's spectacular diplomatic breakthrough helped make the liberal China myth come alive for millions of Americans. For most, the excitement gradually faded as they turned their attention to more local concerns, especially the growing Watergate scandal. Immediately after Nixon's journey to China, three-fourths of all Americans said they approved of the trip. By 1974 (when the Watergate scandal was reaching its conclusion and fewer people were willing to believe that Nixon had ever done anything right), only about half said that they approved of the journey, and a smaller percentage said they had a favorable impression of China.[1] Nonetheless, I will argue in this chapter, the liberal China myth had by now become institutionalized. It had helped to breathe new life into important American institutions — especially academia, but also religion and business — and people closely involved with those institutions thus had an interest in sustaining it.

How did this process occur? I will argue that by helping to revive the American Dream, the liberal master story about China helped to resolve crises in American institutions. To develop this contention, I will have to give a fuller account of the American Dream and develop a fuller theory of American institutions. I will illustrate the argument by examining how three different institutions responded to the opening to China.

Renewing the Dream

As Kissinger suggested in his memoirs, the most important consequence of the new working relationship with China was the least tangible: "The drama of ending estrangement with this great people" was "a breath of fresh air, a reminder of what America could accomplish as a world leader."[2] The new initiative was important, as Kissinger put it elsewhere, because it gave Americans hope.

Hope for what? For nothing less than a renewal of the American Dream. As we have said, this is a dream about individual advancement in a world full of opportunities, a world of open doors. But from the late 1960s on, doors had been closing on Americans around the world. North Vietnamese intransigence had frustrated U.S. military ambitions. The Vietnam debacle was undermining respect for the United States in Europe, and it encouraged nationalistic self-assertion against the United States throughout the Third World. Americans were steadily being forced to recognize, as Kissinger put it, that their power, though great, had limits.

The diplomatic breakthrough with China seemed to reverse that trend. At least in this part of the world, home to a fifth of the world's population, limitations were being lifted, doors were being opened. A favorite American metaphor to describe the significance of the new geopolitical relationship with China was that of "opening"; a characteristic phrase was "the opening of the bamboo curtain" (as in, "Now that the bamboo curtain has been pierced by a Ping-Pong ball. . . .").[3]

The possibility of expanding into new frontiers stirred imaginations throughout the United States. The dreams it sparked were first and foremost ones of individual entrepreneurial success rather than of national glory. In the American Dream, an opening door offers new opportunities for private enterprise. It sets off competition to be among the first to get through the door. Competing in new contests and striving for new goals provide the spice of life in the American Dream. A good society, Americans widely assume, is one that keeps providing such opportunities.

The American Dream is by no means necessarily a dream of rapacious acquisition. Many Americans can be thrilled as much by finding new ways to help others as by finding new ways of profiting from others. Many people who harshly criticized their country's "imperialistic" meddling in Third World nations such as Vietnam became profoundly excited at the prospect of opening new frontiers in China — of being among the first Americans to include citizens of the People's Republic in their circle of friends, to discover new secrets of self-reliant economic development or ancient healing techniques, or to offer effective advice for solving some of China's problems. Other Americans, to be sure, mainly were thrilled at the prospect of making money in China trade. Yet even these businesspeople were often more excited by the chance to expand into a new frontier than by sober calculations of profit. When the Chinese market appeared to open at the end of the 1970s, many American businesspeople rushed into it so hastily that they lost money.[4]

Jan Berris, vice president of the National Committee on U.S.-China Relations and an executive of the organization since the 1971 "Ping-Pong diplomacy," expresses the enormous excitement felt by many Americans involved in the early phases of the U.S.-China relationship — the excitement of opening doors, of rolling back frontiers. The National Committee had been given the responsibility for arranging the reciprocal visit of the Chinese Ping-Pong team to the United States in April 1972. Meticulously organized in cooperation with the American Table Tennis Association (although the National Committee did most of the work) and occurring less than two months after Nixon's trip to China, the visit of the Chinese team was another spectacular media event, with, as Joyce Kallgren put it, "virtually every decision — as to program, travel, translation, as well as other more personal matters — scrutinized and interpreted for insights it might provide into Chinese-American relations."[5] Its highly successful handling of the visit launched the National Committee into the forefront of the complicated new business of managing exchanges between the United States and China.

Echoing sentiments I heard expressed by her colleagues, Jan Berris remembers:

It was exciting to be known as the person who was there at the forefront. I used to feel that it was absolutely astounding for someone from my background — raised in Michigan — getting to know such famous and powerful people. . . . I see what I'm doing more in the sense that it increases the exposure that people have to one another and to one another's society — which helps them understand each other and understand their own society. In the early days of the exchanges — early 1970s — China had a great interest for people. Trips to China were experiences that changed people's lives. And the way the Chinese were treated here renews your faith in America. It was wonderful to see the outpouring of warmth on the part of Americans toward the Chinese. The Chinese saw this too and couldn't figure out how Americans could be so open. They would constantly be amazed at how much time and effort and concern ordinary

Americans showed toward them, taking them into their houses, escorting them around, helping them out. I am very sentimental and romantic and emotional as you can see, and I like to see smiles on people's faces. I see my work as building a core of people on both sides who have had this happy experience of contacting one another, of getting to know and understand one another.

Other people I interviewed about their involvement with the early period of U.S.-China relations may have been less "sentimental" than Jan Berris—they may have been much more concerned with making money than with seeing smiles, for instance—but they were no less enthralled by the powerful hope of expanding themselves, meeting new people, visiting new places, having new experiences in China. Even Americans who did not participate in any direct way could be inspired by knowing that fellow citizens could now expand their frontiers to include China. In the process, their compatriots could vicariously come along with them.

When the first Americans began to go to China in the early 1970s, their hosts were sometimes taken aback by the sheer expansive energy of these foreigners, even when that energy was spent trying to understand and be helpful to the Chinese. It is with a combination of humor and awe that a prominent figure in the Chinese government's Association for Friendship with Foreign Countries recalls the return trip of William Hinton, the dauntless friend of the Chinese revolution whose 1965 book *Fanshen*⁶ glorified the land reform in the north Chinese village of Long Bow: "All day long he went to this place, that place—everywhere—interviewing people. Then he insisted on joining in the farm labor! Every day! Then in the evening he would interview some more people!" At the time of that visit, Hinton's host had only recently returned from a long stint in a "May 7 cadre school," a rural work camp for urban officials, where she had had her fill of manual labor. Though politically correct according to the Maoist ideology of the time, Hinton's exuberant desire to participate fully in the lives of the peasants was more than a little overwhelming to her.

The pioneering American individuals who went to China did not go unburdened, of course; they carried the assumptions of their culture with them. Going into a newly opened China brought immense ego gratification for most Americans, who saw it as a chance to make a little history, to do something important. The peculiar assumptions of their culture stimulated Americans' ambitions about being historical actors and hid from them the difficulties of playing such a role. "The problem with you Americans," several Chinese friends said to me during my visit there in 1988, "is that you have no sense of history." What this observation means, perhaps, is that Americans do not like to think of themselves as being products of history and certainly not as victims of history. But they do like to think of themselves as making history, even when such an aspiration seems naive to people who sense keenly the burden of the past.

The hope engendered by new opportunities to make history was enormously important to Americans, who were increasingly discouraged by signs of a decline in American influence abroad. The urge to see the China relationship as a sign of hope shaped the images Americans discerned in the ambiguous mists of Chinese reality. Thousands of Chinese victims of the Communist Party's capricious brutality regarded their government as an evil monster and their culture as a miasma of corruption and despair. But, flushed with excitement over the opening door with China, many of those cosmopolitan, sophisticated Americans who traveled to China in the mid-1970s did not really want to know about the terrors that lay beyond that door. They focused on the positive side of things. In the Party officials who acted as their hosts and directed their itineraries they saw not Stalinist autocrats but well-intentioned leaders with whom they could cooperate to make a better China. They payed attention not to the cruelties many of these leaders had inflicted (intentionally or unintentionally, directly or indirectly) on the people but to their positive accomplishments: how, compared with the chaotic days of World War II and the Chinese civil war, Chinese society was orderly, most of its people adequately fed and gainfully employed. They saw a hopeful side of the Chinese revolution that even their relatively privileged Chinese chaperones did not see.

It is easy to unearth many books, articles, TV news reports, and documentary films by distinguished and widely respected Americans that in retrospect seem terribly naive about the harsh realities of China. Such materials have been copiously cited in recent publications by Miriam London,[7] Steven Mosher,[8] Simon Leys,[9] Jonathan Mirsky,[10] and others chiding mainstream American China watchers for allowing themselves to be duped about the evils of Chinese communism in the 1970s and 1980s. Why did so many Americans who should have known better allow themselves to be duped? To find an adequate answer, we must consider not only the psychological need some of them may have felt to see hopeful vistas behind the open door — to believe once again in the American Dream. We must consider also the institutional contexts that shaped their motives.

Institutional Revival

The hope inspired by new opportunities in China reinvigorated important American institutions, especially those concerned with the production of meaning. The dynamics of these institutions pressured individuals — especially elites within those institutions — to sustain and indeed exaggerate that hope. To develop my argument about how and with what consequences this exaggeration took place, let me first explain what I mean by institutions and offer a diagnosis of the crisis in American institutions during the early 1970s.

Institutions and the Self. An "institution," as I am using the term here, is primarily a moral enterprise.[11] It is a normative pattern for carrying out certain kinds of activities, a set of rules sanctioned with rewards and punishments for compliance or deviance. American journalism is an institution in the sense that it is regulated by a complex system of written and unwritten rules that specify how journalists should do their work. Chinese journalism is also an institution but one with a different set of rules. American social science is an institution in this sense, and China studies is a part of it. Education, the market economy, religion, diplomacy, the family — all can be thought of as institutions under this definition.

Americans like to think of themselves as self-directors who stand apart from their society's institutions and use the institutions for their own ends. But as my colleagues and I have argued elsewhere, this view of institutions is wrong.[12] We never stand apart from institutions; we cannot keep institutions at arm's length. We live through institutions. They shape our identity, ordering our thoughts and feelings, channeling our ambitions, making us who we are. The fabric of our institutions is the happenstance that stands behind much of our life course, even those aspects of our careers that seem to be the most creative and innovative.

"One thing I found remarkable, as I thought more deeply about it," says one of China's well-known specialists on American society, whom I interviewed in 1988 in Beijing, "was that for all the talk about diversity in America, there [is] a very great deal of consensus about basic values. In America, if your basic values are out of the mainstream, you receive a lot of pressure. There is a lot more consensus about basic values than there is in China." Of course, my Chinese interviewee acknowledged that institutions normally impose much more overt coercion upon their members. But this individual noted with some surprise that American institutions paradoxically impose more apparently *voluntary* conformity than do Chinese ones. American institutions typically channel human action not by forcing individuals to march in lockstep but by encouraging competition among individuals to enact institutional roles. It is this competitive dimension of their institutional life that often leads Americans to think they are not closely tied to institutions but are fundamentally independent of them. Individuals within academic institutions, for example, like to think of themselves as constantly challenging the conventional wisdom in pursuit of their own direct quest for the truth. But it is their institutions that present them with the goal of constantly seeking new knowledge, and it is institutionalized rules of scholarship that determine whether they have in fact triumphed in the competition to find the truth. Often invisibly, institutions provide the sinews of faith, commitment, and consensus that bring order to Americans' desires for individual autonomy.

Crisis of Liberal Institutions. By the early 1970s, American institutions were troubled indeed, their legitimacy cast into doubt, their sense of purpose confused by the controversies of the 1960s. From both the left and the right, critics were assaulting the liberal premises that had been assumed to provide the moral foundation of American institutions throughout the twentieth century.

The norms constituting the major American institutions have been justified on the basis of certain fundamental assumptions about human nature and social value that I have characterized by the term "liberalism." Let me expand and systematize the account of liberalism that I have given in earlier chapters. Among liberalism's main assumptions is the notion that what is most distinctively human is the capacity for instrumental reason, which finds its fulfillment in modern science and technology. Another assumption is that the application of such rationality will lead to constant and universal progress in which the increasing economic abundance produced by a society of diverse but interdependent individuals is complemented by forms of governance that respect the autonomy and privacy of all people. A final key assumption is that individual autonomy — freedom from all external constraint — is an ultimate, universal value. Americans are used to seeing these liberal assumptions as not culturally determined or socially constructed but as self-evident, universally applicable truths about the world.

Some of these key assumptions were explicitly challenged by the Chinese Communists (Mao Zedong even wrote a famous essay, "Combat Liberalism"),[13] who emphasized the priority of social equality over individual autonomy and saw progress as being driven by political class struggle rather than by technological advance. But by the 1970s the ideological challenge of the Maoists was not as important for Americans as the practical difficulties of using liberal assumptions to make sense of an increasingly differentiated and interdependent world. Technocrats who boasted of their reliance on scientific reason had embroiled the United States in a savage and futile war in Vietnam. At home, economic progress turned out to be scandalously compatible with widespread, degrading poverty. Even though American political institutions remained formally democratic, real personal freedom seemed elusive, as individuals faced pressure from massive corporations and a secretive bureaucratic state.

To an important degree, these difficulties had sprung from a decline in the United States' ability to set the terms of its relationship with the rest of the world. Although still the world's wealthiest and most powerful nation, the United States was no longer as dominant as it had been in the two decades after World War II. Increasingly challenged by a rebuilt Europe and a rising Japan, the U.S. economy was unable to expand as buoyantly as Americans expected, raising doubts that poverty and racial tension could be alleviated simply by increasing economic growth. Moreover, Vietnam proved that it was now possible for determined nationalist movements even in technologically backward countries to resist U.S. military power.

Challenges to liberal assumptions threatened the legitimacy of major American institutions. Symptoms of this challenge included turmoil within universities, widespread loss of trust in government (which would reach a high point in the Watergate scandal), and confusion within churches. In the midst of the disorientation and gloom created by this legitimacy crisis, the opening of China offered a ray of hope. It provided a new frontier for creative action in a world where old frontiers had become inhospitable, offering hope that the liberal assumptions of American institutions could be vindicated and the institutions revitalized.[14]

Resolving the Crisis of Institutions. Most Americans who visited China in the 1970s recognized that they were going not simply for their own benefit but also for the benefit of the institutions to which they belonged; whatever good they were to derive from their trip was connected with their ability to improve their institutions. Therefore, they had to ignore less hopeful aspects of Chinese society, especially those that would have cast doubt on the key assumptions of their institutions.

In keeping with the liberal assumption that they are grounded in universal, rationally knowable values, almost all American institutions define their purpose in terms of expansion carried out in the name of progress. Individuals who contribute to an institution's expansion are honored, and it is the drive for such honor (and often its accompanying material rewards) that motivates people to serve the cause of institutional expansion.[15]

Thus, "China hands" who could help institutions expand their scope into China were rewarded; people who dampened the hope for expansion were not. In this way, many American institutions encouraged in their most vigorous, ambitious members an optimism that now seems misguided and irrational; in the name of bringing the United States into closer contact with China, they effectively distracted even very sophisticated Americans from facing up to Chinese realities for a surprisingly long time. Sometimes these institutions maintained this unrealistic optimism even when they seemed to be fostering lively debates.

Three Case Studies

We can see this institutionalized process of embracing illusions most clearly by examining it at work in those institutions focused mainly on meaning, especially the learned professions and religion. Let us then consider the response of three such American institutions toward the "opening of the bamboo curtain": natural science, social science, and religion.

Natural scientists who went to China focused on the triumph of technical reason but ignored the limitations of such rationality in a society as large, complicated, and conflicted as China. Social scientists looked for ways to combine rapid economic modernization with respect for individual integrity, but they averted their gaze from the human tragedy that forced development brings to traditional societies. Religious leaders tried earnestly to detect the presence of their God in a China that defiled much that their faith had taught them to revere.

Natural Science. The opening to China stimulated an extraordinary amount of interest among natural scientists. The National Academy of Science's Committee on Scholarly Communication with the People's Republic of China (CSCPRC) became the main U.S. agency for arranging delegations to China as well as for arranging reciprocal visits to the United States by Chinese scientists. Members of CSCPRC delegations were not "self-selected run-of-the-mill people" with political sympathy for China but rather "first-rate laboratory scientists" (as the former director of the program told me) selected through a peer review process from among the most prestigious members of each discipline.

There were a number of different reasons for American scientists' interest in going to China. Some, such as geologists, oceanographers, and epidemiologists, were looking for new sources of data, new phenomena to study. Here was an opportunity for them to develop their careers by expanding the scope of their disciplines to include data from a hitherto inaccessible part of the world. Others thought they might learn from their Chinese counterparts scientific ideas that had been neglected in the West. For example, some physicians thought the Chinese government's attempt to make its doctors "walk on two legs" by combining traditional medical techniques such as acupuncture with modern techniques might yield new insights about neurology.

Other scientists went to China to expand their reputations. Selection to a delegation was a form of professional recognition, an acknowledgment that one was a leader in one's field. Even when they did not expect to learn much from China, such scholars felt honored by being entrusted with a mission to teach fellow scientists — to begin the process of bringing the Chinese up to world standards.

Senior scientists such as Frank Press, president of the CSCPRC and later the national science adviser to President Jimmy Carter, saw themselves as diplomats of science, indeed almost as missionaries of science. To them, expanding scientific thinking and technological expertise to the ends of the earth was of vital importance to world progress. Science was universal, and one who served science ought to make that universality a reality.

For many Chinese-American scientists, the sense of personal recognition gained by returning to their homeland was especially great. According to a distinguished Chinese-American physicist, part of the reason for wanting so badly to go to China in the early 1970s "was idealism. But it was also because they treated you very well. You were going back to the old country, and they gave you much more lavish treatment than professors [especially Chinese-American professors] are used to getting here in the United States."

At a time when Western assumptions about the importance and efficacy of human technical rationality had come under attack from the counterculture and when American science was being condemned by the left for its complicity with the military-industrial complex, the opening of China was a breath of fresh air. Scientists hoped to find a vindication of reason in the new frontier behind the bamboo curtain. To travel in the name of science on an official high-level scientific delegation to the United States' erstwhile enemy was to demonstrate the ability of science to be a maker of world peace, not a collaborator in the conduct of war.

Through the efforts of Frank Press and its energetic executive director, Mary Bullock, the CSCPRC steadily expanded its budget and its activities throughout the 1970s. The committee's work inspired widespread enthusiasm within both the scientific community and its funding agencies in the U.S. government. It aroused little controversy. Bullock, looking back over her work at the CSCPRC from the 1970s to the mid-1980s, said, "It would be hard to find a job more meaningful than this one."

Still, leading the committee was not without its tensions, especially for someone like Bullock, a historian of China whose work included a book on the Rockefellers' attempts to establish Western-style medicine in China in the early twentieth century.[16] "I feel extremely ambivalent about what we are doing," she said toward the end of her tenure at CSCPRC. Her ambivalence came from her skepticism "about whether Americans can have any long-term influence on China." She reacted very strongly against scientists who tried to work through her committee to exert such influence. Bullock preferred to develop relationships on the basis of reciprocity and mutual interest. In general, she thought natural scientists tended to see their relationships with China in this light, and she took pride in having encouraged that tendency, believing that a harmony of interests among Chinese and American scientists would lead to a convergence of thinking and benefit for all.

The nature of the exchanges between natural scientists seemed to bear this out. In fact, there seems to have been a good fit in the early 1970s between American scientists' desire to expand the scope of their disciplines to encompass China and the interests of their Chinese counterparts. The Chinese scientific community was led by an older generation of individuals, most of whom had been educated in foreign universities and had attained excellent international reputations. They were committed to the idea that science was universal. However, they had suffered grievously from the anti-intellectualism of the Cultural Revolution and from their isolation from peers around the world. In spite of differences in political orientation, they shared with their foreign counterparts a commitment to the universalistic language and values of science.[17]

For these reasons, the new relationship that quickly developed between American and Chinese natural scientists was remarkably harmonious. But would the development of mutual understandings among scientists spill over into the rest of society? Would the triumph of scientific reason in laboratories and universities lead to its triumph in neighborhoods and villages and in the corridors of power? In the early 1970s there were great hopes that this would eventually happen but no data on whether the process had begun. In the 1980s, what is remarkable is how long the hopes continued after the data suggested that they were not firmly founded. It is a testimony not to the power of reason but to the power of faith. The hopes were based on a shared conviction, implicit in the very institutional rules that made possible the practice of natural science as a shared enterprise—a faith that rational knowledge pursued and verified through scientific conventions and extended to a limitless variety of situations could produce universal progress.

Social Science. Social scientists maintained similar hopes based on faith, although they—ironically, especially China experts, whom I will focus on in this section—engaged in more heated controversies than natural scientists about how to understand China. The institutional dynamics of academic China studies determined the nature and extent as well as the limitations of these controversies—for all of the antagonism of the debates, the common view of China emerging from them was in hindsight naively benign.

No group in the United States was more interested in opening a door to China than the China experts. Based, like the natural sciences, on the application of reason to empirical knowledge, American social scientific research thrives on primary data. The institutionalized rules of the discipline reward those who can bolster their theories with as much data as possible. Personally collected data has more weight than data collected by others and reanalyzed by the scholar. Probably the most important institutionalized imperative of social science is to expand the data under its purview. Social scientists who specialized in China were subject to this imperative but frustrated by lack of research access to their area of study. It was hard to be taken as seriously as, say, a specialist on Europe or the United States when one had never actually set foot in China and had to base one's articles on refugee reports, news from the official press, or suspect government statistics. So it was vitally important that a China specialist gain the opportunity to experience China personally—important not only for one's career but also for one's sense of self-worth. As one prominent historian poignantly put it when confronting a suggestion that foreign scholars refuse to go to China because of the Tiananmen massacre of 1989: "Those who want to close off the possibility of going to China have forgotten how keenly frustrated we were before 1972. I will never forget standing on a hill in Macao [in the late 1960s] overlooking China and being reminded of a Jesuit saying: 'Rock, rock, when wilt thou open rock?'"

By 1972 the rock had tantalizingly opened a crack. But Chinese government officials were not especially interested in having large numbers of social scientists—especially China specialists—come through it. Social science in China was in complete disarray in the wake of the Cultural Revolution, and there was no politically acceptable community of social scientists who might have been able to benefit from exchanges with their American counterparts. Moreover, from the Chinese government's point of view there was not much difference between American China specialists and spies.[18]

In response to requests from China specialists that they, too, be allowed to visit China, the CSCPRC laid down a policy that all of its delegations to China should include one China expert. The relevant Chinese leaders accepted, though with some reluctance. But which experts should go? The natural scientists were selected from among acknowledged leaders in their fields; the China specialists should also be acknowledged leaders. This meant that they were to be senior experts from major research institutes.

However, as we saw in Chapter 2, a major struggle had been going on within China studies between younger scholars and their older colleagues, with the young scholars claiming that their greater sympathy for the Chinese revolution and the oppressed in general gave them a better appreciation for China than their mentors possessed. The organizational base of the opposition was the Committee of Concerned Asian Scholars (CCAS).

In 1971, just after the visit of the U.S. Ping-Pong team to China but before Kissinger's secret trip to Beijing, the CCAS scored a triumph. Partly as a whimsical lark, some graduate students working at the Universities Service Centre in Hong Kong—a place from which foreign scholars could do "China watching"—had sent a letter to China requesting permission to visit. Only a few of them were deeply committed activists within the CCAS, but almost all were strongly opposed to the Vietnam War and for that reason at least loosely affiliated with the organization. Accordingly, they proposed to travel to China in the name of the CCAS. In keeping with the spirit of those times, they signed the letter, "in struggle." To their surprise and excitement, the Chinese responded with an invitation.

At that time, officials in the Ministry of Foreign Affairs and the Association for Friendship with Foreign Countries were disposed to invite Americans who were associated with the left. They thought China should stress its support for the left and that, encouraged by visits to China, the American left might influence U.S. foreign policy in a direction favorable to the Chinese government.

As we have seen, the CCAS members were mostly graduate students in the social sciences who studied Asia. They had used their knowledge of China to mount harsh criticisms against their profession, especially the norms that allowed the profession (and their own careers) to be dominated by a handful of senior scholars. Their argument was not a rejection of professional social science but a rejection of the concentration of authority in a few hands. The CCAS claimed that this institutional pattern kept the profession from fulfilling its true purpose: to understand and learn the correct lessons from the Chinese revolution. The elders might claim the CCAS members were naive and untrained, albeit well-intentioned, but these CCAS scholars now had something that most members of the China studies profession hadn't—direct access to the People's Republic, personal experience with the subject of their study. When they were in China, they even were granted an audience with Zhou Enlai.

Although their movements were closely supervised, some of them did get genuine glimpses of the oppressiveness of official control. For instance, a historian remembers noticing a curious boy approach the CCAS group in front of the Beijing Hotel. The official guide accompanying the Americans harshly yelled at the boy, forcing him to steer clear. Now, two decades later, this scholar sees that event as paradigmatic of the way Chinese officials treat ordinary citizens and how they try to hide the truth of their society from foreigners. But this incident was not reported in the book he and his colleagues published after their trip in 1971. That book conveys an extremely positive picture of Maoist China. The historian now downplays his responsibility for the book. It was very heavily edited by some CCAS leaders who had not even gone on the trip — "basically written" by them, he now says — to conform to the CCAS perspective. Nonetheless, he and his colleagues did not fight to have the incident included in their book, and they did not play it up in their public lectures. Perhaps, at the time, they did not fully want to believe it themselves.[19]

The CCAS scholars returned from their journey blessed with a kind of academic charisma. Everyone wanted to interview them. They were in great demand for scholarly lectures. Suddenly these graduate students had more prestige — in some people's eyes, at least — than their mentors had. They seemed to have been propelled to the top of their profession.

Academic radicals were used to thinking of their political activism as a thankless task: Though it was the right thing to do, it was both an expression of their perceived marginalization and a contribution to it. For a brief moment, perhaps, it appeared as though academic radicals — in the field of China studies, anyway — could do well by doing good. Their radicalism would be rewarded by a trip to China, which would put them on the fast track to academic success. But this moment quickly passed.

A year later, in 1972, the CCAS received a second invitation. This time, though, the invitation required the CCAS to select the delegation from among all its members. The first invitation had been tendered simply to those CCAS members who happened to be working at the Universities Service Centre. Some graduate students working there had actually joined the CCAS simply to get in on the trip. But for this second visit, the committee as a whole was to choose the delegation. This set up intense competition, according to one participant in the selection process: "It was considered a very big deal to go, and to be able to go you had to follow the proper ideological line, which also meant being very active in CCAS." The competition entailed all the predictable conflicts over who was genuinely an activist and genuinely a radical. Out of all this came a delegation that was not really unified ideologically; as a result, the visitors squabbled during their trip about how to respond to Chinese authorities and how to interpret what they were seeing.

By this time, though, the Chinese authorities had begun to reevaluate their policies about whom to invite. Because of the relationship established through the diplomacy of Nixon and Kissinger, the Chinese leaders had opportunities to develop productive ties with what they saw to be the mainstream of American life. They began to invite many "old friends" — scholars, diplomats, even foreign missionaries who had lived in China before 1949 and who had good personal relationships with various officials in China, although they may have been critical of Maoist ideology. As one Chinese official in charge of exchanges put it, "From the point of view of China, missionaries were bad. But each individual was different. We saw them as individuals and welcomed them on a case-by-case basis. Some of them were very good friends of China." Because of this change in China's attitude toward foreigners, leaders of the American China studies establishment began to find places on the delegations of natural scientists sponsored by the CSCPRC.

By the time of the third invitation, in 1973, the institutional context of the CCAS's activities had changed. For a China specialist, it was still a prized opportunity to be able to travel to China. Competition for a spot on the new delegation was heavy. The composition of the group was, a former activist now recalls, "one of the big CCAS controversies." But now the Chinese government was (correctly) perceived to be as much on the side of the leaders of the U.S. foreign policy establishment, not to mention the China studies establishment, as on the side of "progressives."[20] Thus, some of the leading CCAS activists argued that there should be no delegation at all to China because China's foreign policy was "incorrect." Observes one member: "In CCAS's view China was supposed to represent a global revolutionary movement. But for reasons of power politics China was against the efforts of the Bangladesh people to secede from Pakistan; they took up Pakistan's side of the conflict, because Pakistan was allied with China against the Soviet Union. . . . In retrospect I think this was arrogant — CCAS trying to 'punish' China for not living up to its expectations." Another CCAS member now speaks of this outlook as the "imperialism of the left," which takes the form of "instruction to other countries about how to be good." The Chinese canceled the trip. There was never again to be an official visit to China by a delegation of the CCAS.

Whence came this "imperialism of the left"? It was not simply the result of the personal predilections of the individuals in the CCAS but a product of the institutional context of China studies in the early 1970s. It was primarily attributable to the way in which the structure of that academic discipline polarized debate and only secondarily a reaction to China. Primarily it represented a reaction of China scholars to one another.

The controversies among China scholars had their origin in ambiguous interpretations of the goals of American academic institutions. The foremost goal, as we have seen, was to achieve progress by expanding scientific knowledge about the world. Scientific knowledge was taken as universal knowledge, basic principles that were valid for all times and places, and as objective knowledge, grounded not in opinion but in systematic empirical research.

How could knowledge of China lead to progress? There were two ways of understanding this. One was to see China as an enemy of authentic progress, the progress that could be achieved under American tutelage in the "free world." This "know thine enemy" rationale was the purpose for much of Soviet studies, and it was the rationale for the National Defense Education Act, which provided funding for many Chinese studies programs. But, in the informed opinions of a wide range of those whom I interviewed, knowing the enemy was never the main purpose of China studies in the United States. As a CCAS member put it — in words that corresponded to sentiments I heard from interviewees on the political center and the right: "The mentality of us China scholars was very different from that of Soviet scholars. We studied about China with people who had loved China . . . people with missionary connections. It was not like the Soviet scholars, who had studied the language and history from people who loved Pushkin but hated much about contemporary Russia. We got from our teachers a profound respect for Chinese civilization and a profound hope for what China might become."

China studies, then, were oriented toward a more positive view of how China could contribute to world progress. Scholars in the center thought the Chinese could learn a great deal from Americans if they diluted their communist ideology with an appreciation of scientific facts about social progress; those on the left thought Americans would learn the secret of genuine progress if only they would listen to Chinese revolutionaries.

Both the center and the left accepted a key assumption of liberalism: that there was in fact a set of universal, rationally comprehensible principles underlying world progress — or "modernization," as it was often called — and that through quasiscientific investigation human beings could discover these principles.[21] But in the circumstances of the mid-1970s, the left's version of this universalism could not compete with that of the liberal center. Activists in the CCAS accused the liberal center of aiding and abetting cultural imperialism because mainstream scholars tried to fit China into the categories of general modernization theory. The CCAS would presume not to teach China but to learn revolutionary lessons from it. But when China didn't have any revolutionary lessons to teach, some CCAS activists presumed to lecture China about the proper political morality of a revolutionary society. In doing so, they discredited themselves and the CCAS, allowing the liberal center to dominate American academic discourse about China.

But suppose that what we think of as progress from a Western, middle-class point of view is not experienced as progress by millions of people whose lives have been uprooted and communities destroyed by modern technology and the modern market economy? Suppose that pressures of modernization — which have been disruptive enough in the West — present non-Western societies with more excruciating dilemmas and engender more profoundly tragic consequences than any of those faced by the West, painful effects that because of the interdependencies of the modern world cannot be avoided? Suppose that in the non-Western world, what we call progress brings out brutal, violent destructiveness among the common people whom we in our democratic idealism see as the beneficiaries? Suppose that in some societies progress produces elites who are more corrupt, cynical, and unscrupulously powerful than any we have had to confront in our middle-class societies? Suppose there are no universal laws of progress, that there is no such thing as progress for all?[22]

If China scholars and other social scientists had asked these questions in the early 1970s, they might have been able to describe the realities of Chinese society more clearly. But then China would have been a much more depressing place to study, and they would have had to rethink the intellectual and moral assumptions behind their professions. Excited by an opening door to China and blessed by considerable ignorance about what lay behind it, social scientists generally stayed away from such uncomfortable and dangerous thoughts. They carried the search for universal laws of modernization into the Chinese frontier.

The institutional pressure to draw hopeful conclusions about the prospects of progress for China even distorted the rhetoric of those liberal centrist scholars with the most astute understanding of China's unique complexities. Consider the account of a 1972 journey to China by John Fairbank, the Harvard history professor who perhaps more than any other scholar was responsible for establishing modern China studies. In his memoirs, published a decade later, Fairbank stressed the ambivalence he felt during that 1972 journey, his first return to China since the Communist victory in 1949.[23] Fairbank had a much clearer sense of the close interrelationship between the bright and dark sides of the Chinese revolution than most younger, radical scholars. He saw clearly that improvements in the rural standard of living had been accompanied by harsh regimentation and fearful repression, especially of intellectuals.

But in an essay titled "The New China and the American Connection," published in the *Foreign Affairs Quarterly* soon after his trip, Fairbank sounded anything but ambivalent:

The people seem healthy, well fed and articulate about their role as citizens of Chairman Mao's new China. Compared with 40 years ago the change in the countryside is miraculous, a revolution probably on the largest scale of all time. . . . The stress and even violence of 1966–69 have now been succeeded, in the aftermath or consolidation phase of this vast movement, by a sense of relaxation and euphoria that makes 1972 a happy time to be in China. . . . From this record, which everyone must balance out for himself, it seems to me difficult not to conclude that the Chinese, despite their blind spots, have the better of the argument. If their highly organized and moralistic efforts at regeneration are to be stigmatized as regimentation, then we must ask whether our own unregimented efforts are equally adequate to our far different needs and circumstances.[24]

In hindsight, revisionist China scholars such as Steven Mosher have accused Fairbank of having Maoist sympathies on the basis of such remarks.[25] The record shows that Fairbank had no sympathies with the brutal side of Maoism.[26] But like most mainstream China scholars of his era, he did want Americans to be excited about China, to see China as sustaining their hopes for the advance of world progress. Twenty years ago it was hard to admit that recent Chinese history could not sustain such hopes.

The explicit goal of American social science was, of course, to produce not hopeful ideas but objective ones, grounded in methodical empirical investigation. The procedures for training graduate students and for rewarding scholarship were based on this goal. But the task of studying China rendered these procedures insufficient for achieving objectivity. Unable directly to conduct research in China, American China scholars had to ferret out hidden shades of meaning in the official Chinese press and radio broadcasts, or they had to rely on the potentially biased accounts of refugees. There were so many ambiguities in this information that younger scholars could easily claim that their mentors' prerevolutionary experience and anticommunist bias were blinding them to the true meaning of the data. The young scholars could also claim that the relationship between their mentors and the U.S. government — most leading China scholars worked, at least from time to time, as government consultants — had biased them against the true meanings embedded in the data, which could only be revealed to those who were sympathetic to China's socialist ideals.[27]

The overall message about China delivered to Americans by social scientific experts was thus a positive one. Academic radicals thought China had done great things; if it had any failing, it was in not being radical enough. The academic center now moved closer to the optimism that had once been the hallmark of the left: In spite of some events of great tragedy in its recent history, China had made great strides toward building a good society and had some important things to teach the West; with the prospects for more openness, the future had become brighter for both societies. In the 1990s, Chinese intellectuals such as Fang Lizhi have chided American scholars for not having recognized the evils of the Maoist regime: "Much of the history of Chinese Communism is unknown to the world, or has been forgotten. If, inside China, the whole of society has been coerced into forgetfulness by the authorities, in the West the act of forgetting can be observed in the work of a number of influential writers who have consciously ignored history and have willingly complied with the 'standardized public opinion' of the Communists' censorial system."[28]

But American China scholars in the early 1970s did not necessarily censor themselves because of careerism. Some of them downplayed the darker realities of the Chinese revolution out of a sense of responsibility to the higher purposes of their work. "We didn't want to discredit the revolution," said one scholar associated with the CCAS. "In our language we buried pieces of knowledge. . . . In our essays there were sentences which were like castors to make things move smoothly along. Somewhere in the work there would be a kind of a sigh." Even those in the center, such as John Fairbank, were concerned that critical remarks about China could fuel the politically destructive hostility toward it that had inflamed the extreme right during the McCarthy era. The future of their professions lay in expanding ties with China. Responsibility toward their professional institutions precluded damaging that fledgling relationship.

For China scholars, then, professionally acceptable understandings of China were based not merely on individual reason but also on socially shared faith and hope, embedded in the purposes and norms of their liberal academic institutions. Institutional differences between social science and natural science made the former more beset by internal debates than the latter. But both institutions sought to expand their scope in the name of progress, leading them to extract a positive, hopeful vision of the future from the dark ambiguities of the Chinese experience.

Religion. This hopeful view of Maoist China was by no means confined to academia. One could find it in institutions that differed markedly from academia in the kind of thinking they encouraged and the kind of people they encompassed. In spite of their enormous differences over how to respond to China, Americans now widely shared a common liberal story about China — a story that imparted a similar focus and direction to the debates taking place within very different institutional spheres.

We have mentioned, for example, the unrealistic optimism that American corporations often manifested toward China in the early 1970s — a subject that is thoroughly, vividly, and humorously considered in Randall Stross's *Bulls in the China Shop.* But to more fully illustrate how a similar hopeful outlook about China pervaded dissimilar institutions, let us consider at greater length the case of American religion.

On the face of it, religious institutions might have been expected to harbor the most critical views of all about China. The Chinese government was, after all, explicitly committed to an atheist ideology. It had expelled all foreign missionaries, cruelly persecuted many of their converts, and during the Cultural Revolution suppressed all religious activity. Although the Chinese government invited some former missionaries to visit as "old friends," it was by no means interested in allowing the resumption of missionary work. Yet among the leadership of the mainline, liberal Protestant churches — which in the 1970s still had the greatest influence among American political and cultural elites — extraordinarily optimistic views of the new China were in vogue.

Like other major Western institutions, the Christian churches are driven by the imperative of progressive expansion: "Go forth and preach the gospel to all nations." For over a hundred years until 1949, American churches had directed their expansive missionary impulse toward China. Now that China was "opening up" — and religious publications tended to use the metaphor of "opening" even more often than secular ones — to the West, how should American Christians respond? Even though there was no hope that missionary activity could resume in the foreseeable future, the churches could not remain indifferent to a whiff of hope that someday Western Christians could bring China within the orbit of their universal mission.

The Chinese revolution had profoundly challenged the Christian understanding of "mission," especially among American Protestants. In the nineteenth and early twentieth centuries, China had been the primary mission field for many of the Protestant denominations. Thousands of American missionaries had devoted themselves to this task using millions of dollars of church money. Yet by 1949 the missionaries seemed to have failed: For all their effort, they had made less than a million converts in China.[29] Then an atheistic regime expelled all foreign missionaries, confiscated their church buildings, schools, and other assets, and persecuted many of their converts. Making matters even more painful to the missionaries, the new Chinese government attacked them spiritually, accusing them of cultural imperialism. There was enough truth to the latter charge to cause pain to the consciences of some missionaries, especially those from the mainline denominations. During the 1950s, the National Council of Churches—the umbrella ecumenical organization for the mainline churches—sponsored a study about lessons to be learned from the mission to China. The report concluded that missionaries had all too often been arrogant, culturally insensitive, and insulated by affluent, privileged lifestyles from the ordinary people of China. However, evangelical Christians (especially those near the fundamentalist end of the evangelical spectrum) were more likely to place the blame for their setbacks on the diabolical stratagems of atheistic communism.[30]

By the mid-1960s the divisions between liberal and evangelical Protestants began to be replicated within the Catholic church. An older generation of Catholic missionaries who had served in China tended to be deeply anticommunist. But by the mid-1960s, inspired by the Second Vatican Council, there had arisen a new generation of Catholic clergy and laity whose views about missionary work in general and China in particular more closely paralleled those of liberal Protestants. Indeed, by the early 1970s, some of these progressive Catholics had begun to cooperate with liberal Protestants, often finding more in common with their Protestant brethren than with fellow Catholics.[31]

These opposing views reflected two ways of thinking about the relationship between the Chinese revolution and the universal mission of Christianity. Leaders in the mainline churches tended to see what had happened in China as the will of God—a perception based much more on their need to sustain their roles within their religious institutions than on any knowledge about China. They needed to see how God was speaking to them through the Chinese revolution. Leaders in the evangelical churches saw the Chinese revolution as the result of human sinfulness and sought to defy the Communist government's repressive policies toward religion. Both shared the belief, so fundamental to the American identity, that the whole world was under the judgment of the God revealed in the Bible and that all of history was part of a single plan of salvation revealed through Christ. If they were serious about their faith, neither mainline nor evangelical Protestants could simply ignore China.

The beginnings of an improvement in U.S.-China relations helped push the mainline and evangelical churches even further apart. The theology guiding the mainline churches led them to perceive an opportunity for reconciliation with a China already filled in some mysterious way with the presence of God. The evangelicals saw it as an opening for a new divinely mandated initiative into a godless territory. As the evangelical Protestant magazine *Christianity Today* put it, "Of great prominence in the foreign-policy views of Christians should be the consideration of what actions are most likely to promote fellowship and evangelism."[32]

The most visible manifestation of the mainline denominations' ministry of reconciliation with China was an ecumenical colloquium held in 1974 in Louvain, Belgium, and cosponsored by the Lutheran World Federation and Pro Mundi Vita, a liberal Roman Catholic research organization based in Belgium. The topic of the colloquium was "Christian Faith and the Chinese Experience." Although the hundred-odd participants in the meeting came from countries around the world (with the notable exception of mainland China), the organization and planning were mainly led by Americans. Because the conference was predisposed to see God's will at work in Chinese history, the tendency was to portray a very happy picture of the "new China." A few of the more extreme papers at the conference even came close to sanctifying Mao Zedong. For instance, in a paper titled "Maoist Ethics and Judeo-Christian Traditions," Canadian theologian Joachim Pillai wrote:

The Christian's task is not to judge or justify, but rather to locate, recognize, participate, and celebrate authentic human liberation wherever it is taking place. Mao's China is certainly a place where during the last four decades God has been at work to liberate and set free nearly a fifth of the human race from the clutches of "sin" (which Mao likes to describe in his own jargon as imperialism, feudalism, bourgeois capitalism, revisionism, and domestic reaction). . . . Like a new Moses, Mao led his people from the bondage of archaism, imperialism, feudalism, and capitalism. One can think of the heroic days of the "long march" of Jiangxi (Kiangsi). Just as on the way to the promised land, during the long desert trek, an ethic of right relations to God, man, and nature emerged in the Ten Commandments, so too in the long and bloody trek of the Red Army, people woke up to a new socialist ethic of right relations to fellow-men and to the People (who are seen as what is most sacred, as what is closest to the heart of God).[33]

The final reports of the conference were not quite so uncritically admiring of Mao's China, but they were rosy enough. As one document put it, China is "a sign of God's wrestling with the world."

What we have witnessed in the Great Leap Forward, the Great Proletarian Cultural Revolution, or the recent anti-Lin and anti-Confucianist Campaigns, etc., are some prominent examples of the turbulences which continue to shake and shape the present and future of China. In this way, the people of China are molding themselves through and being molded by internal forces derived from their messianic vision of a new society and a new world. We believe that God is present in this process of painful struggle, wrestling and agonizing with the people of China to bring their efforts ultimately under the fulfillment of his saving love for all mankind. . . . We believe that here a power greater than China, the power which transcends history and yet works within history, is at work making China a sign to the nations, a sign of God's agony with the wrongs and evils that threaten to erode the foundation of his creation and at the same time a sign that God in his unchangeable love will chart the course of human history, pressing it towards a new creation.[34]

Most participants at the Louvain colloquium did not know much about contemporary China. Only a handful had devoted any time to systematically studying Chinese society. Many of the older members had been missionaries in China before 1949, but by the time of the Louvain meeting most of these had become church administrators—they had little opportunity to study current events in the People's Republic. Even those who had done more formal study of China (notably Ray Whitehead, a Presbyterian minister who was director of the National Council of Churches' China program in Hong Kong and had gone on the first CCAS trip to China) drew their conclusions more from their theology and their church commitments than from any deep understanding of what life was like in China.[35]

Liberal Christian theology, especially its American versions, was committed to the view that God was active in secular as well as sacred history. "The dichotomy between the sacred and the secular has made it difficult for us to understand the meaning of history," the final report of the Louvain conference said. The members of the conference were devoted to overcoming this dichotomy: "Creation is a process with a purpose. From the beginning, humanity is meant to reach fulfillment, history is meant to strive towards its goal. . . . Human response to God's purpose in creation is made in and through decisions in personal, socio-economic, political, and cultural spheres."[36] This view of history saw the hand of God in secular events and commanded humans to fulfill the meaning of their faith not simply by worshipping but also by working to improve the world. It was a theology that resonated especially well with the experience of elites associated with the American mainline churches — well-educated, economically secure people occupying positions of responsibility in most major institutions of American life.

But this theology was not simply a reflection of the interests of the economically and politically successful. The need to find God actively at work in the secular world was coupled with a need to be self-critical. The documents of the Louvain conference castigated Western Christians for complicity with imperialism, racism, and capitalist exploitation. "We have to be conscious of how self-centered our churches still are, how bound to Western cultural, political, and financial ties, how lacking in unity and self-reliance," read one. If God was active in the world, he was especially active outside the United States, at least outside the circles of the rich and powerful in the United States. He was present in the victims of imperialism. From this conviction it was a short, though not necessarily logical, step to conclude that whatever was done in the name of anti-imperialism was good.

The theology articulated at the Louvain conference expressed the mentality of people of action rather than of religious contemplation. Only a small minority of the participants in the Louvain colloquium were professional theologians. Most were directors of various "China study and liaison" projects sponsored by the national headquarters of their various denominations to make local congregations aware of and properly concerned about China. These were individuals who had risen to leadership positions "because they have been dynamic," said one minister, a key organizer of the conference. But he also complained how, once in this position, he and many of his friends had been stifled by the church bureaucracy. His words seem to have captured the self-image of many denominational officials: They saw themselves as progressive, dynamic leaders struggling against bureaucratic inertia on the one hand and against the parochial complacency of local congregations on the other. The minister concluded: "I call [the pastor of my local congregation] 'Pastor Feel Good' because he just wants everybody to feel good. . . . [To keep his job] he has to keep his people happy."

The practical theology of such mainline church officials directed them toward a pessimistic view of their own society and an optimistic view of China. The opening to China was an opportunity to revitalize the true mission of Christianity, which was to expand the kingdom of God. But in their view, the inertia and complacency of the Western churches meant that expansion had to be intensive rather than extensive. Their home churches had to be converted before foreigners. As one United Methodist minister who had been present at the Louvain meeting told me: "In mission we're trying to discover that God is the center, not geography." The task of the church in this view was not primarily to convert large numbers of foreigners to the faith but to deepen the faith of church members by helping them understand themselves critically in light of their relationships with the world.

The willingness to look so uncritically upon China and so critically at the West also represented a theological response to the challenge of the evangelical Christians. By the 1970s, the mainline churches were in decline. Young adults were leaving the churches, especially those who received secular higher educations. At the same time, the evangelical Christian churches were growing.[37] These demographic trends corresponded to changes in levels of self-confidence: The mainline churches were losing self-confidence while the evangelicals were gaining it. Evangelical theology emphasized the need to find the truths of the faith in the Bible, not in the secular history of the world. The primary task of Christians was to follow this biblical word accurately and to preach it to the ends of the earth. It was an emphasis that gave them a strong sense of mission, a powerful capacity to organize collective action to spread the faith to outsiders. After a postwar peak of about 10,000 in 1968, the number of missionaries associated with the National Council of Churches plummeted in the 1970s. (By 1985, there were fewer than 5,000 American mainline Protestant missionaries abroad.) In the same period, the number of evangelical Protestant missionaries was skyrocketing. In 1953, evangelical and fundamentalist Protestant churches sent about 8,000 missionaries abroad. In 1985 they sent 35,000.[38]

In the logic of American denominational competition, the success of the evangelicals pressured mainline Protestant leaders to take theological stances that were the polar opposite of their rivals'. The evangelicals were filled with zeal to spread their faith. Mainline Protestant ministers responded by making extreme warnings about the self-righteousness and ethnocentrism implicit in such zeal and by striving to show that God had already revealed himself in secular history — even in an atheistic social movement such as Chinese communism. As the influential mainline Protestant journal *The Christian Century* reported, "In a period when some Christians see doors opening for the evangelization of China, the predominant mood at the ecumenical colloquium held recently at Leuven, Belgium, was summed up in the words of one of its reports: 'Ask not when the doors of China will open for us. Open first the closed doors of our own hearts and minds.'"[39] Somewhat self-righteously themselves, the mainline church leaders were saying that, unlike their evangelical brethren, they had heeded the Chinese Communists' criticisms about their own self-righteousness during the early part of this century. They could prove that they had done so by embracing the very Chinese Communist regime that had denounced them, thereby strengthening their claim that their competitor churches were guilty of self-righteousness.

The Louvain colloquium's positive view of China was thus driven more by the institutional demands of Western liberal Christianity — especially by its theological rivalry with evangelical Christianity — than by any particular contact with Chinese realities. However, there was an important set of practical connections with China that abetted the tendencies of liberal Christians to celebrate Maoist society, deepening the hostility of evangelicals to that same society and convincing the more extreme among them that liberal Christians were traitors to the Gospel. These were connections with the few indigenous Chinese Christian communities approved by the Chinese government.

In an effort to control all religious activity, the Communist regime had united all Protestant churches into a closely monitored mass organization. The leaders of this "three-self movement" (self-governing, self-supporting, self-propagating), as it was called, were Christian ministers who affirmed their unswerving loyalty to the Communist regime. As part of the proof of their loyalty, they were often called upon to denounce the foreign missionary churches that had taught them their faith. Large numbers of Chinese Christians refused to go along with the three-self movement. However, the mainline Western Protestant churches, with their new emphasis on self-determination, were sympathetic to the three-self movement.[40] Those relatively few former missionaries who had been able to return to China as "old friends" after 1972 usually visited leaders of the three-self movement such as Bishop

Ding Guangxun (K. H. Ting) of Nanjing. They did not meet with any Christians who refused to accept the three-self churches, in part because the Chinese government would not have allowed that. The mainline churches' hope for a productive new relationship with Chinese Christians lay in having a productive relationship with the three-self leaders, who regularly echoed the official government line about China's sacred duty to stand up against Western imperialism and castigated former missionaries for complicity with that imperialism.

Although the American mainline church leaders sometimes agonized about the tension between serving the kingdom of God and serving the bureaucratic structures of their denominations, they remained committed to living within that tension. They were used to associating with people of power within their own societies, and they wanted to continue that association even as they courageously spoke unpalatable truths. Aspiring to an ethic of responsibility, they were committed to carrying on a conversation with the secular institutional centers of their society. In the leadership of the Chinese three-self movement, they saw responsible Christian ministers like themselves, people who struggled to maintain the integrity of their faith within the constraints of a basically legitimate but inevitably flawed political system. Their hope of establishing new relationships with the church in China centered on Chinese Christian groups committed to cooperation with their government, not those opposed to (and opposed by) their government. Mainline Protestants clung to this hope even when Ding Guangxun and other three-self leaders refused to attend the Louvain meeting and denounced it for meddling in Chinese affairs. To the Americans, this hostility was merely another salutary challenge to their God-given capacity to forgive.

The evangelical churches, conversely, looked upon the three-self churches as having compromised their faith. Most of the Chinese Christian communities that had been established by evangelical missionaries before 1949 had refused to go along with the three-self movement and had been bitterly persecuted by the Chinese government — with the approval of spokespersons for the three-self churches. These evangelical communities now carried out their worship underground, without the blessing of the government. For the time being, it was virtually impossible for Westerners to have any direct contact with them, although sporadic news of their dire straits leaked out to Protestant friends abroad.[41]

By eagerly sympathizing with Chinese Christian leaders who had tacitly cooperated with the relentless suppression of their evangelical counterparts, Western liberal Protestants deepened their estrangement with their own evangelical rivals. In a way, however, both sides wanted that estrangement. The institutionalized desire to emphasize their competing theological assumptions was for the time being more important than any deep exploration of the realities of China.

In the midst of the gloom caused by declining membership, one powerful ray of hope for the liberal churches was their contacts with churches in the People's Republic of China. Because of their acceptance of the Chinese three-self movement and their respect for what they perceived to be the accomplishments of the Chinese revolution, mainline Protestants could embark on an inspiring new adventure in reconciliation with China. For the time being, the evangelical churches could do nothing.

Moreover, the liberal Protestants still had the preponderant influence among well-educated middle-class Americans — those who wrote for and read the mainstream press. The liberal churches' passionately optimistic images of China thus helped reinforce the general hopefulness of mainstream public opinion toward China. Every year the National Council of Churches produced a "mission study" on a different geographical region or a major world issue. Church members would spend the year reading about and discussing the issue in local Bible study groups. In 1975 the mission study was on China, and its basis was the Louvain colloquium. Thus, the mainline American churches celebrated the Chinese revolution and criticized themselves for the imperialism and capitalist exploitation that supposedly had made the revolution necessary.[42]

Of course, the ideas expressed by church leaders did not necessarily reflect those of the men and women in the pews. Within the past generation there has developed a much-discussed gulf between understandings of faith at the grassroots and the attitudes of mainline church leaders. As one minister put it, "Men and women move into leadership positions because they have been dynamic. When they get into leadership positions, they talk to themselves." The National Council of Churches' support for Third World revolutionary movements, offered in the name of a "theology of liberation," has been especially controversial at the grassroots. Undoubtedly, the militantly anti-imperialist rhetoric of some of the Louvain documents would have been rejected by many of those who preferred the ministry of a "Pastor Feel Good." But those who directed the 1975 study note that it aroused comparatively little controversy. Though somewhat garishly colored, the picture it portrayed of China had the same outlines as the images being conveyed through universities and the mainstream press. American mainline Protestants might not have wholeheartedly responded to their church leaders' challenge to repent of the sins of imperialism, but most did not utterly reject this message. They seem to have believed that the Chinese experience did indeed contain a lesson — perhaps not one to induce a radical conversion, but at least food for thought. They saw their earnest desire to learn from China rather than preach to it as one of the important marks distinguishing them from those whom they perceived as zealous, intolerant, fundamentalist Protestants.

Thus, the opening of the "bamboo curtain" enlivened many different American institutions, though it did not necessarily produce harmony. Indeed, as we have seen, in academia and religion it produced lively controversy and conflict. But opponents on most sides of the new debates assumed that China presented their institutions with exciting new opportunities to renew themselves. The controversies were about how these opportunities were to be defined and pursued. Although some parties to the debates stressed the negative aspects of Chinese life, the voices that tended to prevail were those that reinforced illusions that China was going in a positive direction.

In this way, the master story constructed by the beleaguered "middle-class and middle-aged" liberal center during the conferences and "teach-ins" of the mid-1960s and popularized and charged with mythical significance by the Nixon journey became an important component of institutional renewal. As a result, influential Americans in many different walks of life began to see themselves as partners with the Chinese in a story filled with hope.

Meanwhile, in China . . .

Before proceeding to the next phase in the American side of this story, let us briefly consider what was going on in China. There, too, master narratives about Sino-American relations were being revised and propagated and used to give direction to a variety of social institutions. But the way this process occurred in China contrasted markedly with the way it happened in the United States, and the contrast can sharpen our appreciation for the distinctiveness of the American institutional context.

If in the United States the new master story rose from a complex of synergistic social practices — from American society, not simply from Washington — in China the new master story descended from Beijing. It was the conscious creation of ideologues within the Communist Party and Chinese government.

In China during the early 1970s, ordinary people had virtually no access to information about the United States other than that provided by Party-controlled media. Within the Party, information about China and the United States was channeled only through a small group of people. Many of the best experts on the United States had been dismissed during the Cultural Revolution. The job of providing information to China's top leaders was in the hands of a small cohort of perhaps a half-dozen specialists.

The job of interpreting the United States to the Chinese public was in the hand of ideologues who took their understanding from orthodox Maoist premises.[43] According to those premises, the United States was the world's foremost imperialist power. Its political leaders (e.g., Richard Nixon) were warmongers and tools of monopoly capital. U.S. imperialism was aggressively aimed at dominating the Third World, which was led in heroic defense by the people of China under the leadership of Mao Zedong. After Mao Zedong and Zhou Enlai decided for strategic reasons to seek a rapprochement with the United States, ideologues had to develop a rationale. David Shambaugh summarizes what they did:

At first, no doubt responding to cues from central authorities, the principal Chinese media organs ceased their overtly hostile attacks on the United States. In their place, more subtle references to "imperialism" appeared, which could easily be distinguished from its twin "social imperialism" (the USSR). This new pattern of references was reinforced by delegate Deng Xiaoping's speech to the Sixth Special Session of the United Nations General Assembly. . . . the first major sign of ideological revisionism in the foreign policy domain in the wake of China's turn westward.[44]

According to this revised ideological line, the United States was a waning imperialist superpower. To lead the Third World to victory against imperialism, China, following the strategic principles that had enabled it to unite temporarily with the Guomindang in the war against Japan, could join this weaker of the two major imperialist powers in a broad "united front" against the most pressing threat.[45]

But in rationalizing a fundamental reversal of the government's official policy toward the United States, Chinese ideologues probably only furthered their loss of credibility. That credibility had been strained to the breaking point by the Cultural Revolution and then dealt a devastating blow by the failed attempt of Lin Biao, Mao's chosen successor, to usurp power from Mao in 1971. China was entering a period when any story concocted by officials was becoming suspect in the minds of a disillusioned populace. Not a few Chinese were now willing to believe that if officials said one thing, the truth must be just the opposite. Thus, some were willing to imagine that if the ideologues said the United States was a problem-riddled imperialist power, it must be a very good place indeed.

Although few Chinese outside of official circles had information that might give substance to that notion, the number of knowledgeable people was slowly beginning to increase. Gradually, experts on the United States were recalled from internal exile in "May 7 cadre schools"; staff at research institutes was increased; journalists from the New China News Agency were dispatched to New York to cover the United Nations; and a number of Chinese traveled to the United States on delegations arranged through agencies such as the National Committee on U.S.-China Relations. Most of the work of the government researchers was conducted in secret, and observations of journalists and delegation members were written to correspond to the ideological line.[46] But very slowly, widening circles of Chinese were getting information about the United States that contradicted the dogmas of official ideologues, and more people were willing to use that information to get beyond these dogmas.

It was precisely this awareness of how their understandings of the United States had been manipulated that enabled some Chinese to be surprised by their encounters with Americans and actually to learn something from them. A wide variety of Americans looked toward China through the lenses of their major institutions and saw not China but, as in a magic mirror, a flattering vision of themselves. However, some Chinese were able to look toward the United States through the cracks in the lenses of their institutions and to glimpse something truly new that forced fundamental reconsideration of their relationship with their society. Zi Zhongyun, a former director of the Institute of American Studies in the Chinese Academy of Social Sciences, gives an example:

[In the early 1970s], wherever an American gave a talk in China, he invariably lectured to a full house. Even the contents of his talk spread far and wide. For instance, William Hinton, an American agricultural expert and author who zealously helped China with agricultural mechanization, gave a report describing his experience of operating the equivalent of 700 to 800 mu of land [about 117 acres], at the same time setting aside ample time for travel and writing. This was certainly an eye opener for Chinese used to a small scale peasant economy. His report was printed and widely circulated. For a while Hinton's farm was on the lips of the leaders of numerous units across the country as well as in Beijing. Even more surprising to the Chinese was the fact that even though he owned so much land, Hinton still could not make ends meet and had to go into debt; he and his wife survived on incomes from other sources. This was totally at variance with the Chinese image of the "big landlord." This example is cited to show how little ordinary officials, including people in leadership, knew America. As far as understanding America is concerned, this was a new enlightenment. Soon this sense of novelty was followed by a strong new desire to know everything about the United States.[47]

What was at issue in this new knowledge about the United States was not whether it was a good place or a bad place or even whether and how Sino-American relationships could be normalized but whether China's political controls and theoretical dogmatism had blinded it to important aspects of reality. Hinton was highly critical of American capitalism and very much in favor of a collectivized, socialist agriculture. In that respect he reaffirmed what his Chinese listeners had been hearing from their propaganda apparatus for years. But his revelations about his farm showed his listeners that they did not know much about the economics of agriculture in a complex industrial society. Perhaps inadvertently, Hinton cast doubt on an educational system that had fostered such naivete.

For many Americans, the opening to China helped postpone reconsideration of some of the increasingly problematic assumptions underneath their major public institutions. For some Chinese, the opening to the United States helped hasten such reconsideration. In both societies, nonetheless, new knowledge of the other mainly provided the means for a discourse about the self.

In the United States, the new relationship with China helped to rekindle self-confidence and to inspire a sense of mission within public liberal institutions. This revitalization helped many Americans to believe once again that they still had something to teach the rest of the world, even if some believed that, after having taken to heart the Maoist message, they might now teach others the true meaning of the Chinese revolution.

Most Chinese, conversely, were not interested in teaching anybody anything but merely sought to recover from the devastation of the Cultural Revolution. In China, new glimpses of the United States helped further to discredit Maoism's grip on the Chinese consciousness — without, however, producing any clear sense of what could replace Maoism.

In both the American and the Chinese cases, the knowledge was superficial. Americans looking to China usually saw what they wanted to see, or more precisely what their institutional commitments led them to see. Chinese looking at the United States were allowed only a few tantalizing glimpses of American life, which made them want to learn things that might fundamentally challenge their self-understandings. These patterns continued even when more profound interchanges between the two societies became possible after normalization of U.S.-China relations in 1979.

By the late 1980s, though, the encounters between American and Chinese institutions were bringing about changes that neither side had anticipated and that challenged each side to understand the other more deeply while coming to terms more critically with itself. In the next three chapters I will describe the emergence of these challenges from both the American and the Chinese sides.

5

Diplomatic Normalization

Moral Challenges to the Liberal Myth

Even as American institutions were steadily building up hope for expansion into China in the years following the Nixon visit, relations between Washington and Beijing were deteriorating. The deterioration was largely the result of instability in both governments. In 1972 Nixon had promised the Chinese leaders that he would seek to normalize relations with them during his second term in office; the Watergate scandal made this impossible. In 1976 Zhou Enlai and Mao Zedong both died, setting off a succession struggle that led to a triumph of Deng Xiaoping's forces over the "Gang of Four," who had supported Mao during the Cultural Revolution. It took Deng Xiaoping two years to consolidate his power fully, however. Finally, in December 1978, at the Third Plenum of the Eleventh Communist Party Central Committee, Deng's forces had secured enough control over the Party to turn the Chinese government dramatically away from the policies of the Maoist era. A program of "four modernizations" was to replace the revolutionary class struggle. Moreover, in pursuit of modernization, China would open itself to Western investment and, even more important (although the Chinese government leaders did not intend it this way), to Western ideas and cultural influences.[1]

Meanwhile, President Jimmy Carter took office in 1977, the first president elected since Nixon's forced resignation. By 1978 the Carter administration was ready to begin negotiations on normalization. The negotiations were completed in December, and the United States and China normalized diplomatic relations in January 1979. With that, popular American hopes for China — and popular Chinese hopes about the United States — blossomed into full flower.

The Moral Price of Normalization

Yet on both sides the efflorescence of hope contained seeds of disillusionment, manifested in the doubts and controversies that clouded the achievement of normalization in both countries. These problems arose from moral dilemmas inherent in the new U.S.-China relationship. Rather than being resolved, these dilemmas were partially obscured by the hopeful excitement attendant on normalization; in the end, they posed fundamental challenges to the liberal China myth. In this chapter and the next, I will discuss these challenges from the American point of view. In subsequent chapters, I will discuss them from the Chinese side.

To the small group of U.S. officials who secretly carried out the negotiations over normalization, the issues were very complex: Asia-Pacific security issues; the transference of technology that could be put to military use; the resolution of claims by U.S. companies on property confiscated by the Communist regime; and China's membership in a host of international organizations. But to the American public these technical factors were not of major consequence. The crucial issue was stark, simple, and moral: What should be done about the U.S. commitment to Taiwan?

The government of the People's Republic of China had always demanded that, as the basic price of normalization, the U.S. government would have to break its diplomatic relations and defense treaty with the Republic of China, reversing its policy of thirty years. By 1978 the Carter administration was willing to do that. Specifically, the administration agreed to sever all official diplomatic relations with Taiwan (although both the United States and Taiwan could replace their embassies with unofficial agencies); to sever its mutual defense treaty with Taiwan (but after a year's notice rather than immediately, as the PRC initially demanded); to withdraw all military forces from Taiwan (although it was tacitly understood that the United States could still sell some defensive weapons to Taiwan); and to acknowledge that how and when the PRC was reunified with Taiwan was an internal affair (although the United

States government was able to state unilaterally that it wished the issue to be resolved peacefully).

The Carter administration experts who negotiated the normalization agreements did not consider the Chinese government's price steep; indeed, it was far outweighed by the long-term, tangible benefits the United States would reap from the resumption of formal diplomatic relations with the People's Republic. Although the Chinese government was unwilling to renounce its right to liberate Taiwan through force, U.S. intelligence analysts considered a PRC invasion militarily infeasible, at least in the near term. So from the point of view of the policy experts, the U.S. government gave up few of its practical interests in return for conceding in principle the People's Republic of China's right to assert sovereignty over Taiwan. At the same time, the United States gained increased cooperation with the Chinese government in maintaining a strategic balance of power with the Soviet Union, and it opened the door to vastly expanded trade with the People's Republic.[2]

In the policy experts' calculations, the benefits clearly outweighed the costs. "In fact," remarks Michel Oksenberg, the National Security Council staff member who was chiefly responsible for coordinating the normalization efforts, "one legitimate criticism of the China policy during the Carter administration was that everyone was for it. It might have been better, have led to a more realistic policy, if there had been some critical voices." However, "everyone" consisted of only about a dozen officials and their expert advisers. The negotiations had to be closely held, especially because of concern about adverse congressional reaction to the treatment of Taiwan.

Indeed, when the normalization agreements were announced, intense debates ensued in Congress over legislation necessary to implement them. The main issues were whether the United States should retain an official diplomatic presence on Taiwan or (as the PRC government and the Carter administration insisted) only an unofficial agency, the "American Institute in Taiwan," staffed by officials who had temporarily retired from government service; whether the United States should make a firmer and more explicit commitment to defend Taiwan from any military attack by the People's Republic; and whether it should back up this commitment by officially declaring that it would allow the sale of weapons to Taiwan.[3] Congressional criticism of the normalization agreements and attempts to modify them in Taiwan's favor were driven by special interests. Many members of Congress were angered because they had been kept uninformed about the negotiations. Some had received support from the China lobby connected with Taiwan. Others were dependent on support from the defense industry, which encouraged them to advocate continued weapons sales to Taiwan. Republicans were happy for an opportunity to discomfit a Democratic president. But the rhetorical cement that unified these various interests and allowed them to mount a powerful opposition was an argument about the morality of the agreements — about whether it was right, as Senator Jesse Helms put it, "to sell Taiwan down the river."[4]

The moral rhetoric drew on a strong current of public opinion. As John Fairbank put it in a 1978 *New York Review of Books* essay published before the normalization agreement was concluded: "[W]e should not underrate the American emotional attachment to Taiwan, the part of China that seems to be coming our way [even though at the time Taiwan was ruled by an authoritarian, one-party state that kept many political prisoners], that still receives our missionaries and their good works, sends us students, welcomes our tourists, and grows apace in our international trading world. Taiwan is not a place with which the American people will willingly break off contact."[5]

Playing to this generalized public concern, George Bush, who in 1974–1975 had been the first representative (a quasi-ambassador) in the U.S. liaison office in Beijing, wrote that the deal with the PRC was "all cost, no benefit."

Personally, I have long felt that in spite of the totalitarian nature of the Chinese government, it was in our own national interest to improve relations with Beijing [Peking]. But the critical question was the terms on which the recognition was initiated. . . . The terrible truth is that the United States now stands exposed to the world as a nation willing to betray a friend. . . . For President Carter, who professes a strong belief in Christian ethics, it should be a tormenting thought that by his hand the United States has put an entire people adrift in a cruel, hostile sea — and for scarcely any purpose.[6]

Other critics used rhetoric even more powerfully redolent with biblical and civic republican themes. As David Pietrusza wrote:

The sudden decision to recognize fully the People's Republic of China and to abrogate unilaterally our twenty-five year old Mutual Defense Treaty with the Republic of China (or "the People on Taiwan" as they are now known in 1984-style Newspeak) struck many as yet another giant stride in America's global retreat. The Beijing [Peking] government tendered no new concessions; in fact it seems Washington insisted on none, as we jettisoned yet another ally. In place of lost honor, the administration dangled before the public the chimera of trade with the mainland, the allure of "a billion new customers," the clank of thirty pieces of silver. . . . Americans did want a link with Beijing, but were not prepared to grovel for it or to relegate one of our oldest allies and one of Asia's most progressive societies to an uncertain future as part of the bargain.[7]

The negotiators of normalization, such critics alleged, were weak of character, which made them willing to "grovel" and led them to commit the sin of disloyalty. Tough-minded geopoliticians such as Richard Nixon, of course, did not see the normalization agreement as a groveling act of weakness. When the pact was finally concluded in December 1978, Michel Oksenberg was sent by President Carter to brief Nixon. Nixon blessed the deal with the words, "Your politics have been very tough — but the public won't necessarily see it that way." Interpreting Nixon's message, Oksenberg said, "The toughness of our policy, the brutality of it toward Taiwan, came from the fact that we were consolidating our position over a long period of time. It may have been that it would have been to our short term benefit to hold on to our relationship with Taiwan. But it would not have been to our own long range benefit."[8]

President Carter, though, had come into office at least partially on the strength of promises not to imitate Nixon in the conduct of foreign policy. As Carter put it in one of his campaign statements, "The question, I think, is whether in recent years our highest officials have not been too pragmatic, even cynical, and as a consequence have ignored those moral values that had often distinguished our country." In his inaugural address he quoted Micah 6:8: "What does the Lord require of thee, but to do justly, and to love mercy, and to walk humbly with thy God?"[9] Why then did the Carter administration conduct itself toward China in a way that would have made Nixon proud?

Part of the answer, certainly, is to be found in the dynamics of bureaucratic infighting within the Carter administration. There were differing perspectives within the administration on how the costs and benefits of normalization should be calculated. For those like Secretary of State Cyrus Vance, who saw the benefits especially in terms of China's potential role as a stabilizing force in the Asia-Pacific region, there was a closer balance between the cost of cutting relations with Taiwan and the benefits of normalization. A too precipitous withdrawal from Taiwan might cast doubts about U.S. resolve in capitals throughout Asia. Normalization, though good in itself, would have the side effect of antagonizing the Soviet Union, perhaps stalling arms control negotiations and prompting further conflict with the Soviets around the world.

Vance, therefore, favored a slower pace of normalization, and he was willing to try to extract somewhat larger concessions from the Chinese on the Taiwan issue.[10]

However, for those who, like Zbigniew Brzezinksi, Carter's national security adviser, saw China mainly in terms of the global power balance, normalization was a "card" that could be played in the great strategic game with the Soviet Union. Normalization could be used to threaten the Soviet Union, to punish it for misbehavior elsewhere in the world, and to pressure it to be more forthcoming in negotiations over the Strategic Arms Limitation Treaty (SALT). From this geopolitical perspective, the benefits of normalization rather decisively outweighed the cost of cutting relations with Taiwan.[11]

A trip to Beijing by Vance in August 1977 ended in some frustration because, as Brzezinski wrote in his memoirs, Vance "was not in a position to cross the Rubicon insofar as U.S. relations with Taiwan were concerned."[12] By early 1978, Brzezinski, at the National Security Council, had gained the upper hand in his bureaucratic battles with Vance at the State Department. One rhetorical weapon he had used against Vance and the State Department was that the foreign policy of the first year of the Carter administration was "flabby." This adjective referred not only to real international problems allegedly caused by weak U.S. responses to Soviet provocations but also to the public perception that the administration was willing to yield too much to old enemies. For instance, some officials in the State Department were arguing that the United States should normalize diplomatic relations not only with China but also with Vietnam and Cuba as part of a doctrine of "universal recognition"—that for pragmatic reasons the United States should extend diplomatic relations to any government that had control over its population, without attaching any moral praise or blame to the act of diplomatic recognition. Whatever the benefits of this policy in the abstract, it was seen as spineless by many ordinary Americans.

But for Brzezinski, recognition of the PRC was fundamentally different from recognition of Vietnam or Cuba. It was an act of strength, not of weakness—a bold, aggressive move against the Soviet Union. On this rationale, Brzezinski pushed hard for a fairly rapid normalization in 1978. In May 1978, he got himself sent on a mission to Beijing to announce that "the United States has made up its mind"— that is, that it was willing to pay the Chinese government's basic price. From there on the path toward normalization moved smoothly forward.[13]

The virtue of Brzezinski's stance toward normalization was that it made the surrender of Taiwan into an act of U.S. assertiveness. U.S. normalization with the PRC was deeply disturbing to the Soviet Union, which feared a Sino-American alliance against its interests in Asia. Normalization became the "China card" to be played against the Soviets. Brzezinski seemed to gain a visceral pleasure out of playing the card. Consider his account of how he notified the Soviet ambassador about the normalization:

Dobrynin arrived full of cheer at 3 P.M. . . . . At first I chatted pleasantly . . . and then out of the blue I informed them that we are announcing tonight initiation of diplomatic, full-scale relations with the People's Republic of China. He looked absolutely stunned. His face turned kind of grey and his jaw dropped. He didn't say anything but then he recouped and thanked me for the information. I added that it wasn't directed against anyone and that American relations with China would then have as normal a character as Soviet relations with China. Formally, a correct observation; but substantively, a touch of irony.[14]

Although an insider's account of such bureaucratic maneuvering can help explain the pace and timing of the normalization process and some of the terms for which the United States was willing to settle, it neglects that which was most salient and most obvious to many ordinary Americans — the moral ironies embedded in the process.

At bottom, the debates about normalization — those within the corridors of power as well as those out in the public forum — were about the fundamental values that ought to shape American society, especially the value of freedom. How could normalization be reconciled with the American Dream — with the myth that the United States was defined by its commitment to universal freedom, leading to progress and justice for all?

Freedom and Order for Whom?

America was supposed to stand for freedom; the cold war against Soviet communism was justified in terms of the preservation of the "free world." But to win the cold war, the U.S. government had to establish domestic and international structures of order, predictability, and stability. In such a context, the freedom the United States sought to preserve looked different to those at the top of the mechanisms of order than it did to those at the bottom. For those at the top—chiefs of state and their staffs, chief executive officers of multinational corporations, and the like—freedom meant the ability to maneuver flexibly to maximize the efficacy of their organizations. For those at the bottom it meant freedom from being manipulated to the advantage of those on top.

In finishing the diplomatic process begun by Nixon, Jimmy Carter enhanced the U.S. government's freedom to maneuver in the global superpower competition with the Soviet Union, and he enhanced the freedom of large corporations to maneuver flexibly in pursuit of investment and trade with the most populous country in the world. But he enhanced this freedom by sloughing off "sentimental" commitments with a loyal ally. This was what David Pietrusza called "the clank of thirty pieces of silver."

The Carter administration argued that the enhanced freedom of the United States in the international arena did not amount to a betrayal of Taiwan because for all practical purposes nothing bad was going to happen to Taiwan. Indeed, the new international order made possible by normalization with China would produce a geopolitical stability and Asia-Pacific economic vitality that would indirectly benefit Taiwan. Such are the arguments usually made by technocratic elites in both government and business in their version of the American Dream: More freedom for them will produce economic and political benefits that will trickle all the way down the social scale.

Pietrusza was appealing to a populist rendition of the American Dream, a tradition that does not trust claims of benevolent political power and technical expertise. This tradition held that expertise worked for the benefit of ordinary people only if experts were bound by moral loyalties to such people. Freedom of the rich and powerful had to be balanced by moral ties to the weaker members of society—as long as the latter constrained their quest for absolute, uninhibited freedom with a reciprocal responsibility to work hard and participate honestly in the political system.[15] By the standards of such a moral tradition, the United States had betrayed Taiwan; and if it did so without compunction, might it not also betray its own citizens? By Pietrusza's standards, a nation's real strength is based on its moral character, on the capacity of its citizens to do what is right even when that is not expedient—to refuse to grovel for the sake of some material gain.

Throughout most of the twentieth century, the gap between the elitist, technocratic view of freedom and the populist, moral view has not been unbridgeable in the United States. In spite of their disagreements, both elitists and populists could see themselves as sharing the same American Dream. The gap between elitists and populists has indeed been much narrower here than in most societies in the world, because the distinction between elites and masses is unusually fluid in this country. Possibilities for mobility make the "common man" much more likely to achieve uncommon distinction in the United States than virtually anywhere else. Many of our elites, especially those who have advanced by acquiring professional expertise, had ancestors who were poor and lowly just a few generations ago. Thus, American elites tend to retain more sympathy for and more of a sense of moral responsibility toward ordinary people than do elites in most other societies — especially China.

Moreover, common people in the United States have been more willing to trust in the good intentions of their technocratic elites than have common people in less "modern" nations. (American populists have a hard time imagining how brutal and destructive the masses in less fortunate societies can become when mobilized by nationalistic passions or memories of class exploitation. Likewise, American elites have difficulty imagining how unrestrainedly arrogant elites in a more hierarchical society can become.) An important contribution to diminishing the gap between elites and populists has been made by American churches and synagogues, which for all their disputes and conflicts have provided Americans with a powerful common moral language with which to discuss their differences.

In his election campaign, Jimmy Carter had appealed to the populist sensibility, promising to create a government "as good as the American people." Once in office, though, he consistently followed the advice of his technocratic experts, especially in the conduct of foreign affairs. Sometimes, there was such a great contradiction between what he had promised to do and what he actually did that he became very vulnerable to charges of inconsistency and even hypocrisy. He had pledged to make concern for international human rights a centerpiece of his foreign policy, but for geopolitical reasons he was inconsistent in applying pressure on human rights violators. At other times, the gap between his stated aspirations and the realities of geopolitics seemed to leave him confused, so that he vacillated between conflicting policies and exposed his administration to charges of incompetence. Perhaps his perceived failures came about because he fell victim to the particularly American illusion that the differences between elites and masses in their understanding of freedom and social order are really in the end just differences in perspective or differences in emphasis, not fundamental differences in interests that might necessitate making tragic choices.[16]

Walter Russell Mead colorfully portrayed the moral contradictions implicit in the Carter administration's foreign policy: "Under Carter, American foreign policy was like a sinner in search of what theologians call 'cheap grace' — like a brothel owner offering to improve working conditions and wages to gain respectability. The United States would put itself at the head of the world's genuinely progressive forces — at no cost to the United States. Absent from American rhetoric was any specific idea about what the United States would do to meet the aspirations of the peoples in revolt."[17]

But in the case of the Carter administration's China policy, these contradictions seemed resolvable. Although opinion surveys revealed profound reservations about withdrawing diplomatic relations and breaking the defense treaty with Taiwan, on balance the polls suggested that the public supported the president's decision.[18] The majority of Americans, it seemed, wanted to believe that normalization was a benefit, not just for manipulative elites playing geopolitics but ultimately for almost all ranks of Americans and for Chinese on both sides of the Taiwan Strait. It was as if, in the face of a challenge to the American Dream, they embraced all the more firmly the liberal China myth that seemed to confirm that dream. In spite of public wrangling over the terms of the agreement, a groundswell of euphoria about the future of U.S.-China relations seemed to arise within American society, reaching a peak during the visit of Deng Xiaoping to the United States a few weeks after the normalization agreement took effect in January 1979.[19]

"The Deng Xiaoping visit," wrote Carter in his memoirs, "was one of the delightful experiences of my Presidency. To me, everything went right, and the Chinese leader seemed equally pleased."[20] As Brzezinski described it in his memoirs: "On Monday morning, January 29, Deng made his first appearance at the White House. The atmosphere was charged with electricity, and I could not recall a comparable sense of excitement in the White House."[21] The day ended with a formal dinner at the White House — in Brzezinski's judgment, "probably the most elegant dinner given at any time during Carter's four years in the White House"[22] — and with a gala, televised reception at the Kennedy Center. At at the end of the reception, as Carter noted in his diary for that day:

Deng and I, his wife, Madame Zhuolin, Rosalynn and Amy went on the stage with the performers, and there was a genuine sense of emotion when he put his arms around the American performers, particularly little children who had sung a Chinese song. He kissed many of them, and the newspapers later said that many in the audience wept.

Senator Laxalt, who has been a strong opponent of normalization, said after that performance that we had them beat; there was no way to vote against little children singing Chinese songs.

Deng and his wife genuinely seemed to like people, and he was really a hit with the audience present and also the television audience.[23]

It is difficult to reconcile the image of the warm, friendly, people-loving Deng Xiaoping of that happy night at the Kennedy Center in 1979 with the image of the dictatorial Deng Xiaoping of that horrible night in 1989 when hundreds of protesters were shot around Tiananmen Square. The fact is that the harsher edges of Deng's character should have been known in 1979 to anyone who had studied a little modern Chinese history and were in any case amply revealed to Carter and his advisers during Deng's visit in 1979. For just before that gala evening at the Kennedy Center, wrote Carter,

Deng requested that we leave our large group of advisers so that he could discuss a more confidential matter with me. Fritz, Cy, Zbig, and I went with Deng and the interpreters from the Cabinet room into the Oval Office, and listened carefully as the Chinese leader outlined his tentative plans for China to make a punitive strike across the border into Vietnam. When he asked me for my advice, I tried to discourage him. . . . The Vice Premier thanked me for my comments, and added that it was highly desirable for China that its arrogant neighbors know they could not disturb it and other countries in the area with impunity.[24]

As it turned out, the Carter administration kept Deng's plans confidential. When the three-week-long invasion of Vietnam was launched, the U.S. government publicly deplored it but did nothing to stop it or to punish the Chinese government for it. As Brzezinski put it, "The Chinese learned in the course of the three critical weeks that they now had a reliable friend: they could confide in us, we could keep a secret, and our public reaction — formally critical but substantively helpful — was firm and consistent. We learned that the Chinese trusted us, that they were not easily intimidated, and that their determination could be strategically helpful."[25] From the geopolitical point of view, the new relationship with China made excellent sense for the United States. Throughout 1979, Brzezinski and his aides moved to solidify this strategic relationship, especially by beginning a process of technology transfer that would increase the threat of China toward the Soviet Union.

But the romantic aura manifested in the public reaction to the Deng Xiaoping visit continued to color perceptions of China and to affect even the hardheaded geopoliticians at the top of the Carter administration. The Chinese leadership was predominantly understood in terms of virtues rather than vices. Jimmy Carter, the pious, high-minded moralist, remained "favorably impressed with Deng. He's small, tough, intelligent, frank, courageous, personable, self-assured, friendly, and it's a pleasure to negotiate with him. . . ."[26] According to Walter Russell Mead, "The military overconfidence of the Kennedy-Johnson years led the United States to a military impasse in Indochina. The moral overconfidence of the Carter team had a similar result. . . . Like Carter, [the American people] preferred to comfort themselves with illusion—to believe that the truly hard choices need never be made."[27]

Before the end of the Carter administration, the basis for such illusions was shattered by the Iranian revolution and by political upheaval in Central America. But the illusions were sustained for a decade by changes taking place in China — at least, as such changes were perceived through the hopeful lenses of American institutions.

Illusions and Interests

What sustained these misperceptions was a combination of elite and popular interests mediated through the values of American religious, academic, and professional institutions.

Consider the formation of American illusions about China's progress toward greater respect for human rights. Carter had come into office pledging to pressure countries dependent on the United States to improve their conduct on human rights. To this end, the Carter administration set up a human rights office in the State Department headed by Patricia Derian, a lawyer who had been active in the civil rights movements of the 1960s. The Chinese government's record on human rights was atrocious, a fact clearly demonstrated by an Amnesty International study published in 1978.[28] However, Darien's office was kept from addressing the Chinese human rights issue by the Carter administration. In the view of the White House, normalization and the establishment of a firm strategic relationship with China took precedence over human rights. The United States even voted to sustain the claim of the murderous Pol Pot regime to Cambodia's seat in the UN because the Chinese government supported that regime.[29]

When asked in 1988, a year before the tragedy of Tiananmen Square, about the Carter administration's policies on Chinese human rights, Michel Oksenberg became uncharacteristically defensive.

On the question of human rights, I personally would say that we were and we have been concerned about human rights in China, and that we have tried to do something about this. People like Pat Darien would disagree with me, however. She would say that we would make an exception with regard to human rights in China. I had some difficult times with her. I was responsible for monitoring her speeches and I excised various statements from her speeches concerning human rights in China.

Human rights are advanced in different countries in different ways. It is very difficult to get a country to make improvements in its human rights situation if you don't have relations with it. In my view, we have had as intelligent a program of human rights with regard to China as any country in the world.

Oksenberg and other Carter administration officials based their China policy on the assumption that the best way to get the Chinese government to improve its human rights record was, paradoxically, to leave the issue of human rights out of the negotiations. Doing so would encourage Chinese leaders to build closer relations with the United States, allowing American institutions to gradually work their magic on the Chinese. This stance toward the human rights issue was plausible only if one believed firmly in the liberal myth about China. According to Oksenberg: "An important contribution to human rights in China has been made by institutions like the Ford Foundation and their legal studies program. This is helping to establish a legal framework for human rights in China. The exchange programs have also made a great contribution by exposing Chinese students to the United States. The USIA through its educational programs has also made major contributions to human rights in China."

As Oksenberg summarized his case, "We have improved the human rights situation in China by letting it come from within." A demand for a government that would better respect basic human rights did indeed come from within China in the decade following normalization, but it did not come from within the Chinese government. It came from sectors of China other than those with which Oksenberg, Brzezinski, and Carter negotiated, and it threatened the stability of China and damned the honor of precisely those officials whom Carter had found it "so pleasant to deal with" and on whom his administration had placed so much hope. After 1989, it forced the U.S. government and the American public to confront an uncomfortable question: Are we on the side of the people who demand human rights or of the government that can ensure order?

Powerful economic and political interests sustained the belief within the Carter administration and within elite circles of American society that China would steadily, inevitably, and naturally make progress in human rights. We can see these interests at work in the rationalizations made by the administration to Congress in its case for granting most-favored-nation (MFN) trading status to China. Under U.S. law, MFN is supposed to be reserved only for countries with free market economies and basic civil and political rights, especially the right to emigration. In 1978 China obviously met none of these conditions. Still, soon after normalization, in accordance with promises made to the Chinese government during the negotiations, the Carter administration proposed that China receive MFN status.

There were persuasive commercial and geopolitical reasons for this proposal. Granting China MFN status would provide potentially lucrative opportunities for corporations anxious to undertake trade there. It would also strengthen ties between China and the United States, to the disadvantage of the Soviet Union. But the Carter administration could not frame its case to Congress solely on the basis of these pragmatic considerations. It had to suggest that China was now fundamentally different from those Soviet bloc countries that the MFN designation had meant to sanction and to isolate. The administration asked for a waiver of the Jackson-Vanik Amendment (legally requiring that to be granted MFN status a nation had to allow freedom of emigration) on the grounds that the PRC's emigration policies were moving in the right direction. Moreover, it encouraged a belief that, by opening its doors to the United States, China was on its way to developing free institutions. As Representative Charles Vanik, who led the support for the administration's position during the debate in the House of Representatives, put it, "I would hope that . . . the extension of MFN to the PRC would stimulate a broadening of human rights." Echoed Representative Bill Alexander, "Seeds of democracy are growing in China." Thus, China morally deserved MFN.[30]

Such rationalizations, so convenient to geopolitical strategists and corporate elites, were in the end plausible to millions of ordinary American citizens as well. Where did the plausibility come from? One important source was the dramatic shift after 1978 in Chinese policy on educational exchanges with the United States. Until 1978, the Chinese government had kept students carefully isolated from the West. Although a few senior scholars had the opportunity to travel on fact-finding tours of the United States, there were no opportunities for ordinary students to travel abroad for an education. Suddenly that changed. The impetus came in July 1978, soon after the serious, secret negotiations on normalization had begun, when the Carter administration sent to China what Brzezinski called "the most high-powered science/technology delegation ever sent by the United States to any foreign country."[31]

Led by Frank Press, the president's science adviser, the fifteen-person delegation included the heads of NASA, the National Institutes of Health, and the National Science Foundation. It was intended to send a "powerful signal" to the Chinese government. However, different members of the president's staff had different perspectives on what that signal meant. Brzezinski saw it in its strategic context: The United States was willing to transfer some of its technology to China so that China could become "strong and secure" in a way that would discomfit the Soviet Union.[32] President Carter, according to a close adviser, saw it in less strategic terms. A nuclear engineer by training, he had a general faith in the value of science and technology as a way to involve people in the rational pursuit of mutual self-improvement. Frank Press took this faith even further. One acquaintance said he possessed a "messianic vision" of the value of scientific and technological exchange for elevating the level of rationality in human discourse and reducing differences between the developed and undeveloped worlds. More practically, he also hoped, in the words of Denis Simon, "that various cooperative programs could provide the lubricant to facilitate the sale of equipment and technology by U.S. industry. Similarly, by training a whole cadre of Chinese managers, it was hoped that these individuals would be more inclined to favor U.S. products and ways of operating."[33] In any case, Press used his toasts at formal dinners in China to communicate a message of world interdependence.

The reaction to the Press delegation was unexpected and enormously exciting to the Americans. During the trip, the Chinese government announced that it was planning to send its first group of students abroad to the United States since the founding of the PRC. In return, some Americans would be allowed to study in China. The announcement sparked a tremendous amount of enthusiasm in the United States. American universities scrambled over one another to offer admission and financial aid to PRC students. After the arrival of an initial group of fifty Chinese students, the flow from China, to the astonishment of all, quickly turned into a torrent. By 1990 there were over 40,000 students from the PRC in the United States.

The willingness of the Chinese government to send students to the United States helped deepen a hopeful belief in the liberal master narrative about China. The pattern of expectations went like this: China would not just take our technology to use for its own political and economic purposes (which is exactly what the Chinese leaders actually intended to do). China would learn our values from us. The United States would help train the next generation of Chinese leaders. China might be a harshly repressive, economically backward society today, but once it opened itself to American ideas it would change steadily for the better.

American scholars sometimes published thoughtful papers in 1979 and 1980 warning about the perils of overenthusiasm over such academic exchanges, sometimes citing the mistakes and disappointments of early twentieth-century missionaries and social reformers.[34] But often these same scholars participated vigorously in hosting visiting delegations, preparing the way for Chinese students to come to their campuses, and expanding relationships between their universities and "sister schools" in China. It was considered the mark of a good scholar to express reservations about a headlong rush to establish academic ties with China; but it was considered the mark of a good member of the university community to participate wholeheartedly in that rush. Scholars worried as individuals; their institutions pulled them collectively forward to sustain hopeful illusions.

In the preceding chapter, I discussed how major American institutions subtly induced their members to respond hopefully to the "opening" of China as a way of reaffirming those institutions' values. Now that the door to China seemed to have flung open dramatically, the pressure to hope reached a peak. However, as Americans passed through the door and began to experience the complexities of real life in China, the spirit of hopefulness began to erode. The encounter with China engendered new controversies over the meaning of the central values of American religious, educational, and professional institutions—new challenges to the American Dream. I will now discuss some representative controversies and show how they arose out of encounters with the practical realities of China.

6

Missionaries of the American Dream

Putting the Liberal Myth into Practice

From the point of view of Washington, normalization of U.S.-China relations was meant to serve a variety of strategic and diplomatic purposes. But most American citizens who turned their attention to China had different interests than their government officials. As I have argued before, the most widely shared interest was cultural. The normalization of relations with China seemed dramatically to give new life to the American Dream. It verified the liberal master narrative central to the legitimacy of American institutions. Normalization seemed to confirm and amplify the hope that China would now become part of a revitalized liberal world order, beneficently and progressively presided over by the United States; a world in which economic growth would be unleashed by the transformation of China's socialist system into a market economy fully open to world trade; a world enlightened by reason and held together by common understandings grounded in scientific knowledge; a world in which democratic values would eventually triumph.

This hopeful story was embedded not just in the minds of individual Americans but also in the fabric of major American institutions. The latter are legitimated by the claim that they represent universal values, and they reward people who seem to be successful in proving that claim. Thus, these institutions inspired energetic Americans to try to transform China, to be missionaries of the American Dream.

Chinese propagandists called this "cultural imperialism." Yet central to the legitimating myths of American institutions is the assumption

136

that their universalistic aspirations are *not* imperialistic. Imperialism is based on force. The American claim to universalism rests on the premise that central American values will be accepted by rational people anywhere by virtue of their intrinsic persuasiveness. For instance, it is a contradiction in terms to hold that you can *force* someone to be a democratic citizen. Normalization of U.S.-China relations, coupled with the Chinese government's new policies of reform and opening, seemed to give American institutions a chance to demonstrate the intrinsic persuasiveness of their values.

Randall Stross's *Bulls in the China Shop*[1] vividly and entertainingly shows how American business institutions instilled in their members the hope that they not only would profit from China but also would turn Chinese socialists into born-again consumer capitalists. In this chapter, though, I will focus again on American institutions that claimed to represent more fundamental values than making money: religion; the "knowledge professions" of academia and journalism; and the more practically oriented "development professions." I will show how, in spite of their differences and occasional antagonism, these institutions drew on a common liberal myth about China. I will also show how tensions and frustrations arose from inadequacies within that myth.

Missionaries of the Gospel

"My interest in China was kindled when I was a small boy during the 1930s, studying about Baptist missionaries there," wrote Jimmy Carter in his memoirs. "From the slide programs put on by itinerant missionaries on furlough I was taught to look upon the Chinese as friends in urgent need of hospitals, food, schools, and the knowledge of Jesus Christ as their Savior. Our fellow Baptists working in China were considered an elite group — exalted in our eyes above those 'in the foreign field' in other countries."[2]

As a young man, Carter himself had served briefly as a Baptist missionary among Spanish-speaking people in Massachusetts. After he became president, Carter continued to believe that missionary work was good not only for his fellow Baptists but for the United States as a whole. In 1978, the head Sunday school teacher at his church in Washington quoted him as saying: "I don't want to wake up ten or fifteen years from today and find a country that is friendly to us that has turned to another side just because some missionary did not do the job he could have done. I would like to be part of being able to turn that country back to God and back to our side and I'll hope that someday that's what I'll get to do."[3]

Not surprisingly, then, during the banquet to honor Deng Xiaoping's visit to Washington, Carter asked his guest about the possibility of missionaries returning to China.

[Deng] reluctantly admitted that some good missionaries had come to China. However, he insisted that many of them had been there only to change the Oriental lifestyle to a Western pattern. I reminded him of all the hospitals and schools that had been established, and he said that many were still in existence. He was strongly opposed to any resumption of a foreign missionary program and said that the Chinese Christians agreed with him, but he listened carefully when I suggested that he should permit the unrestricted distribution of Bibles and let people have freedom of worship. He promised to look into it. (Later he acted favorably on both these suggestions.)[4]

Some of Carter's aides, who fancied themselves hardheaded strategic thinkers, seemed embarrassed that he would make such a request of Deng. Like many secular scholars, perhaps, they saw Carter's missionary concerns as a distraction from the real business of government: geopolitics and the promotion of commerce. Yet Carter was more attuned to the self-understandings of most ordinary Americans — over 90 percent of whom say they believe in God — than many of his expert advisers.

For most ordinary American citizens, geopolitics is impossibly arcane, and patterns of international trade are difficult to understand and are important only insofar as they affect job prospects. What does excite many Americans, however, is the perception that their most cherished beliefs and values are on the march, being respected and accepted around the world — witness the success of American religious missionaries in their global outreach. When powerful elites make deals to further their own political and economic interests, the fruits of that success do not necessarily trickle to the bottom of the social hierarchy. But when these deals seem to open the way to a broad diffusion of American beliefs and values, ordinary people share in the triumph. They take satisfaction in the thought that their spiritual superiority has been acknowledged; they think they gain the ability to trust distant strangers; they feel more confident that the powerful will accept a sense of responsibility toward the weak; they think they can trust that the poor will rise through responsible, disciplined hard work rather than class warfare;

and they hope that rich and poor individuals will temper their demands for absolute freedom by voluntarily accepting moral responsibility for the common good. Carter's hopes for the new spread of Christianity in China were widely shared among the American population. Though Deng Xiaoping's government continued to bar foreign missionaries, hopes of evangelizing China once again stirred within the institutional fabric of the United States' Christian denominations.

Such hopes were widely shared among all manner of Christians, which helps account for the breadth of popular support for the normalization agreement in spite of the voices crying that Taiwan had been sold out for thirty pieces of silver. But corresponding to—indeed, undergirding—differences in elitist and populist perspectives on the American Dream are differences in religious understandings of the relationship between faith and social life.

Churches and Sects in Mission. These differences are embodied in what Ernst Troeltsch called the "churchlike" and "sectlike" forms of religious community. In sociological parlance, a church is an institution that aims to save the world by accepting it as it is, hoping that the world will then listen at least partially to its message. In order to change the world, the church compromises with it. The church allows diversity in its membership; it does not expect its members to agree fully in their beliefs; and it welcomes people with different degrees of religious commitment. The church is hierarchical because, given its openness to all kinds of people, it must recognize some as more learned or spiritually advanced than others. With its celebration of hierarchy and its tolerance of established social structures, the church most readily appeals to elites who have been successful in worldly terms.

A sect hopes to save the world by confronting it. It strives to save the world's good people by isolating them from the bad. Thus, a sect demands a homogeneous membership: Everyone who belongs to it should firmly believe the same things and adhere to a single high standard of virtue. Within its boundaries, the sect is egalitarian and eschews hierarchy. The sect especially appeals to those who have been unsuccessful in worldly terms.[5]

In the United States, the church-sect distinction cuts across religious denominations. That is, most denominations exhibit both churchlike and sectlike tendencies. Struggles within religious institutions are driven by chronic disputes between those who think their faith should be more churchlike and those who think it should be more sectlike. Churchlike religiosity is stronger in the mainline Protestant denominations than in the evangelical denominations.[6]

For both mainline and evangelical Protestants, the normalization of U.S.-China relations stirred up powerful hopes. For leaders of the former, prone to a churchlike understanding of Christianity, the opportunity was at hand for a grand new ministry of reconciliation and for fruitful cooperation with secular authorities to build a better society in China. For the latter, there was an opportunity for a challenging new ministry of conversion. The mainline effort drew upon what might be termed "inherited capital," the legacy of assets returned with normalization and of old friendships developed in the first part of the twentieth century, and this effort was supported by official PRC policy regarding the practice of religion. The evangelical effort drew upon the zeal and financial sacrifice of American Christians in the present; it was carried out in violation of official PRC policy, and its success depended on the initiative of the evangelists and the intrinsic appeal of its pietistic message to a population weary of accommodation with the secular powers of Chinese modernity.

The United Board for Christian Higher Education in Asia. The mainline Protestant agency with the most churchlike response to the new opportunities in China was the United Board for Christian Higher Education in Asia. The United Board was put together in the early part of the twentieth century as the interdenominational agency responsible for governing the Christian colleges established by American and Canadian Protestant churches in China. The establishment of such colleges was itself a very churchlike way of carrying out missionary work. The colleges were open to all, Christians and non-Christians alike. (In fact, many important Communist leaders were graduates of such colleges.) Their goal was not to provide an explicitly religious education but rather to impart a broad, Western-style liberal education that, it was assumed, would implicitly carry Christian values.[7] The headquarters of the United Board were in New York City. Its trustees were drawn mostly from the "Eastern establishment" ("About twenty-five people on our board are Republicans," said one of them to me in the early 1980s, "but they wouldn't vote for Reagan") and included such names as Nathan Pusey, retired president of Harvard, and Elisabeth Luce Moore, the daughter of Henry Luce (who founded Yanjing University, the most famous of the Christian colleges) and the sister of Henry Luce II (the founder of Time-Life). The Luce family, in fact, was one of the United Board's most important sources of support.[8]

After the establishment of the People's Republic, the Communist government nationalized China's Christian colleges, confiscating all of their property. The board then began to establish Christian colleges in locations throughout Asia, including Taiwan (Tunghai University) and Hong Kong (Chungchi College). In the late 1950s, there arose a heated dispute within the board about whether to press claims against the PRC for compensation for confiscated property. The argument against filing claims was basically about turning the other cheek, coupled with a sense that, though formally owned by foreigners, the colleges had been set up for the sake of the Chinese people and truly belonged to them. The United Board, however, was implicated in secular institutions that could not operate on the principle of turning the other cheek. Its legal counsel finally determined that since the board was chartered as an educational institution within the State of New York, it was legally bound to file a claim to such property.

One of the issues negotiated with the Chinese during normalization was that of compensation for American assets seized by the government. As part of the overall settlement of such claims, the United Board received about $9 million (a fairly small fraction of what its property was really worth). The question then arose of what to do with this money. The board decided to use it to become "helpfully related to higher education in the People's Republic of China."[9]

A United Board delegation, which included Elisabeth Luce Moore and Nathan Pusey, went to China in 1980 to try to establish the new relationships. Their Chinese government hosts, badly in need of money to modernize education, welcomed them but firmly insisted that the United Board's efforts not be used to proselytize the Chinese people in any way. This request was felt by the United Board to be completely consistent with its mission: "The Board is aware that all education in China is under the guidance of the Communist Party and is offered within the context of Marxism, with its particular views of religion. The Board believes, however, there is an opportunity for effective Christian witness in serving Chinese scholars and students in their search for truth and professional skills. In this the Board sees itself as faithful to its original purpose."[10]

"The ultimate reason why we are working for these exchanges . . . is to do what Jesus taught us to do," said a director of the board. "He taught us to serve in the name of Christ. And that is the reason for our involvement with China. Our Board feels very strongly that apart from any effort to make Christians out of these people—and there is some care about that—we must simply devote ourselves to serving them." But the service was not utterly disinterested. "Quite apart from the service motive," the director said, "there is the possibility of being of some indirect influence on the Chinese people. . . . We did not have a lot of illusions about our ability to influence Chinese education. . . . They are in control of their country—we can't hope to influence that. But indirectly we could influence them through our friendship."

For the most part, though, the United Board hoped to influence not individuals but rather Chinese institutions, especially academic institutions. Like secular American educational institutions, the board hoped to help the Chinese conform their academic system to international standards in teaching and scholarship—that is, the standards followed in the United States. But unlike some secular American educators, who hoped to bring Chinese scientific and technical education up to world standards, the United Board wanted to promote classical ideals of a Western liberal education, in which the study of science and technology would be balanced by study of the humanities and social sciences. Leaving the development of science education to other institutions, the United Board throughout the 1980s used its resources in China to rebuild and develop programs in the social sciences and humanities.

Because the Chinese government deemed these programs less important to modernization than science and technology, the humanities and social sciences were indeed in special need of help. The United Board provided aid by supporting Chinese scholars studying for master's degrees in American universities and by paying for some American professors to teach in China. The board also helped improve libraries in various Chinese universities. It concentrated its efforts on lesser-known universities in relatively remote areas, with the idea that such schools needed aid more than central, prestigious ones. The board did not attempt explicitly to preach Christian doctrine, but the overall effect of its programs was to bear witness to convictions common among American mainline denominations: that scientific knowledge needs to be complemented with understandings about the nature of society and discussions about the meaning of life (though the church should not dogmatically insist on its own current view about these issues); that poorer communities need to be attended to as well as rich communities (but the poor should work within the social system established by legitimately constituted authority); and that a spirit of service is one of life's most important values (though if the service is effective it should produce results that are pleasing to the giver).

Did this message have a positive influence on those who received it? There was almost no way to measure. The ability to exercise beneficial influence was taken on faith rather than gauged objectively. "We have a basic faith that the Chinese have a strong self-identity," said a United Board director. "They can make use of ideas from the outside to fashion their own society. They won't blindly imitate outside ideas like other cultures have done." Whether or not good works carried out in the practice of faith communicate that faith to the recipient, they usually strengthen faith in the giver. In the 1980s, the attempt to serve the Chinese in the name of Christ intensified the United Board's conviction that providing such service was good—that it was good in itself and good because in a small but significant way it was influencing the Chinese people for the better.

What kind of people was it hopeful of helping its Chinese beneficiaries to become? Board members naturally envisioned the development of leaders with liberal virtues like those professed by the American mainline Protestant establishment. Such virtues are evoked in a board director's description of the students sponsored by the board in the mid-1980s. Though few of the students were Christians, they had "a serious sense of responsibility," and when they came to the United States, they "worked their heads off." They also saved most of their money. "It is amazing to see how much they save on food and housing—crowding into small apartments and skimping on food—so that they could buy books and other educational materials to take back with them. They do of course buy some consumer goods—but that's understandable. But most of their money . . . goes back into materials for continuing their education and for helping them be better teachers of others."

Besides being imbued with the work ethic, "they show a great open-mindedness about things. They're not dogmatic people rigidly adhering to some party line." The students dared to think and speak for themselves. "Last year during the 'spiritual pollution' campaign in China, the Chinese students and scholars at Harvard got together and read the riot act to the officials at the Chinese consulate about the campaign. 'How could you expect us to study in the United States,' they said, 'if you are going to threaten us with criticism for having absorbed spiritual pollution from the West?'" But, in this board member's view, their open-mindedness was balanced by a strong sense of moral propriety. "They make a discernment rather quickly about what is good and what is bad about this culture. What is good about China: no crime and drugs. What is bad: lack of culture, movies, works of art, etc."

This combination of ambition and open-mindedness with moral discipline and a strong sense of social responsibility was precisely the pattern of virtue that the American Protestant establishment saw as the moral basis of a democratic society. Though decrying the erosion of these virtues in the United States, United Board members delighted in perceiving them in the Chinese who partook of their programs, even if the Chinese had presumably learned them from their own culture without benefit of any contact with Western Christianity.

As the 1980s progressed, however, the intractable realities of Chinese society began to shake the view that American mainline Christianity might exert a beneficent influence upon China. Ironically, as we will see in more detail in the following chapter, academic exchange programs like the United Board's were helping to undermine those moral virtues that board members delighted in discerning in their Chinese visitors.

One of the most troubling facts faced by morally concerned people who ran educational exchange programs like the United Board's was the reluctance of many visiting scholars to return to China. In 1984 the United Board director could say: "We've had a few older professors [from China] who were egocentric — more like American scholars. There was one professor, for instance, who wanted to extend his stay beyond the two years allotted to him. He put up quite a fuss about this. This was a selfish thing to do, because if he stayed it would be depriving another Chinese student from having a chance to participate in this program." By the late 1980s, however, it was not simply a handful of "egocentric" Chinese scholars who wanted to stay in the United States. Many, perhaps most, scholars in all exchange programs were interested in extending their stays.

Most American leaders, and for that matter most Chinese leaders, were surprised and somewhat puzzled by this turn of events. Both Americans and Chinese had expected from the beginning that a few disgruntled individuals would not want to return to China. But no one anticipated the flood of applicants for extended visas and permanent resident visas. It was not simply that the Chinese visiting scholars were more "selfish" than American benefactors expected. The problem was that students and scholars who had come to the United States often were subjected to frustration and harassment when they returned to China. The talents they had cultivated abroad often went unappreciated in their home country. And by the late 1980s, the problems China faced in carrying through its reforms had become so mind-boggling that many Chinese intellectuals despaired that anyone, no matter how intelligent or well-intentioned, could find solutions.

For a scholar who had gained a skill that qualified him or her for a job in the United States, staying there was not necessarily an act of unpatriotic selfishness but was definitely one of common sense. (By 1990, one saying that made the rounds of the Chinese students in American universities was: "A green card is a patriot's safe-conduct pass.") American exchange programs, like that run so devotedly and generously by the United Board, might open a few minds—perhaps even save a few souls—but they could not do much to bring about a humane outcome to China's struggles for reform, and indirectly they may have helped hasten the spread of the cynicism, loss of self-confidence, and cultural despair that had swept through China's urban youth by the end of the 1980s.

The virtues the United Board sought to cultivate were unsupported by the social and political realities of modern China. By the end of the 1980s, it seems in retrospect, a Chinese intellectual might have had to leave the PRC to have effectively practiced such liberal virtues. But, until 1989 at least, American members of the United Board, prisoners of the churchlike liberal hope that motivated and gave direction to their religious institutions, would have resisted such pessimistic conclusions.

"We depart greatly heartened by what we have experienced here," said Paul Lauby, outgoing director of the United Board, in his speech at the conclusion of a United Board–sponsored colloquium on education and social progress held in Nanjing in the fall of 1988. "We leave with a faith that this great social experiment you are undergoing is going to be a great blessing to the world." Lauby was speaking for all twelve American participants at this international conference, which was the culmination of years of United Board effort. The United Board considered the colloquium "the beginning of a process of dialogue and consultation which will deepen educational relationships and enhance the quality and value of educational exchange."

But the leaders of the Chinese institutions with which the board had to interact seemed reluctant to engage in such dialogue. The American colloquium delegation was warned: "From the beginning of its China program in 1980, the United Board has wanted to engage Chinese educators in substantive discussions about issues of common concern. The Board has always viewed itself as far more than a funding agency, rather an organization intimately involved in the Asian educational enterprise.

Initial attempts to engage in such discussions have been far from successful. A concerted attempt to arrange a conference in 1986 met with some resistance on the part of the Ministry of Education (now the State Commission)."[11] The State Commission on Education apparently wanted the United Board's money much more than its ideas.

Finally the commission relented, perhaps sensing that if it did not agree to an exchange of ideas, money might not continue to be forthcoming. The colloquium itself was very lively, with a variety of frank critical discussions of China's educational system presented by the Chinese and some thoughtful papers presented by the Americans. A comprehensive report of the proceedings was published in the *Guangming Daily,* the Beijing newspaper aimed at intellectuals. But the context in which the colloquium was given — increasing disarray in the Chinese economy, increasing anger on the part of Chinese citizens against government corruption, and increasing repression of intellectuals — did not offer great cause for hope. The United Board's idealistic earnestness, moreover, was challenged by the eagerness of some of the Chinese organizers to grab as much foreign currency from the enterprise as possible. Some (but not all) of them seemed willing to engage in a dialogue about ideas only in order to make some easy money.

For all their need to be hopeful, the United Board members, as Lauby put it, "leave this conference with a sense of overwhelming burden. We face a great deal of unfinished business as we wrestle with our gigantic problems. . . ." The United Board's efforts represented the best of mainline religious idealism, the hope that, through rational efforts at least partially sustained and motivated by faith, well-intentioned men and women from different cultures could work out common problems together. But by the end of the 1980s China was too conflicted, too unsettled, for the kind of genteel dialogue envisioned by the United Board to bear much fruit. Perhaps the Chinese government officials were right, under the circumstances; perhaps the United Board's money was much more important than its ideas, no matter how good and well-meaning those ideas might be. In churchlike fashion, the United Board had hoped to change the Chinese world by adapting to its official structures and compromising with its leaders, engaging them in open, rational dialogue. But by the end of the 1980s, China's official leaders had frustrated churchlike religious hope and made open, rational dialogue seem useless.

Evangelism and China. Though it tried the faith of American mainline missionary religion, the bewildering, overwhelming complexity of China's problems encouraged the missionary hope of sectlike religious institutions. "I'm very disturbed at the electronic preachers and their approach to Asia, especially to China," the director of the United Board told me. "Jimmy Swaggart just did a movie. . . . It shows him walking along the streets of Shanghai and going up to some man on the street and saying to him, 'Do you know Christ?' and the man in the street looks at him like he's crazy and says no, he doesn't know Christ, and then Swaggart uses this to tell the American people how steeped in sin and darkness the Chinese people are and how they need to donate money so that he can beam the gospel to the people of China." What irked my liberal Christian interlocutor more than the theological wrongness, from his point of view, of Swaggart's approach was the *success* of that approach. For televangelists such as Swaggart had indeed raised large sums of money from their viewers for ministries to China.

They used the money to beam religious radio programs — often Chinese translations of their own American broadcasts — into China and sometimes also to smuggle Bibles into the country. Besides fundamentalist Christians such as Swaggart, other evangelical Christian denominations raised a great deal of money to proselytize in China and sometimes spent it in very sophisticated ways. A Christian study center in Hong Kong interviewed Chinese coming out of the mainland to ascertain their views about religion and their receptiveness to the Christian faith. Associations were set up to prepare missionaries to get jobs in China as English teachers and use their access to carry out evangelical work. Large-scale efforts to smuggle Bibles were organized.

Such efforts, of course, were vigorously denounced by the Chinese government and by the Chinese Christian churches in the three-self movement, which functioned in cooperation with the government. The Chinese Christian communities with which the American evangelical missionaries interacted were "house churches," which carried out their worship outside the law in private homes rather than in the church buildings that had been officially approved by the Bureau of Religious Affairs. During the Cultural Revolution, virtually all churches were closed, and almost all Chinese Protestants who dared to practice their faith had to worship in homes. But by 1979 the Chinese government had begun to relax its restrictions against religion. It proceeded to open and even rebuild church buildings and allowed worship within them by those who accepted government supervision. But some Christians refused to accept government supervision and continued to operate house churches, even when officially opened church buildings were available in which they could worship. In the Chinese context, such house churches were sects standing against the world. Spokespersons for the three-self movement, such as Bishop Ding Guangxun (K. H. Ting), condemned these sectlike churches for daring to break Chinese laws and for undermining the foundations of the new China.[12]

The leadership (though not necessarily ordinary churchgoers) of the mainline Protestant churches in the United States turned receptive ears to the churchlike message of Bishop Ding, who on his several trips to North America during the 1980s was welcomed to preach in strongholds of liberal Protestantism such as the Riverside Cathedral in New York City. Bishop Ding called the efforts of evangelical Protestants to smuggle Bibles and missionaries into China another attempt at cultural imperialism.[13] Mainline Protestants stressed the need for reconciliation with the Chinese revolution and the new China. Conversely, many leaders (though not necessarily the rank and file) of the evangelical churches were strongly anticommunist. (Saint Paul's statement that all are brothers in Christ does not mean that you should let "Communists deal you cards from under the deck," said one such minister at a rally in San Diego.) Evangelical missionaries with "a burden for China," as some of them put it, also took an assertive, zealous stance toward their calling. One evangelical minister averred that he would not "crawl on my belly in front of the Chinese."

The evangelical churches saw themselves as giving vital resources for the establishment of sectarian Christianity in China. They saw themselves as committed to a higher law than the laws of the Chinese government forbidding their activities. They were willing to judge any government for failing to act in accordance with that higher law and saw communist governments as less legitimate than the U.S. government. The American mainstream press ignored them. The mainline church leadership derided them but tended to underestimate them, often believing that the evangelical churches were too culturally insensitive to get far in China. The worst the evangelicals could do, mainline leaders assumed, was to cause a negative reaction against religion on the part of the PRC government, which would stifle the growth of the three-self churches as well as the house churches. Such assumptions may prove incorrect. Accurate statistics are very hard to come by, but it seems that the house churches grew steadily during the 1980s, in some places outstripping the growth of the three-self churches.[14] This growth is part of a widespread expansion of evangelical sects throughout East Asia, Latin America, Africa, and the former Soviet Union.

Strangely and ironically, the behavior of American evangelical missionaries who went to China in the guise of English teachers was more acceptable to many Chinese—even Chinese officials—than that of secular American teachers and scholars who prided themselves on their cultural sensitivity. The evangelical Christians who went to China were usually willing to work for very low pay and tended to be well disciplined. They did not get into trouble with sex or drugs. They could be relied upon to work hard and not complain too much about the conditions of their employment. Whereas some secular teachers and scholars developed a fondness for the fancy foreign hotels that sprang up in the big cities, many more of the evangelical missionaries—unable to afford such luxuries anyway—were willing to put up with the hard conditions necessary to reach ordinary Chinese citizens. Chinese officials may have disagreed with evangelical Christians' proselytizing efforts and made vigorous efforts to suppress them when they distributed literature denouncing the three-self movement in front of churches, but the officials sometimes seemed pleasantly impressed with the evangelicals' lifestyle.

The theology of the sectlike missionaries was surprisingly appealing even to the Chinese associated with the three-self movement. When Bishop Ding sent seminarians to study at Union Theological Seminary in New York, the visitors were shocked at the secular activism of American liberal Protestants and by their predilection for the theology of liberation—which to the Americans meant not only the liberation of the proletariat but also the liberation, in the name of "multiculturalism," of oppressed ethnic groups (such as the Tibetans), women, and gays and lesbians. As described by a somewhat frustrated staff person in the headquarters of the National Council of Churches:

The official position of the Chinese Church is that they are a post-liberation society. They don't need liberation theology. . . . The kind [of liberation theology] preached by a lot of North American theologians is very aggressive. The Chinese are put off by the manner and interpretation of it within the Church. This is perhaps an American tendency, to be very aggressive for pushing for change around the world. . . . Certain aspects of [the theology of liberation] probably are similar to their commitments at least in the early parts of the Chinese revolution. But they have felt a need to deepen their spiritual emphasis. Though spiritual, the liberation theologians have a political dimension that is so pronounced that the spiritual sometimes gets lost.

In summary, according to this mainline Protestant church worker, "the Chinese church is very pietistic. Some of them are kind of shocked by the international ecumenical movement. They see it as too secular, too political. They are threatened by the radicalized feminism that is part of it and by the emphasis on gay and lesbian rights."

Common Conundrums. The frustrations of missionary work in China were perhaps felt more deeply by the churchlike mainline Protestant missionaries (or "fraternal church workers," as they preferred to call themselves) than by the more sectlike evangelicals. Their efforts to adapt themselves to the main structures of Chinese society led them to work closely, cautiously, and politely with elites—heads of universities, heads of the ministry of education, and so forth—who were sometimes being damned for their rigidity and corruption by a new generation of Chinese boldly demanding fundamental changes in the system. These were just the kinds of people that, elsewhere in the non-Western world, American mainline church leaders were embracing in the name of the theology of liberation. There was a deeper, more tragic conflict going on within China than the mainline churches were prepared to understand.

Evangelical missionaries felt more confident, less confused in their sense of mission to China. They had lower expectations about the possibility of converting Chinese society as a whole. In spite of official government harassment, their efforts bore a surprising amount of fruit. Yet to what avail were their efforts at saving a few souls in the face of the immense problems of China?

Although American mainline and evangelical missionaries profoundly disagreed with and sometimes even despised one another, when they actually worked together in China they developed surprisingly good relations. As one liberal Protestant who worked alongside evangelical Christians on a Chinese campus put it: "Often the experience of confronting the complexities of China, of dealing with particular personal relationships with Chinese people rather than with abstractions, helps to bridge doctrinal gaps." This bridging of gaps seems not to have been a true reconciliation of ideas but rather a kind of personal unity born of shared frustrations at confronting a Chinese reality that only very ambiguously confirmed the expectations of religious missionaries. Eventually, the frustrations of working in the real China might force them to seek a deeper understanding of themselves.

The churchlike and sectlike missionary styles represented different poles in the approach not only of American religious institutions but also of secular American institutions toward China. Much of what I have said about Protestant churches' approach to China after normalization can be applied analogously to the approach of the American knowledge institutions—academia and the press—and the practical professions, especially those devoted to economic and social development.

Missionaries of Knowledge

"Recognition of the People's Republic," as Michael Hunt put it, ". . . set long suppressed dreams of a return to China swirling in the minds of educators (the legatees of the missionary impulse)."[15] Like their missionary predecessors, American educators soon found their dreams broken by the complexities of China; but the nature of their frustrations differed according to whether they had a churchlike or a sectlike understanding of their academic institutions. The frustrations of China intensified the conflict between those having these different understandings of their academic calling.

The Tar Pit of Educational Exchange. In retrospect, the level of enthusiasm generated among American academic leaders surprises even those who were swept up in it. "It was like a tar pit," recalls Kenneth Prewitt, who was head of the Social Science Research Council in 1979, describing the forces that suddenly pulled his time and energy into arranging the initial stages of the American research presence in China. Today he still finds it somewhat difficult to understand why he and so many other American academics reacted with so much excitement and with such a sense of urgency to the opportunity to send scholars to China. Perhaps, he muses, it had something to do with a "Pearl Buck syndrome," an abiding sense of wonder, lodged deep within the American psyche, about the infinite subtleties of Chinese culture and society.

In the initial agreements concluded on the eve of normalization, fifty Chinese scholars were to come to the United States and five American researchers were to go to China. Quickly, though, the numbers of students and scholars going in each direction mushroomed spectacularly: twelve thousand Chinese students and scholars were in the United States by 1985, forty thousand by 1989; by that year there were about four thousand Americans studying in China.[16]

In addition, hundreds of American scholars traveled to China to lecture and teach. Moreover, American universities and other academic institutions established a number of training programs within China, such as the program to train graduate students in sociology at Nankai University and the programs at the Johns Hopkins–Nanjing Center for Chinese and American Studies.

Even when budgets were tight, it was often surprisingly easy for faculty members to coax money for these programs from university administrators. One professor from an East Coast university who was active in establishing exchange programs in sociology in the early 1980s says that, from the hindsight of 1990, his motives appear "naive and imperialistic." Like many American scholars at the time, he justified expenditures of money for his program on the grounds that "our doctorates will occupy leadership positions in Chinese society." He now recognizes that this rationale was based on several blind assumptions: that the theories and methods of American social science were easily applicable to the study of Chinese society; that those who gained mastery of such theories and methods would naturally rise to leadership positions in Chinese academia; and that those who came to the United States to study would want to return to China to improve Chinese academic institutions.

These assumptions are not as plausible now as they once were. Chinese students trained in the West have often striven to master those theories and methods that would give them most prestige in the West, not those that might be most relevant for use in Chinese society. In the process such scholars have become alienated from their peers in China. By the late 1980s it was becoming apparent that many Chinese students in the United States wanted to do everything possible to avoid returning to China. One could make a strong (though still inconclusive) case that American academic institutions have been used by ambitious Chinese students to leave China and advance their personal career goals as much as these institutions have changed Chinese society for the better. Like the churchlike form of religious organization, the American secular university was primarily concerned with establishing a presence in Chinese society and accepted on faith that such a presence would influence China for the better.

Therefore, American academia in its churchlike manifestation was willing to make considerable compromises with Chinese officials in order to maintain such a presence. For the sake of having their values triumph in China, American academic leaders might be willing to compromise some of those values, at least temporarily. It turned out, for example, that many high-ranking Chinese government officials were eager to have their children study in the United States. Anxious to cement their exchange programs with China, university administrators sometimes facilitated admission for such individuals even when admission would not have been warranted strictly on the grounds of academic merit. (It was easy to rationalize such favoritism, because it was so difficult to ascertain in the Chinese context who was well qualified to study at an American university and who was not.) Later, officials' ability to place their children in universities abroad became a prime target of Chinese dissidents' complaints about government corruption. From the dissidents' point of view, it exposed the hypocrisy of official appeals to socialism.[17]

Churchlike and Sectlike Ethics of Research. For American academia, establishing a presence in China meant not only hosting Chinese scholars in the United States but also sending American scholars to China. Indeed, the former was a condition of the latter, because Chinese officials, traditionally wary of exposing the secrets of their domestic life to outsiders, were willing to accept American scholars only in exchange for the valuable opportunity to send their own students abroad.

There was an asymmetry in the flow of students across the Pacific. The Chinese authorities wanted to send students to study American science and technology to help in the modernization of their country. American academic interest mainly centered on social scientific research, but the Chinese government had been very reluctant to permit such research. It required a direct negotiation between Jimmy Carter and Deng Xiaoping to persuade the Chinese leadership that they had to allow Americans to do social scientific research. It was taken on faith by the Americans that their ability to do direct research in China would lead both to major advances in scholarship and to greatly enhanced international understanding. There was such a powerful faith in this idea that American academic leaders were willing to sacrifice (at least temporarily) the quality of the actual content of research in order to establish a strong research presence in China.[18]

Within two years after the normalization of U.S.-China relations, this churchlike aspiration was disturbed and some of its limitations dramatically illustrated by the case of Steven Mosher. A graduate student in anthropology at Stanford University, Mosher was a member of the first group of American research scholars placed in China after normalization. After spending part of 1979 and 1980 doing fieldwork in a Guangdong village, Mosher published — originally in the spring of 1981 in a magazine on Taiwan, later in an American scholarly journal, and finally in a much-discussed book[19] — a sensational article about how callously coercive some local Chinese officials were in enforcing family planning, compelling women as much as eight months pregnant to have abortions and creating a climate in which some parents felt pressured to practice female infanticide. The Chinese authorities responsible for managing the exchange program with the United States accused Mosher, even before he had published his article, of having engaged in serious improprieties while conducting his research, including traveling to restricted areas of China without a permit, illegally importing a van into China, and illegally bringing out restricted documents. Chinese authorities eventually demanded that Stanford punish Mosher and cited his case as one reason to deny long-term fieldwork access to anthropologists and sociologists seeking to study Chinese communities.

After an investigation carried out in consultation with senior leaders in the field of Chinese studies (most of whom seem to have agreed that Mosher had been, as one of them put it in a private conversation with me, "like a rogue elephant"), Stanford did expel Mosher from its graduate program. The university claimed it did so not because Chinese government officials wanted Mosher expelled but because Mosher had violated professional ethics and transgressed Stanford's own rules for graduate student conduct. He allegedly lied to his dissertation committee about how he was doing his work and was spending his research funds; manipulated local Chinese people into cooperating with him; and violated the confidentiality of some of his research subjects. If these allegations were true (which is impossible for an outsider to tell because the university's deliberations were conducted in secret), then Mosher's expulsion would have been justified even if his research had not had disturbing political implications. But because of its political context, the Mosher case became the focus of a debate on the broader issue of how American academia should relate to China.[20]

The Mosher case became one of the most widely publicized academic controversies of the early 1980s. Newspapers spanning the political spectrum — from the *Wall Street Journal* to the *New York Times* to *The Nation* — denounced Stanford and defended Mosher. The *Wall Street Journal* editorialized in July 1983:

We smelled a rat when Steven Mosher was expelled. . . . It's clear . . . a good part of the American social science establishment, fearful that research opportunities in China would otherwise be closed off, had joined in the stone throwing. . . . If Mr. Mosher had discovered forced abortions in South Africa or Chile, perhaps even violating local law in the process, he might have been given a medal of honor by the academic establishment. Unless Stanford can say more about just what Mr. Mosher did that was so outrageous, it is difficult to avoid the conclusion that he was singled out for special moral scrutiny solely because his unpleasant truths were too shocking for his fellow academics to bear.[21]

The Role of the University. At issue in such comments was not just an understanding of China but also a vision of the mission of the modern university. Should the university's role in American culture be that of a church or that of a sect? Stanford was criticized for being more interested in accommodating the desires of the Chinese government and maintaining exchange relations than with reporting the truth. Some academic supporters of Stanford stressed the responsibility of an anthropologist not to "foul the nest" — that is, not to ruin research opportunities for succeeding generations of scholars. In the view of such academics, whether or not Mosher had committed the specific transgressions that Stanford used to justify his expulsion, he deserved censure because his reckless pursuit of academic glory had destroyed opportunities for a long-term American research presence in China. These scholars would never have said that American researchers should cover up human rights violations in China simply to preserve good exchange relations with China. But some would have said that responsible scholars should be cautious about offending official Chinese sensibilities — in short, that they should compromise with Chinese officials and suppress sensationalistic findings so that the groundwork might be laid for a deeper understanding of China in the long run.

The critics of Stanford, by contrast, wanted academia to take more of a sectlike approach — to make no compromises in search of the truth, even if that meant taking a strong stand against the powers of Chinese society. They wanted to know about the lives of individuals, especially downtrodden individuals. They did not want to hear about bloodless "social structures," ineluctable "social forces," and abstract "social contexts." They wanted academic knowledge that would help concrete persons, not gradually transform society. And a new generation of China specialists were finding that there were a lot of people who needed help in China.

The new opportunities for American scholars to live and study in China for long periods of time very quickly exposed many of them to the harsher realities of Chinese society: the oppressiveness of the Chinese bureaucracy, the widespread corruption of Chinese officials, the arbitrariness of authority, the intolerance toward any political dissent, the almost paranoic cruelty of the Party toward intellectuals, the oppressiveness of many Chinese men toward women. Any foreigner who, like

Steven Mosher, could speak Chinese and was willing to step outside the official norms guiding the activities of foreigners could meet plenty of individuals whose lives had been senselessly destroyed by the Chinese political system.

Moreover, many of these unfortunate individuals would be people for whom middle-class foreign intellectuals would naturally feel sympathy. Every society — the United States certainly included — has its share of horror stories. Any American middle-class intellectual who spent some time in the south Bronx could find plenty of lives tragically ruined by a corrupt, unjust social system. But such victims, of a different status and probably of a different race than the middle-class intellectual, would not necessarily elicit the kind of sympathy that a refined Chinese intellectual with an analogous horror story would elicit. In China, foreign scholars could find many people similar to themselves in status, learning, and articulateness who had suffered terrifying cruelties. The stories of such people could provide the material for poignant reportage. The first American journalists allowed in China after normalization, most notably Fox Butterfield of the *New York Times*[22] and Richard Bernstein of *Time*,[23] wrote very popular books filled with such stories.

Journalistic Ethics versus Academic Ethics. Newspapers like the *New York Times* sympathized with Mosher because he had published work very similar in muckraking sensibility to what their own reporters had written. The main difference between Mosher's and the journalists' work was that Mosher wrote mostly about the plight of peasants, whereas the journalists had highlighted the difficulties of intellectuals. Mosher experienced very different consequences than did the journalists, however. The journalists were widely acclaimed in the United States, though denounced in China. Their books sold well and, though they could not return to China, they went on to distinguished careers in journalism, mainly covering domestic news. Conversely, Mosher's academic career was destroyed. Although he eventually got a job at the Claremont Institute, a conservative think tank near Los Angeles, he was effectively barred from teaching in universities because he had no Ph.D., and he was shunned by most mainstream China scholars.

The difference in these outcomes was due to the differences in the institutional contexts of journalism and academia. After normalization, American journalism quickly gained a stable presence in China. The normalization agreements specifically allowed each country's major newspapers and news services a presence in the other's capital. Even if the Chinese government did not like what American journalists wrote about their country, it was not going to bar journalists from China, as long as it maintained diplomatic relations with the United States. The Chinese government had been very reluctant, however, to admit research scholars, and in the early years after normalization, as demonstrated by the Mosher case, it could quickly shut down opportunities for meaningful research. Thus, the mishaps of a few scholars could — or so it seemed in the early 1980s — severely harm the access of American academics to China.

Understandably, then, the American academic community reacted strongly against scholars whose actions threatened that fragile access. Moreover, academia, as an institution, legitimates itself by claiming to produce knowledge of long-range consequence. It emphasizes research that will not necessarily produce immediate results but will pay off in the long run. Journalism, by contrast, promises quickly delivered news on the important events of the day. The problem faced by American journalists when they went to China in the late 1970s was that there was not much late-breaking news to be had from official sources. Government bureaucrats either completely ignored journalists or handed them press releases consisting of blatant propaganda. To produce vivid news stories, journalists had to go outside official channels. In the furtive whisperings of the most desperate, most alienated members of Chinese society, they found apparently authentic voices. Their status as journalists rose when they reported on those voices. And when, following the career pattern of foreign correspondents, they were rotated back to the United States, they found good assignments waiting for them on the basis of their bold investigative reporting in China.

It was easier, of course, for a foreign journalist to act boldly in speaking the truth about China than it was for a Chinese citizen. If the foreign journalist irritated Chinese officials, the worst that could happen was expulsion. For a Chinese, the punishment could be imprisonment or even execution. The dissident Wei Jingsheng was sentenced to fifteen years in prison officially for "giving state secrets to foreign journalists." And after Richard Bernstein, the *Time* magazine reporter, published some information that a man named Lu Lin gave him, the informant was sentenced to six years in prison.[24]

For academics, the challenge was to capture the larger social and political contexts of China. Academic reviewers who criticized Steven Mosher's revelations about forced abortion in Guangdong did not dispute the accuracy of his reporting, claiming instead that he failed to place the events in a larger context: He did not show whether the forced abortions he witnessed were typical or indicative of broader trends. His writing was therefore "sensationalistic" or "journalistic" rather than social scientific.[25]

In churchlike fashion, then, the typical position of American academic leaders was that China faced grievous problems but that, with the benefit of policy reforms and openness to the West, its government would gradually solve them. In compromising with the world in the hope of someday saving it, American scholars had to refrain from antagonizing the Chinese government and endangering the ties they had finally been able to reestablish with China.

Missionaries of Development

The American practical professions, especially those devoted to fostering societal development around the world, also split between a churchlike and sectlike approach. The Ford Foundation perhaps best represents the churchlike aspirations of the practical professions and has done the most to enable those aspirations to be realized in China. In the late 1970s, says Francis X. Sutton, a retired program officer who is writing a history of the organization, the Ford Foundation's professional staff

saw China as typical of [the foundation's] international engagements. We felt we had something to give to the rest of the world: modernization, education, bringing people out of age-old prejudices. We had a moral obligation to do something about these. In the old days, giving people like the Chinese religion was enough. Now we were believers in the development ideology — we all believed that if we could only transmit to other societies the ideology that had made us rich and great, poor societies would be able to develop themselves also. It was assumed that there were two classes of society, those relatively well off that shared a sort of common ideology stressing the importance of economic development and various kinds of free institutions, and those that were not. . . . On the whole the kind of people I have known at the Ford Foundation have been very typical Americans — optimistic, can-do Americans. . . . They had a faith that if things were managed right, things would go right. . . . The idea was that if you've got a problem, there's an answer to it. People now, however, don't share this positivist faith. They have begun to doubt.

For some Ford Foundation experts, the possibilities that opened in China in the early years after normalization inspired enough hope to assuage such doubt. Beginning in 1979, the Ford Foundation began to spend millions of dollars to support the training of Chinese experts in economics, law, and international relations. The guiding hope behind these programs was, as Sutton described it, "that these kinds of exchanges will ultimately have a liberalizing, democratizing influence." By the mid-1980s, the foundation had established an office in Beijing to direct its efforts. When I visited it in 1988, the interior of the office contrasted markedly with the cramped, austere interiors of similar Chinese offices in Beijing. The Ford Foundation office was comfortably large for the number of people who worked there. Computer terminals flickered in each office. A light grey synthetic fabric rug covered the floor. Soft indirect lighting suffused the room. Attired in a fashionable red dress, the secretary looked more like an office worker from Hong Kong than one from Beijing.

"The Ford Foundation's assumption," said Peter Geithner, the director of the Beijing office, "has always been that the keys to development are good people and good institutions." In Geithner's view, developing good institutions in China required realism: "There is a question of how far you can go to hurry up the path to development. Societies have to pass through stages. To some extent you can short-circuit the development path. But you probably can't short-circuit it too much. . . . Social problems are institutionally determined. You have to work through the specific existing set of institutions to solve them. You have to be realistic about what, under a given set of institutional circumstances, constitutes an adequate response." In this view, being realistic meant conforming to the prevailing customs of China in order to establish a firm institutional presence for the Ford Foundation. At a time when many foreigners in China were worried that their mail would be opened and read by the Bureau of Public Security, the Ford Foundation marked its envelopes "OPEN HERE FOR POSTAL INSPECTION."

For many at the Ford Foundation, it was, as Peter Geithner put it, "a trouble . . . to deal with a totalitarian state like China." But there was a silver lining to this trouble: "In China, ironically, it's easier to get things done [than in a place like India] because the society is closed. If you have access to the right person and he makes a decision, then things will get done. If China became more open, it could complicate things — more groups would be demanding a say in how Ford did things. But in a broader, more pragmatic sense, the whole purpose of all this is to make things more open."

The foundation's churchlike approach was apparent in its response when an association of Chinese political science students in the United States, funded by the Ford Foundation, elected as their president Hu Ping, a student dissident whom the Chinese Communist Party had labeled a "counter-revolutionary." The Ford Foundation had helped establish this organization because it was concerned about the number of Chinese students who were seeking to stay in the United States rather than return to China. Like the United Board for Christian Higher Education in Asia, the foundation favored letting Chinese students study in the United States with the hope that these students would come home to reform Chinese institutions. If the students remained in the United States, they undercut the foundation's purposes. Foundation-sponsored organizations such as the Chinese political science students association were to provide moral support that would encourage the students to keep their attention focused on their homeland. That association, though, was, in Geithner's words, "tarred by some of its members," who used the organization to denounce the corruption of the Deng Xiaoping regime and elected the notorious dissident as their head. As a result, the Ford Foundation cut off its funding.

"Unlike many foreigners," a well-connected director of an important academic institute in Beijing said about this incident, "Mr. Geithner understands us." Geithner in fact did not speak Chinese and was not especially well versed in Chinese history and sociology. What the director meant by "us" was "Chinese officials." And what he meant by "understand" was that Geithner accepted the point of view of such officials. The Ford Foundation, as represented by Geithner, was determined to accommodate the wishes of Chinese officials in the hopes that they would gradually be persuaded to undertake top-down institutional reforms that would benefit all of China.[26]

After the Ford Foundation withdrew its funding, the political science students received new funding from the Soros Foundation. This was a foundation established by George Soros, a Hungarian immigrant who had made a fortune as a financier in New York. Soros had used some of his money to set up "Funds for Democracy" in Eastern European countries and finally in China. These funds paid for reading rooms and helped advocates of democracy in those countries to study, write, and discuss how to transform their societies. The China fund supported a series of "salons" where young people discussed how to change the Chinese system. It was George Soros himself who made the decision to support the Chinese political science students after the Ford Foundation had withdrawn. "That undid three years of work," sighed a person who had once been connected with the fund's professional staff and who had tried to work, Ford Foundation–style, to slowly build credibility with Chinese officials. In any case, this was part of a pattern of actions taken under the impetus of the assertive, entrepreneurial director of the Soros Foundation — "typical of someone with first-generation money," said one of the foundation's churchlike critics — toward China, aimed in good sectlike fashion at creating enclaves of people with strong democratic values and setting them apart from and against their world.

Institutional Entanglements and Moral Confusion

Within the churches, within the knowledge professions, and within the development professions, debates about whether to accommodate or to confront the established structures of Chinese society were debates about how properly to enact a common faith: a belief that American liberal values were universal and that, having been exposed to them, Chinese society would eventually adopt them.

But by the end of the 1980s, China was frustrating the hopes of American cultural institutions, both elitist churchlike ones and more populist sectlike ones. Mainline church administrators and theologians bent over backward to adapt their message to the "liberationist ideology" of Chinese communism, only to find that China's "revolutionary" leaders did not want to hear about the theology of liberation or the political mission of the church — and that their three-self church counterparts wanted nothing more than an old-fashioned pietistic theology. The American academic establishment expended large amounts of resources to train the future leaders of Chinese society, only to have many of those trainees settle permanently in the United States. Social science researchers had to wrestle with uncomfortable ethical, even epistemological dilemmas about how to find and whether to tell the truth about Chinese society. The practical professions, as represented by the Ford Foundation's Chinese development program, saw some of their major beneficiaries turn away from the gradual, patient reform of Chinese institutions; other development programs began to get undermined by official corruption in China.

The sectlike efforts of American cultural institutions encountered fewer frustrations. Sectarians expect that things will be difficult and consider small victories a triumph. Evangelical missionaries to China encountered many of the expected hostilities from government officials but gained better entree to Chinese society and gleaned more converts than they might have predicted. Those in the knowledge professions who took a sectarian approach found plenty of poignant stories of individual oppression to write about and often gained a wide audience for their writing. The sectarians in the practical professions found heroic collaborators in the struggle against the established authorities of China.

Nonetheless, Americans with sectlike aspirations encountered the same frustrations they usually do. Evangelical Christian converts had to carry on a furtive existence, and for all their growth in numbers remained a tiny, beleagured minority. The outrages uncovered by the journalists continued to exist, and publicizing the outrages did not alleviate the burden faced by China's unfortunate and in some cases increased it (for instance, by resulting in the arrest and imprisonment of those who had provided information to the journalists). And the dissidents encouraged by the sectlike practical professions were powerless to effect the fundamental transformations in the Chinese system to which they aspired, partly because they themselves were so factionalized and partly because their ideas were so unrealistic.

The normalization of U.S.-China relations breathed new life into some of the major institutions of American liberalism, encouraging them to reaffirm their central myths by spreading their supposedly universal values to foreign lands. But as the institutions engaged themselves in Chinese realities, they encountered puzzlements—a society that would not follow the plot of the master story, that would not fit into their categories, that would not validate their hopes.

Let us listen now to the people who were the objects of the missionaries of the American Dream. What did the normalization of U.S.-China relations mean to the Chinese? What did the Chinese aspire to receive from their new relationship? And what frustrations and puzzlements did they encounter?

7

Openness and Emptiness

Chinese Reactions to the Liberal Myth

Since 1979, Chinese society has changed rapidly, profoundly, and dramatically. Most of this change has been caused by internal forces, the most important of which was a powerful reaction against the inhumanities of the Cultural Revolution. But at least some of the change has been a consequence of increased contact with the outside world, especially with the United States. During the 1980s, missionaries of the American Dream often attributed these transformations to American efforts, even when the changes were probably the result of indigenous forces. In any case, Americans assumed that contact with their institutions was leading Chinese society toward becoming a liberal democracy and thus validating the American Dream.

But the changes have been more convulsive and their outcomes more ambiguous than most Americans anticipated. For instance, the U.S. officials who negotiated the normalization agreements had little respect for China's communist ideology and were happy to see it challenged by Western ideas. But insofar as they imagined any scenario for the future, they looked for a peaceful, orderly transformation, gradually embraced by a responsible, enlightened leadership as well as by ordinary people — a blending of the best aspects of the West with the best aspects of Chinese culture.[1] What occurred during the 1980s, however, was a devastating loss of self-confidence among urban intellectuals, widespread discontent among workers in the state sector, a profound sense of moral disorientation on the part of many urban young people, and rampant corruption on the part of government officials.

By 1989, many Americans knowledgeable about China were puzzled at these unwelcome developments and dismayed at the turmoil attendant upon them. Was Chinese society impervious to the American Dream? Or had Americans failed to propagate their values effectively enough? In the next two chapters I will argue that many Chinese, especially relatively elite urban Chinese, were influenced by some American values and did embrace part of the American Dream. However, most missionaries of the American Dream would find the consequences of their success disturbing because they challenged important elements of the liberal myth about China. What happened, I will argue, was similar to what philosopher Erazin Kohak says of his native Czechoslovakia:

> The unfortunate truth is that as the former subjects of the Soviet empire dream it, the American dream has very little to do with liberty and justice for all. . . . The Americans of Czech popular imagination are people who never have to deny themselves anything. . . . Most of all, they live in a land which is totally dedicated to the unlimited expansion of individual material affluence. That is approximately what most Czechs unthinkingly assume the dream of freedom to be, seldom pausing to reflect that it is a dream made up mostly of irresponsibility, unreality, and instantly gratified greed.[2]

I will argue that it was mainly because of indigenous social and cultural circumstances that some Chinese thus interpreted the American Dream — but it was also, to some degree, because of unresolved contradictions within the American Dream itself, contradictions that most Americans have usually not wanted to face.

Let me first describe what the American Dream looked like to various influential sectors of Chinese society and why they saw it that way.

Official Ambivalence and Unofficial Acceptance

The official view of American society promoted by the Chinese government's propaganda apparatus has been ambivalent. *Meiguo,* the Chinese word for America, literally means "beautiful country." When the Communist Party's propaganda apparatus denounced "American imperialism," it rendered that term in a kind of Chinese shorthand — *"Meidi"* — which literally means "beautiful imperialist." In his book by that title, David Shambaugh carefully documents this ambivalence in the writings of China's officially sponsored "America watchers."[3] He cites as a representative example an article written in 1984 by New China News Agency Washington bureau chief Li Yanning entitled, "America—A Country Full of Contradictions." The article notes, "This country's education is so developed . . . on the other hand 26 million Americans are illiterate or semiliterate." Later, Li observes, "Americans spend a lot of stress on keeping fit; . . . on the other hand, so many people become addicted to drugs and do not hesitate to destroy themselves. . . ."[4]

With the commencement of the period of "reform and opening," the official view was that Chinese needed to learn American technology and methods of economic management but should beware of "spiritual pollution" from unenlightened and antisocial American values. According to the long tradition that defined Chinese culture as the only true standard of civilization, China, the Middle Kingdom, was morally superior to the West. In spite of its poverty and technological backwardness, China had a great deal to teach the West about social justice and personal virtue. China had a more just society: It shared its wealth more equitably and, unlike Western capitalist societies, provided basic housing and medical care for all. China also had a more temperate society: It had an extremely low divorce rate and was unafflicted by the scourges of prostitution and drug use. In short, unlike in the United States, Chinese culture held liberal individualism in check by a strong, collectively shared sense of social responsibility. It was the job of the Chinese government's propaganda apparatus to convince Chinese citizens of their culture's superiority, and it was, among other things, the job of China's public security apparatus to stifle the expression of decadent, socially disruptive Western ideas.

As contact with the United States widened, however, the preaching of the propaganda apparatus increasingly fell on deaf ears. As I noted in Chapter 4, many Chinese were so disillusioned by the Cultural Revolution that they assumed the truth must be just the opposite of what the propagandists said. By this principle, if the propagandists said the United States was bad, it must be good indeed. Even those who were not so cynical, however, often found American values powerfully seductive—witness the middle-aged couple who, on visiting their graduate student daughter in New York in the mid-1980s, asked to be taken to a porno shop in Times Square so they could see "the dark side of capitalism." In their unofficial capacities, even many of China's ruling elites—including those connected with the propaganda apparatus—found themselves swept up by some of the values they denounced in the United States. In so doing, they further discredited their propaganda.

Values such as democratic self-government proved attractive as well, and some Chinese became willing to risk their lives for these. But many Chinese found it hard to discriminate between the darker and brighter sides of the American Dream. Learning about the United States gave them a feeling of liberation and generated a thirst for autonomy. But this autonomy embodied self-indulgent, greedy impulses together with aspirations for new kinds of personal discipline and voluntarily accepted social responsibility.

Most missionaries of the American Dream surely recognized that there were darker sides to American-style freedom, that the American Dream carried with it antisocial vices as well as democratic virtues, and they probably assumed that these vices would find their way into Chinese culture as well. But most Americans, perhaps, assumed that these sins would not be too disruptive of Chinese social life and that, in any case, the more beneficent sides would prevail. It is this set of liberal expectations that the Chinese experience called into question.

Although, as we shall see, the American Dream was perceived differently by Chinese of different generations, social statuses, and institutional affiliations, there were important commonalities of experience among those who encountered American values. Let us first explore those commonalities before discussing the differences.

Awakening

Many Chinese whom I interviewed in 1988 spoke of their exposure to Western culture as an "awakening" — a sudden, startling opening of the imagination to new possibilities. This process seemed beyond the control of those who underwent it. It came, first of all, not from conscious study of big ideas but from small, ordinary experiences.

Those who underwent such experiences most intensively and extensively were students, especially students who were sent to the United States or who flocked to classes in English and Western culture in China. For instance, Su Wei, a literature student who studied at UCLA and Harvard in the mid-1980s — and later ended up on a Chinese government "most wanted" list for the role he played in the Tiananmen demonstrations — describes the culture shock of his first encounter with American academic life. When he went to register for his courses, he was confronted with a bewildering array of choices. In China he had never had such a thing; the curriculum had always been neatly laid out for him, with no electives. When he asked his adviser whether he could take a particular course, the answer was: "Just try it." He had never been encouraged to try something out for himself in China. When he finally attended a seminar, he was confronted with an assignment to produce a paper that expressed his own ideas. This, too, was a shock. "While people here have every week been producing their 'own ideas,'" he reflected, ". . . how many of their 'own ideas' have the whole Chinese people produced over the past several hundred years?" Immersed in an American academic context, he was not merely reading about some of the ideas of Western liberalism, he was living them. It was the living rather than the reading that had the most profound effect on him. He found the whole experience disturbing but also exhilarating.[5]

I have heard many similar testimonies about awakening among Chinese students exposed to an American style of life. "I feel so free when I'm in class with my [American] English teacher," said a graduate student in China. This feeling came about because the teacher encouraged free expression in her students and posed no threat of using what they said against them. Such practical experiences taught far more powerful lessons than theoretical learning did.

A more subtle way of acquiring American values was by adopting new modes of communication. Take, for instance, the reaction of those within the Chinese government's propaganda apparatus to the new requirements for communicating with the West. Before 1978, the propaganda agencies made no serious effort to communicate broadly with Western publics. Under the suffocating control of the Party, they vacuously spoke *at* the West rather than to it. As late as 1978, the director of the office of Radio Beijing that broadcast propaganda to North America couldn't speak English and was unwilling and unable to make the broadcasts intelligible or appealing to an American audience. Broadcasts directed toward the United States were simply stilted English translations of material that had appeared in the *People's Daily*. After meetings of the Party Central Committee, for instance, the radio announcers were required to read in English the names of all elected members of the committee — listed in order of the number of strokes in the Chinese characters that made up their surnames. Even if the radio station interviewed some English-speaking "friend of China" for broadcast to the

United States, the Radio Beijing staff would first have to translate the interview into Chinese so the director could go over it and edit out any statements that didn't fit the current Party line.

After U.S.-China normalization, these practices changed. New directors were gradually put in charge of China's news organizations, and new personnel were employed on their staffs with the charge of revising the format of outwardly directed news coverage to make it credible to foreign audiences.[6] A good example of these efforts was the establishment of the *China Daily,* a new English-language newspaper that first appeared in 1981. Planning began in 1979 for this newspaper, designed to meet the needs of the Western tourists and businesspersons who began flocking to China under the new Chinese policy of openness. Some government officials had originally suggested producing an English-language version of the *People's Daily.* But, as one of the founding editors of the *China Daily* put it: "The *People's Daily* is an official organ of the Chinese Communist Party; its intended readership is Party members. An English version of this paper would not meet the needs of foreign visitors. Our purpose in writing for these people is not to convert them to Communism but to promote mutual understanding. . . ."

Some of the key senior editorial staff of the new publication were journalists who had had experience working with American publications such as *Time* and *Life* in the 1930s and 1940s. Aided by fellowships from American foundations, the *China Daily* also sent some of its younger staff members for training in the United States at institutions such as the Columbia School of Journalism, the University of Missouri, and the University of Hawaii. The new publication also benefited from the help of "foreign experts," especially young journalists from the United States, who spent a year or more at the paper's headquarters, located inside the *People's Daily* compound in Beijing.

The result was a newspaper strikingly different in appearance from a Chinese-language paper. It was the first paper in China to use computers for its composition, the first to print unedited dispatches from foreign wire services such as UPI, the first to devote 25 percent of its space to advertising, and the first to make liberal use of photographs. It *looked* like an American newspaper. The purpose of the *China Daily,* however, remained different from that of an American newspaper; it remained a Party-controlled propaganda organ, albeit a different kind of propaganda organ than its predecessors. As the *China Daily*'s editor told me:

In China we have a different concept of freedom of the press than you do. Foreigners like to call Chinese news "propaganda," and they think that is a bad thing. But in China "propaganda" is a good word. It was only Dr. Goebbels from the Hitler days who made it a bad word. In China, the purpose of propaganda is to explain the Party's policy to the masses of people and to convey feedback from the masses to the Party. Since the Party and the people in China are working together [a notion that many alienated Chinese citizens would certainly disagree with], we have freedom of the press. But it is a different concept of freedom than given in your country by the First Amendment.

The editor went on to criticize journalists such as Fox Butterfield and Richard Bernstein for writing books critical of China. His complaint against these books wasn't that the facts they cited were untrue but that they were excessively negative, designed simply to turn sentiment against "China." It was partly the government's own fault, he mused, that these books were written. When the PRC admitted foreign correspondents, it erred in not giving them sufficient access to government spokespersons. As a result, the foreign journalists didn't have enough to do. "Where were they to collect news? From the man in the street! They listened to rumors. Now we realize that we have to help them to cover the news. So each unit now has a spokesperson from whom foreign journalists can get news releases." This policy, he thought (the interview was held before the Beijing Spring of 1989), was solving the problem. Guided by a helpful government public relations apparatus, the foreign journalists would generally write pieces favorable toward China. The editor of the *China Daily* still saw himself as a propagandist responsible for communicating to foreigners; he was merely concerned with communicating that propaganda more effectively. Thus, he needed to adopt the techniques of the Western public relations specialist rather than those of the old-fashioned Party *apparatchik*.

However, the very necessity of clothing propaganda/public relations in Western garb helped to undermine some of the values the propaganda was meant to serve. "Journalists here and in your country," he said to me, "have a lot of similarities based on their professional standards." The effort to adopt some international professional standards gradually induced him — and, to a much greater degree, his younger staff — to pull away from rigid Party control. "When Reagan was shot," he said, "we ran a picture of the assassination attempt on the front page. The editor of the *People's Daily* criticized us: 'Why run a big picture of a leader being shot?'"

In adopting the journalistic conventions practiced by Western newspapers, the *China Daily* was distancing itself from the traditional standards of Chinese propaganda organs and introducing new conceptions of acceptable political discourse. The desire to adopt at least some global standards of professional journalism also meant *China Daily* reporters could not simply concoct stories to meet the needs of political leaders. They insisted on using uncensored excerpts from international wire services. They might work hard to put a "spin" on the facts to accord with the political interests of the Chinese leaders, but they could not grossly distort the facts or simply make them up—if for no other reason than that the foreign readers of the *China Daily* would eventually have access to other news services that would expose and render incredible any crude distortion or fabrication. Liberal notions of professional objectivity and autonomy thus entered into a Chinese institution and began to change how Chinese journalists understood their mission. These values only moderately influenced the *China Daily's* senior editor, but they sometimes had a profound influence on younger generations of journalists. One of the prominent groups of demonstrators who marched on Tiananmen Square in the spring of 1989 was a contingent of journalists with a banner: "The news media should tell the truth!"[7]

The morning after the Beijing massacre, the English-language service of Radio Beijing broadcast the following short message: "Please remember June the Third, 1989. The most tragic event happened in the Chinese Capital, Beijing. Thousands of people, most of them innocent civilians, were killed by fully-armed soldiers when they forced their way into the city. . . . Radio Beijing English Department deeply mourns those who died in the tragic incident and appeals to all its listeners to join in protest for the gross violation of human rights and the most barbarous suppression of the people. . . . Because of the abnormal situation here in Beijing there is no other news we could bring you. We sincerely ask for your understanding and thank you for joining us at this most tragic moment."[8] If the adoption of new forms of internationally oriented communication could partially awaken even propagandists to Western ideals of professional autonomy and make them demand protection of human rights, the adoption of such modes of discourse must have had similarly profound effects on managers, technicians, scientists, lawyers, traders, and artists.

Such changes were just what many missionaries of the American Dream would have wanted: the insinuation of a taste for the most positive aspects of individual autonomy into the most articulate and influential strata of Chinese society. But to assimilate new values in a beneficial way, people need a fund of self-confidence. They need to feel they can absorb the new without completely destroying their old identity. They need to believe they already have something valuable to build upon. This is especially true when the new value being acquired is that of personal autonomy. As anyone who remembers the turmoil of adolescence will recognize, the quest for personal autonomy can become disorienting. Without a base in any taken-for-granted certainties, this quest can be positively debilitating, even self-destructive.

When many Chinese first encountered American values in the 1980s, they lacked a firm basis for self-confidence. The Cultural Revolution had destroyed much of that, and the propagation of the liberal American Dream helped undermine what little was left. Bereft of self-confidence, many Chinese all too often fell prey to the most negative consequences of American liberalism.

A Bankruptcy of Confidence

Although ordinary citizens may have been widely disillusioned before the opening to the West, many of the Chinese elites who were initially able to travel to the United States or interact with Americans carried with them a firm sense of dignity, based on their confidence that their traditional virtues were superior to those of the West. One of the Chinese officials who accompanied Deng on his visit to the United States remembered his bemusement at encountering a Hungarian refugee security guard who told him, "I never want to go back." He proudly contrasted this Hungarian's attitude with that of a distinguished scholar who visited the United States in 1979 and was asked by someone at the University of California at Berkeley, "Would you like a chair here?" "I prefer standing in China!" was his reply. Such a spontaneous response was evidence, according to the official who told me this story, that Chinese culture was much stronger and therefore morally better than Hungarian culture and indeed better than the individualistic culture of America. "We have a saying: 'I live a Chinese, I die and become a Chinese ghost.' I have faith that Chinese culture is a cohesive force." But by 1989, even this privileged, politically loyal official had become disillusioned. He has left China and now lives in the United States.

How did propagation of the American Dream further erode the cultural self-confidence that might have enabled Chinese discriminatingly to adopt the best of American ideas? Cultural self-confidence is grounded in a notion that one has something to teach as well as to learn from others. But as far as American culture was concerned, it increasingly appeared to many Chinese that they had nothing of value to teach — in part because most Americans they met did not really seem to want to learn from them. Often enough, when Chinese made contact with American society, they encountered a kind of socially embodied pride.

"Americans are extraordinarily proud," says Jan Berris, the associate director of the National Committee on U.S.-China Relations. "For instance, we take a delegation to see Mayor Koch of New York and he tells the Chinese: 'Welcome to the greatest city in the world.' We do have a great sense of pride in our history and in our technology and I find myself guilty of the sin of pride in showing the Chinese around our country." Unlike less culturally sensitive Americans, Berris works hard at overcoming that fault. "I don't think that our culture is superior to that of the Chinese. I do think that we can learn from each other. I do think that there's a lot they can learn from us, about technology especially; and there's a lot we can learn from them."

But is it possible that the pride many Americans naturally have in their country could have intimidated some of the Chinese they encountered, especially because that pride was often manifested so spontaneously and ingenuously? Despite the efforts of people like Berris, on balance, I will suggest, the overall message Chinese received from their encounters with American institutions was that Americans did not believe they could learn much from Chinese culture. Could this message have contributed to the lack of self-confidence that made the Chinese unable to blend the best in their own culture with the best in American culture?

Chinese who gave me their impressions after traveling in the United States often expressed amazement at the energy and enthusiasm of Americans. The level of affluence and the degree of technological development also surprised and moved them. In the words of a Chinese journalist who had worked in Europe in the 1970s and covered the United States during the early 1980s: "To tell you the truth, I was surprised by the extent of the wealth — the extent of the wealth was quite amazing. Also, the uniformity of the service. For instance, the phone system — wherever you go in America, you can pick up a phone, and it works! And you use the same procedures to dial wherever you are!"

The visceral impression received by Chinese such as this journalist (who had read quite a bit about the United States before going there) from direct exposure to the United States was one of shock at how far the West was ahead of China and what a daunting task it would be for China to catch up. Increased contact suddenly made the contrast between China and the West painfully visible.

By the mid-1980s, such visceral awareness of this contrast affected not just Chinese who traveled abroad but all who lived in major Chinese cities. The prideful spirit of the West came to China embodied in material artifacts, especially the buildings built by and/or for Westerners. Dozens of hotels and skyscraper office buildings sprang up throughout major Chinese cities. These buildings were up to international standards of comfort and efficiency—not to mention price. At the beginning of the 1990s, for example, the price of a room in one of Beijing's new luxury hotels was over $150 a night—the equivalent of about two months' salary for a Chinese university professor. The Lido Hotel in Beijing (part of the Holiday Inn chain) featured a medium-sized shopping mall like those found in American suburbs, with designer boutiques and gourmet ice cream shops. In the mall, all signs were in English; throughout the hotel there was almost no Chinese writing to be found. The Shangri-la Hotel in Beijing featured a discotheque—called the Xanadu—in its basement. Next to the door of the disco was a sign in Chinese, one of the few not accompanied by an English translation. The sign stated that the disco was "for foreign guests only"—no Chinese allowed.[9]

The foreign users of these hotels demanded a staff that was up to international standards of efficiency: waiters and reservations clerks who could speak English, cooks who could prepare Western food, janitors and housekeeping staff who conformed to Western standards of cleanliness. Service personnel in Chinese establishments were notorious for lethargy and inefficiency. To get qualified employees, the managers of Western hotels offered salaries that were extraordinarily generous by Chinese standards, though minimal by standards of industrialized countries; they hired applicants carefully (usually demanding that they speak English); and they put their workers through intensive training programs. A room service worker in a major Beijing hotel could easily make more money than a senior professor at a Chinese research institute.[10] By the end of the 1980s, much to the consternation of their parents, some of the brightest of China's teenagers were seeking service jobs in luxury hotels rather than going on to a university.

Ordinary people in China were thus confronted with gleaming towers for foreign habitation, temples to consumer values, in their midst. I have heard grumblings that these new places were like the public parks built exclusively for Europeans in the prerevolutionary treaty ports. Unlike the old foreign concessions, however, the new hotels and office buildings tended to provoke more shame than resentment. The new buildings did not represent colonial enclaves forced on China by gunboats. They were lucrative sources of foreign investment, examples of the efficacy of advanced Western construction technology, that had been eagerly invited into China by the Chinese government in the name of the Chinese people. Yet for most Chinese, especially state workers and peasants, they represented standards of consumption that were infinitely out of reach. (High Party officials and a rising class of nouveau riche private entrepreneurs could afford them, however.) They could never hope to stay in one of those places, even to eat a meal in one. The closest they might get was to land a job in one as a servant; and a mere servant connected with one of these foreigners' establishments could earn more than the highest-paid and most prestigious Chinese professionals. The foreigners' grand new hotels and office buildings towered over the Chinese urban landscape, gleaming reminders that the Chinese were now part of an international world of communication and commerce — and that they stood so close to the bottom of that world's stratification system that they could never hope to climb near to the top in their lifetimes.

Some Chinese maintained an attitude of moral censure toward the wastefulness and perhaps decadence of Western styles of life. ("Americans actually keep dogs as pets — and they even feed them meat!" a Beijing resident exclaimed to some guests at a dinner party in the mid-1980s.) But in the end, the images of the good life represented by the modern hotels possessed an enormous attractive power, especially to urban youth. Not only, then, did it increasingly appear that Americans had nothing to learn from China, but the seductiveness of consumerism took away those virtues — self-discipline and social responsibility — that Chinese had been taught to believe were their special contributions to world culture.

The most attractive parts of the American Dream were those about limitless self-expression through consumption of material goods. In the early 1980s, when Chinese first started reading American books in translation, the books they most frequently read and most widely craved were not works of political philosophy or even highbrow literature. Rather, what became immensely popular in China, especially among young urban readers, were works of popular literature by authors such as Taylor Caldwell, Jackie Collins, Irving Wallace, Sidney Sheldon, and Louis L'Amour.

According to a Chinese scholar who translated and promoted the publication of many of these novels, the kinds of books that sold the best and made the most profound impact on young readers were those that didn't make high intellectual demands and could be read just for fun. Avant-garde novels did not go over well in China. A best-selling book for the Chinese audience "must be written in a fairly realistic way. It has to have some suspense and to include a love story and some sex — but not too much." This Chinese translator, in fact, saw himself as providing an important service for Chinese young people by introducing them to American books that provided some (but not too much) description of sex. "People in China are so ignorant about sex. They must be enlightened, even about sex. Otherwise such books will just go underground." What was important for young people to know, he thought, was simply the variety of ways that sex can be enjoyed and the fact that it can be enjoyed for its own sake.

He summarized the moral revolution that such pulp fiction had helped to engender: "Young people," he said with great feeling, "suffer a lot from feudalism. We used to criticize the bourgeois way of life, but the young people have begun to realize that feudalism is really much worse." What American popular novels taught them, he thought, was the antifeudal idea that good books don't have to be morally uplifting. American popular books begged to be read just for pleasure. Doing something purely for individual satisfaction was an immensely liberating experience for people taught from their earliest years to submit their wishes to the collective good.

But once Chinese rejected the validity of moralistic feudalism and began thinking of the American consumerist way of life as morally superior, what did they have to teach to the rest of the world? So long as they stayed in a country as poor as their own, they could never hope to attain the quality of individual self-expression celebrated (and, of course, exaggerated) by American popular fiction. They now believed that they were not just inferior technologically but inferior morally as well.

The embrace of consumerism sent cultural self-confidence on a downward spiral. The more Chinese accepted the logic of consumerism, the less reason they had to feel that they had important values to teach the rest of the world, and the less self-confidence they had. The less self-confidence they had, the more they tended to rush blindly after short-term gratification.

Symptoms of Bankruptcy

The bankruptcy of self-confidence created public moods that were not at all conducive to a measured acceptance of the public-spirited virtues that hold liberal democracies together. The younger generation in the cities especially seemed lost and confused. One of the few American novels of high literary quality that did sell very well when translated into Chinese was *The Catcher in the Rye.* "The style and tone of that book reflects the spiritual dilemma of our young students," said its translator. "The young people are beginning to lose faith in everything. Their feelings are perhaps like those Americans [for whom *The Catcher in the Rye* was written] who after World War II lost faith in the future because of the atom bomb."

Overreacting to the symptoms of this alienation and cultural confusion, the Communist Party leadership deepened it by waging campaigns against "spiritual pollution" in 1983 and "bourgeois liberalism" in 1987.[11] These campaigns were primarily directed against those who were demanding political freedoms. Playing on what it perceived to be popular ambivalence about the importation of foreign culture, the Party tried to connect political liberalism with cultural decadence, manifested in activities ranging from disco dancing to pornography and prostitution. The Party might have been more convincing about the need for Chinese to resist the more extreme forms of Western self-indulgence had it not claimed that such behavior was intimately connected with all criticism of the government — and if Party leaders had not themselves hypocritically succumbed to the blandishments of the cruder forms of Western consumerism. Ordinary Chinese could not hope to taste the sweetness of the good consumerist life represented by the gleaming, modernist, "international style" steel and glass towers, but high-level government officials and their children could. These officials seemed to think the dignity of their office required that they possess at least some of the symbols of success of their foreign counterparts.

Exchanging rumors about the lavish, decadent lifestyles of leading officials became one of the favorite leisure activities of many urban Chinese. Actually, by international standards these lifestyles seem relatively modest. The houses of high-level officials (ministry heads and army generals) that I have visited are about as large as, but more run-down than, an ordinary middle-class suburban dwelling in the United States, and, though well appointed with imported electronic equipment — Japanese-made televisions, VCRs, and stereos—rather shabbily furnished. By the standards of ordinary Chinese citizens—a whole family in Beijing is lucky to get a few hundred square feet of living space—such living accommodations are indeed extraordinarily luxurious. But by comparison with the living standards one would associate with the CEO of a major American corporation or cabinet-level official in the U.S. government or with elites in many parts of the Third World, the Chinese leaders' living standards seem quite unpretentious.

Participation in an international community includes competition for individual status as defined by symbols of consumption. It was perhaps inevitable that Chinese officials would pursue international standards of consumption when they began to participate in the world community. Perhaps because they simply didn't have access to as much money as elites in the rest of the world, their personal dwellings were not luxuriously furnished by Western standards. However, they could and unwisely did use public funds for flashy automobiles.[12] By the mid-1980s, the car of choice was the Mercedes Benz. Hundreds of thousands of these automobiles were imported into China. After top officials became accustomed to using them, lower officials demanded them too and used their offices' funds to get them. By the end of the decade officials as low as county secretary were being chauffeured around in black Mercedes Benz SLs.[13]

Most Chinese commuters could afford no more than a bicycle. The fondness of high officials for Mercedes became the subject of many bitter comments by ordinary citizens, and during the mass protests of the 1989 Beijing Spring it was explicitly cited by demonstrators as a symbol of government corruption. For some critics, what was at issue was not just officials' taste for luxury but their conspicuous consumption of *imported* luxury. "Even Soviet leaders," one intellectual remarked to me, "travel in Soviet-made limousines." If the foreign exchange used to import all of those Mercedes had been used to modernize China's own automobile assembly lines, the Chinese population may have received considerable benefit. But high officials scrambled to meet foreign standards of consumption rather than invest in the good of the nation.

One result was prevalent, anguished questioning on the part of ordinary Chinese citizens about why their culture had failed to produce the kind of moral leadership that would work together for the public good. Another result was a widespread, cynical suspicion that those officials were in a way correct—that despite all their pious warnings about "spiritual pollution," the life of self-indulgent consumerism was indeed the good life that every individual should grasp if it ever came into reach. The sum of all these results was the widespread feeling of doubt that Chinese culture could make any moral contribution to world culture — that the people of the Middle Kingdom had anything anymore of which they could be proud.

A Shift in International Perspective

Connected to this bankruptcy in self-confidence was a widespread shift in popular understandings of China's place in the world system. During the Maoist era, Chinese citizens were taught to identify China's cause with that of the Third World. Mao Zedong was considered the world's leading thinker about the potential and destiny of the Third World. According to Maoist theory, China would prove its national greatness by uniting the poor and oppressed nations of the earth against the mighty and wealthy superpowers, just as the Chinese Communist Party had led China's peasants against its capitalist-dominated cities.[14] But in the 1980s, Chinese widely began to reject the Maoist theory of the Third World. For instance, by the end of the decade, the basic course in international relations at Beijing University contained mandatory readings about Maoist theories of the Third World, but it mainly set them up as straw men to be overturned by the latest Western international relations theories. In none of the major international relations research institutes that I visited did I meet scholars who seriously considered Maoist Third World theory better than "scientific" international relations theory.

Moreover, foreign diplomats and correspondents who have lived in China generally agree that there was widespread disdain at almost all levels of Chinese society toward Third World diplomats and students residing in China — especially those from Africa. (In the late 1980s, there were several widely publicized incidents of violence against Africans studying in Chinese universities.) In the new popular perspective, China was part of a world dominated by the industrialized West, but it was near the bottom of that world, and its position was getting worse rather than better.

For most Chinese elites, the four modernizations were an attempt to break free of the poverty and ignorance that characterized the Third World by excelling at the science and technology characteristic of the

First World. They realized that it would be a long time before they could catch up with a society such as the United States. But many of them developed high hopes of emulating the "little dragons" of Taiwan, Hong Kong, South Korea, and Singapore. One of the most popular American social science books read in translation during the mid-1980s was Alvin Toffler's *The Third Wave,* which argued that poor countries did not necessarily have to follow a classic development path leading through light industry to heavy industry to high technology but could, through the application of modern science, leapfrog the earlier stages and move directly toward an economy based on high-tech industries.[15] *The Third Wave* sold over a million copies in China because it held out hope that China, through the brilliance of its intellectuals, could quickly move to the status of a developed country. Zhao Ziyang, the Party's general secretary at the time, invited Toffler to China for personal conversations.

If the third wave existed, however, most of China never managed to catch its crest. Aided by an immense influx of capital and ideas from Hong Kong, the Guangdong region did indeed begin an industrial take-off, followed by other southeastern coastal areas such as Fujian and Shanghai. Even in these successful regions, however, development was uneven; pockets of poverty persisted in villages lacking good communication with industrializing centers. Throughout the 1980s most of the rest of China grew relatively slowly; even though urban standards of living underwent a steady improvement, Chinese perceived a widening gap between their society and the developed world. Dissidents such as Liu Binyan would score powerful rhetorical points by citing United Nations' statistics showing that China's per capita income was 126th out of the nations of the world — and that its ranking had actually fallen since the beginning of the decade.[16]

The dominating spirit of this new world increasingly seemed to be one of relentless, merciless economic competition. American society, in the view of many Chinese who traveled there, was perhaps the most vivid manifestation of this spirit, dramatically exemplifying both its benefits and the penalties for refusing obeisance to it. "Competition, competition, competition" was the lesson one member of an international relations policy institute learned about the nature of American society during two years spent in Berkeley. Remarked this individual, "Even the beggars were competitive when they appealed for your spare change." For other Chinese who spent time in the United States, the beggars also represented a warning about the fate of those who fail to live up to the demands of competition. Says a journalist who was in the United States when the members of Jim Jones's "People's Temple" committed mass suicide in Guyana, "I felt I could understand the People's Temple members better [after I had lived for a while in the United States]. I could understand the kind of pressures that would produce such actions. The competition. If you had the ability in America you could become very wealthy. But you could also lose everything." For some Chinese, the competition that drove American society was a model for the competition that drove the world economy. In such a world, nations who were unable to compete would indeed end up as self-destructive beggars. As one well-respected scholar summarized it, "The market will not forgive us."

The Cultural Segmentation of Chinese Society

I have been describing a widespread crisis of confidence, partially engendered by exposure to the American Dream, that paradoxically made it psychologically difficult for many Chinese to adapt the best aspects of the American Dream to their social and political needs. The crisis of confidence, though, was not equally felt by all sectors of Chinese society. The differences were a function of the degree to which members of different institutions could plausibly believe that they still had important things to teach as well as to learn from the West. Let us now describe some of these differences and show how they affected the capacity of sectors of Chinese society to put to good use the best aspects of Western liberalism.

Christian Communities. The Chinese Christian churches, for instance, seemed both to assert their own distinctive Chinese identity and to grow in self-confidence as a result of new relations with the West. The first message the three-self churches communicated to their brethren in the West after 1979 was a strongly nationalistic one: The religion propagated by missionaries had been too closely connected with imperialism; the founding of the People's Republic of China had allowed the churches to cut themselves free from foreign domination and to develop their own Chinese understanding of their faith; Western Christian concern for the Chinese church was appreciated, but not if that concern masked an attempt once again to subordinate the Chinese church to a Western Christian agenda.[17]

A second message was a warning to the Western churches about the incompatibility of Western liberalism with some of their fundamental beliefs. "Freedom always has two sides: The negative and the positive," said Chinese Protestant leader Shen Yifan at a 1981 conference in Montreal, which for the first time since 1949 brought together mainland Chinese and Western Christians (both Catholic and Protestant) for theological dialogue. "On the negative side, it means 'free from' and on the positive side it means 'free to.' It means that we have been freed from sin, in order to return to our harmony with God and man. Evidently, freedom is not an end in itself. To look upon freedom as an end, and to advocate freedom for freedom's sake, can easily become a pretext for licentiousness."[18]

Mainline Protestants in the United States and in Europe were put on the defensive by such declarations of self-determination and spiritual superiority. By the 1980s, the theology of the Western mainline churches committed them to such community self-determination, and that theology had always warned against confusing the negative, individualistic freedom celebrated by popular versions of the American Dream with the positive "freedom of the sons of God." Thus, it was relatively easy, as a Roman Catholic observer unkindly put it, for Chinese Protestant leaders such as Bishop Ding Guangxun to "guilt trip" Western Protestant leaders.

The Western churches were ready to provide aid — money and technical expertise for printing new editions of the Bible in Chinese, for example — to the Chinese deferentially and with few strings attached. When they did advertently or inadvertently try to attach strings, Chinese leaders successfully shamed them into removing the strings. For instance, when the United Bible Society tried to raise money among Western Christians for the printing of new Bibles in China, Bishop Ding objected strongly to the tone of their advertisements, which made it sound, he asserted, as if the Chinese church would be totally helpless, completely unable to preach the gospel, without foreign help. If the United Bible Society was going to solicit donations with advertisements written in this patronizing tone, Ding said, the Chinese church did not want its money. The United Bible Society changed its advertisements.

The Chinese Protestant churches could be so assertive because they did not think of themselves as second-rate in comparison with their Western counterparts. Although they did not have the theological sophistication of their Western brethren, they had something that even Westerners had to admit was more important: a faith that had been tried and tested by enormous hardships over the past thirty years. In steadfastness, courage, and pastoral ingenuity, they were more than equal to any Western church.

They were, to be sure, materially poor and in need of technical assistance. In 1985 they set up an organization called the Amity Foundation as a channel for contributions of money and personnel from the Western churches. Unlike the prerevolutionary mission boards, this foundation was dominated by Chinese church leaders. Western money came to China on Chinese terms — at least, in this case, on the terms of the leaders of the officially approved three-self churches. With this help, the Chinese churches established a printing press in Nanjing with state-of-the-art equipment, enabling it to produce almost a million Bibles a year. Funds given to the Amity Foundation also enabled the Chinese churches to expand services to the poor, the sick, and the disabled. Such activity contributed to a new vitality within the Chinese church, which grew from about a million members to perhaps five million in the 1980s. Here was a case where a Chinese institution was able to increase its self-confidence through renewed contact with the West, because it was able to teach its Western counterparts the kinds of spiritual lessons most important to it while receiving much-needed material and technical aid.

Entrepreneurs. An analogous spirit of self-confidence could be found among local entrepreneurs in those coastal areas that had been opened to foreign investment. In Guangdong province, for example, economic development was driven by capital and expertise imported from Hong Kong. This influx of outside help — which wasn't, after all, as culturally "outside" as help from the United States — created a wealth of opportunities for local entrepreneurs to exercise their creativity. A colorful cast of characters, consisting, in Ezra Vogel's typology, of economic "statesmen, scramblers, and niche seekers," cooperated with Hong Kong investors to set up a dynamic mix of factories and trading centers. The local economy — especially the local entrepreneurs — profited handsomely. Without such local initiative, the foreign capital would have been fruitless. The "statesmen, scramblers, and niche seekers" could take great pride in their creativity and flexibility. Though they sometimes exasperated their foreign partners, they frequently earned their respect by achieving what the foreign partners themselves valued: economic success.[19]

Of course, the achievements that were the basis for their self-confidence were very different from the spiritual achievements of the Chinese Christians. Like the nouveau riche elsewhere, the new entrepreneurs often flaunted their wealth in crassly materialistic ways, and they were often rumored to be fond of gambling, promiscuous sex, and other vices.[20] For this they incurred the opprobrium of more moralistic Chinese, though less than was reserved for high officials. I have often heard various Chinese make the judgment that the entrepreneurs were at least helping China's economy, whereas officials were just parasites.

Intellectuals. At the other end of the self-confidence spectrum, though, were Chinese intellectuals. In general, their scientific and academic institutions were simply not up to world standards. In the early 1980s, American delegations of scholars duly noted this deficiency in their reports, and Chinese students discovered it for themselves when they pursued higher education in the United States and other Western countries.

When they went abroad in the early 1980s, many Chinese students seemed to have genuine intentions of returning to serve the motherland by blending the best in Western culture into revitalized Chinese academic institutions. But by mid-decade, many had decided to stay overseas, and those who did return often wished they hadn't. Part of the problem was their reverse culture shock at having to endure the low salaries and poor living conditions of their own country. But this would not have been intolerable if they could hope that their new learning would be respected in their native land and that their quality of life might eventually improve. Most of the first contingents of candidates for Chinese Christian ministry who went to study in American seminaries, for instance, were for just these reasons generally anxious to return to their home churches. Similarly, some entrepreneurial Chinese who studied in American business schools passed up lucrative job offers in the United States to return to China and set up enterprises there. The Shanghai stock exchange, for example, was established by several such students.

But students in the sciences, and to an even greater degree in the humanities and social sciences, had less hope that their talents would be utilized and rewarded back in China. In academic institutes, senior scholars who had not been abroad—or who had received their foreign training in the Soviet Union—quite understandably felt threatened by young upstarts returning with incomprehensible new ideas and a host of foreign contacts. As a result, these senior scholars all too often made life miserable for returnees.[21] Such a cool welcome came as a bitter shock to bright young intellectuals who through hard study had come to feel accepted by their peers in foreign graduate schools. The kind of work that had won them praise and acceptance in the United States, it seemed, brought them nothing but grief in China. To make matters worse, they felt cut off from their foreign professional peers once they returned to China, not necessarily by political pressure but by economic necessities. "People write to me from America," lamented one brilliant young scholar with a Ph.D. from Harvard, "and they ask me for a copy of my dissertation. But to copy and mail the dissertation would cost me as much as a month's salary. . . . I recently received a letter to Harvard alumni, asking for a donation. I thought it was a bad joke."

Achievement of an advanced degree placed Chinese students within an international professional community whose norms of collegiality and standards of excellence were incompatible with those of Chinese academic institutions. Even though, as smart individuals, such students could rise to the top of their professions if they stayed in major research centers abroad, they were prone to feeling that, as members of Chinese society and heirs of the Chinese cultural tradition, they had nothing of value to contribute.[22]

When faced with similar circumstances, talented students from newly industrializing countries such as Taiwan and Hong Kong and from countries throughout the Third World often opted to stay in the West. The difference between the experience of those countries and that of China was that the exodus of the best and brightest Chinese students happened so abruptly, after so many years of isolation from the West— and that it happened in a society of people that had been taught to think of their culture as unique, cohesive, and attractive. According to Chai Zemin, the Chinese ambassador to the United States at the time of normalization, "Deng Xiaoping said it would be no problem if a few hundred students would want to stay abroad. But we did not anticipate how many would want to stay." As it became apparent by the mid-

1980s that massive numbers of them wanted to remain abroad, Chinese intellectuals' assumptions about the cohesiveness of their culture were severely challenged.

Chinese leaders had justified the opening to the West as a way for China to acquire modern technology, which could then be grafted with the best of Chinese culture to create a powerful and prosperous nation. Intellectuals expected to play a major role in this process. Now, the hope of a modernization effort led by intellectuals disappeared, as the young professionals who could have brought modern technology back to China elected to stay away. Although Chinese intellectuals had abandoned their ideology of solidarity with the Third World, they now found themselves in circumstances all too typical of a Third World country: Their students wanted to emigrate to centers of learning abroad; their leaders adopted lifestyles appropriate for the world's metropolitan centers; lavish buildings for the enjoyment of foreign visitors sprang up in the midst of the humble dwellings of ordinary citizens; and the country as a whole retained one of the lower per capita incomes in the world, although pockets of local entrepreneurs, in cooperation with foreign capitalists, got ostentatiously rich by taking advantage of cheap labor to produce goods for export.

Heirs to a moral tradition that taught them to consider with anxious concern the fate of their society as a whole, intellectuals thought they and their nation deserved better. For all of its cruelty and incompetence, the Communist Party had held out to them a vision of national greatness. A generation past, even powerful world figures such as Nixon had come in awe to China and considered its leader a "colossus." Now, with the new opening to the West, even that sense of national pride was revealed to be an illusion. If one pointed out to dissident Chinese intellectuals that their government did not seem as corrupt or ineffective as the governments of many Third World countries—the Philippines, for instance—their common answer was that their tradition of socialism had held out the promise of a much better way of life. Several dissident intellectuals responded to me in this vein, even when they argued that China should completely abandon socialism. People who have never had any hope for a glorious future perhaps can fatalistically numb themselves to a harsh reality; people who have had such hope, only to see it taken away, are driven to despair. As a widely respected middle-aged scholar put it: "No foreigner can understand the depth of our pain."

The Fragmentation of Chinese Culture

By the late 1980s, as different segments of the society reacted in sharply different ways to the opening of new cultural horizons, Chinese culture became increasingly Balkanized. During the Maoist era, common national political movements — often terrible events such as the Great Leap Forward or the Cultural Revolution — imparted a commonality of experience to Chinese society. Now, however, a diversity of responses to the West produced a wide diversity of experiences, a mosaic of discordant social worlds out of communication with one another. "Don't eat in those little restaurants [run by independent entrepreneurs] on the street outside of our institute," a member of the Chinese academy of social sciences warned me in 1988. "The hygiene there is terrible. We never eat there ourselves." His relation to the bustling commercial life of the street was like a tourist's to the natives of a foreign land. Intellectuals often bitterly accused entrepreneurs of being dishonest and selfish. Entrepreneurs, for their part, criticized intellectuals for their timidity, their dreamy impracticality, and their ineffectual hand-wringing.

Usually, American visitors did not comprehend the depth of the segmentation of Chinese society. Diplomats, journalists, scholars, and businesspeople tended to think that the attitudes prevalent within the social circles they frequented were common to China as a whole. This perception was perhaps partly due to a common naive assumption that all societies can balance unity with diversity as naturally as the United States has done. Sophisticated Chinese had no illusions about this. They marveled at the United States' exceptional accommodation of diversity within a common culture. "America is not anarchic," one of Beijing's leading experts in American studies exclaimed with not a little amazement and envy. "In America there is a spectrum of ethics and customs that few people deviate from." China, though, did not have a single culture anymore, in the view of this scholar. Therefore, "China has to go through a difficult period — to come up with a Chinese set of ethics." There was no way of avoiding this difficult period. "There has been a rapid worsening of the situation" since the mid-1980s, he said. "There has been a loss of control, a worsening of people's morals."

Although some segments of China's increasingly fragmented society seemed more confident than others about the value of their distinctive way of life, all seemed to have lost confidence in the possibility of integrating their society as a whole around any common framework of values and meanings. What members of China's differentiating segments shared was a sense that there no longer was any such integrating framework. Even if they could be proud of themselves and happy about their personal prospects in life, they could not be proud or happy about the public circumstances within which they lived. Though as individuals they might be capable of blending the best of Western values with their Chinese culture, they were at a loss as to how to bring these values to bear on the public sphere.

For many of the urban Chinese with whom I spoke in 1988, the behavior of people on buses was one of the most powerful symbols of the breakdown in public values. During rush hour, people at bus stops forwent all queuing up, and entrance to a bus was accomplished with great pushing, shoving, and cursing. Inside the bus, riders commonly made liberal use of knees and elbows to get into one of the scarce seats or force themselves toward the door. Fistfights between angry passengers were a daily occurrence. From an outsider's point of view, the behavior on the buses seemed no worse than in most poor countries with overcrowded buses. The behavior was not much worse than that on subways in New York City, and it was very similar to the behavior I experienced in Taiwan in the early 1970s. But the mainland Chinese seemed to expect better of themselves. "The shock was tremendous," said a senior Chinese scholar of his return from a year and a half in the United States in the mid-1980s. "The manners on the public buses were appalling; the level of corruption was so great; the situation was rapidly worsening. . . ." Chinese citizens became obsessed with what they perceived to be a spirit of petty acquisitive selfishness overtaking their culture.

I have argued that the loss of self-confidence among some Chinese was due partially yet directly to the opening of their horizons to the West, which resulted in the sense that they had everything to learn from the West and nothing to give. However, the decline in public spirit I have just described was only indirectly related to cultural contact with the West, in my view. It was more directly related to internal changes, especially the rise of economic competition in a society that was not used to it and morally unprepared to keep it under control.

The uncivil public behavior seemed to symbolize the problems inherent in striking a balance between cooperation and competition in the new society. The Chinese people need to compete more with one another, many Chinese economists agreed. As one young economist put it: "The [classic Confucian] Doctrine of the Mean is a big problem for

China. It means that people don't want to stand out, don't want to live up to their full potential." Competition is not a bad thing, this young economist said, because Adam Smith's "invisible hand" will make the actions of competitive individuals work out for the good of all. But this was abstract speculation; in real life, this young economist also complained about the buses.

The buses represented all the ugliness of unbridled competition for scarce resources. "Since the opening to the West, people are finding themselves for the first time," said a scholar in Guangdong. He meant that they were gaining a new sense of assertive, individual identity, which was linked, he thought, to new assertive regional identities such as that of Guangdong. But in the environment of increased competition, people were also losing themselves. As this intellectual put it, the increased competition had its yin and yang: It led to increased creativity but also to moral self-destructiveness. This declining morality was manifest, he and many like him thought, in increased drug use and sexual licentiousness — pornography and prostitution, not to mention casual extramarital sex — and in the cheating and price-gouging practiced by some entrepreneurs. Young people were becoming especially disoriented, he and many middle-aged Chinese said; all that seemed to count for the young was how fast they could make money and how much pleasure they could acquire. In the search for easy money and instant gratification, many young people were dropping out of school, losing any interest in pursuing long-term careers. They were becoming jaded and cynical. They represented an antisocial individualism.

Between Choice and Creation

Most of the Chinese with whom I talked in Beijing concurred that the despair began to set in around 1985. By then it was apparent to many in China that their rapidly rising expectations were not going to be quickly satisfied. It was true enough that certain areas of China, such as the Guangdong region, were indeed reaching an economic takeoff point. But it was equally clear that, in the short run, these regions were not going to pull the rest of the country forward. Regional prosperity would not translate into national prosperity, because those with vested interests in maintaining the inefficient state-controlled industries were not going to allow these industries to be fundamentally reformed.

As the rate of growth began to slow and become uneven, Chinese citizens needed more than ever an overarching vision of what they should commonly strive for, a framework of purposes with which to legitimate development priorities and to justify the inevitable sacrifices that would have to be made in fulfillment of China's long-term goals. But one thing that the American Dream did not give, as interpreted by a disillusioned, confused people, was a coherent moral and political vision. As we have seen, it engendered intellectual and moral pluralism while destroying the self-confidence of many Chinese — especially intellectuals, the one group that might have been able to produce a new vision.

"We are standing in the space between choice and creation," said a social scientist in Guangdong in the late 1980s. This was an indeterminate, unstructured sort of psychological space, a field of ambivalences: conjunctions of hopes and fears, apparent liberations that also looked like entrapments. Intellectuals were now faced with an array of new personal, social, and political choices, but there was no way of knowing which of the choices would lead to happiness and which to disaster.

No wonder, then, that existentialism became an intellectual fad, especially among young people, in the early and mid-1980s. No wonder the intellectuals Zhang Xinxin described in an essay about the increasing prevalence of divorce in China all read "newly translated, if not new books. The reporter Guo, in the course of his divorce, read Niccolo Machiavelli's *The Prince* over and over again, and he thinks it changed his whole outlook on life. Zhu . . . is reading Nietzsche and Milan Kundera. . . . The life path of our generation is continually defined by such books and theories."[23] And no wonder that one of the most popular poems written in the 1980s was the dissident poet Bei Dao's "The Answer," with the oft-quoted lines: "Let me tell you, world / I-do-not-believe! / If a thousand challengers lie beneath your feet / Count me as number one thousand and one."[24]

American observers of Chinese society in the 1980s tended to see such expressions of angst as a positive sign, proof of a lively intellectual ferment that would eventually lead to a better society. But Americans perhaps have difficulty appreciating how their cherished intellectual pluralism fulfills its creative potential only by being subtly held in check by a multitude of taken-for-granted institutional restraints. "Our problem is not that we have no ideas," said one of the leading figures in the

Chinese Academy of Social Sciences. "Everyone has plenty of ideas. Our problem is that nobody has the same ideas." He and his colleagues noted with envy the degree to which major American public institutions could distill common beliefs out of the swirl of millions of individual ideas. China simply could not do so in this phase of its history.

"I see so many problems in our society now," blurted out a middle-aged woman from the foreign affairs office who had accompanied me to a meeting with some Guangdong scholars at the end of my 1988 stay in China. "There are the problems . . . of gambling, disco halls, prostitution, drugs, kids giving up school. It seems that the only thing that matters to people anymore—the only thing they care about—is money." The senior professor with whom I had been speaking had been arguing that he was basically optimistic about the future direction of China—that the pursuit of vice among some sectors of Chinese society was simply the immediate and temporary result of the release of constraints after years of social repression and that preoccupation with unhealthy things would diminish once Chinese got used to the new social openness. His response to the foreign affairs officer's outburst was simply: "I remain optimistic." And there the matter stood—an unresolvable difference of opinion, summarizing what I heard throughout five months of living in China and have continued to hear in even sharper terms during more recent visits.

The differences of opinion did not just separate individuals—they battled internally for possession of reflective individuals' hearts. Even those Chinese who were most sanguine about the benefits of learning from the West were prone to episodes of irrational (from a cosmopolitan Western point of view) fears about suffering the consequences of Western vice. The possibility of catching AIDS particularly terrified them. One of the most ardent admirers of things American whom I met in China was an early-middle-aged woman who came to see me often to confide her feelings about Chinese society and her yearning to go someday to the United States. "Everybody in China knows about AIDS," she said. "They are afraid of foreigners because of AIDS. A lot of my friends tell me, 'Be careful of associating with foreigners, because you might get AIDS.'" She said that although the swimming pool at the International Club was open in the summer to some local Chinese as well as to foreign guests, most of her friends were now afraid to go because they were afraid of catching AIDS by swimming in the pool. She did not seem convinced by my assertions that it was impossible to contract AIDS this way.

At that time, few Chinese residents of Beijing had contracted AIDS, although the disease now shows disturbing signs of spreading in parts of China. But for some, at least, the disease seemed to have become an emblem for the mysterious perils accompanying contact with the West. The transliterated word for AIDS in Chinese is *aizibing* — which in one of its renditions literally means "Love-Capitalism-Sickness."

Perhaps, in ways that my Chinese friend did not explicitly articulate, the AIDS disease is indeed a good metaphor for China's predicament. There are many socially destructive tendencies in American culture — the ruthless competition demanded by a capitalist economy, the callousness toward the losers in that competition, the irresponsible self-expression encouraged by an economy that persuades people to strive constantly for ever-increasing levels of consumption. But the United States and most Western societies still have a strong cultural immune system that enables them to keep the destructive forces of capitalist individualism under control. By the time China encountered Western culture in the 1980s, however, its cultural immune system had been gravely weakened. Because of the moral and political traumas of the Cultural Revolution and perhaps because of years of isolation from the outside world, Chinese culture did not possess the sense of discipline and purpose that would have immunized it from some of the worst tendencies of Western liberal individualism. Social "diseases" that are kept within manageable limits within the West thus threatened to overwhelm Chinese culture.

The predicament faced by China has been a common one during the twentieth century. Theodore H. Von Laue has written:

As a largely invisible ingredient the West's spiritual discipline has never effectively spread around the world as part of the outpouring of Western material culture. Where imitation of Western power is a matter of political survival . . . , the built-in social restraints of Western culture have to be externally — and often counterproductively — imposed. Elsewhere, in the run of non-Western societies (Japan excepted), society continues in violence and crisis, while heads of states typically call for more discipline. Ignorant of the causes and consequences of its expansion, the West has left the interdependent world of its creation without guidance, without a rational explanation on how to cement the fragile life-supporting unity into a true community.[25]

8

Searching for a Dream

Chinese Creations of Their Own Myths

In spite of all the problems discussed in the last chapter, there are still grounds for hope. As a senior Chinese expert in American studies told me while gloomily assessing his country's breakdown in public confidence in the late 1980s: "Without opening, the country would have been dead. Sterile." The new policies, he believed, had saved Chinese society from even worse fates that might have befallen it. Much had been accomplished that might form the building blocks of a better future.

For instance, even amid the obvious self-doubt and anguish that afflict intellectuals, one can discern, if one looks in the right places, signs of a generative creativity, hints of a capacity to synthesize the best parts of Western and Chinese culture into mature new visions for China's future. Perhaps the most ambitious and influential example of this creativity has been the production of *Deathsong of the River*, a six-part television series broadcast in 1988.[1]

The first segment was entitled "Searching for a Dream," and the whole series in fact was a search for a viable Chinese dream, a new Chinese master narrative linking the legacies of the past with hopes for the future. In the course of this search, *Deathsong*'s creators also had to grapple with the American Dream. Their efforts point the way to new forms of cross-cultural dialogue in which Americans and Chinese might more critically understand themselves in the light of each other. To end this discussion of Chinese encounters with the American Dream in a hopeful manner, let us discuss the message of *Deathsong* in its social context.

Culture Fever

By the late 1980s, Chinese intellectuals talked often about the "culture fever" sweeping their circles.[2] They meant by this that the topic of Chinese culture had become an object of extraordinarily widespread, heated debate. This fever started around 1983 and steadily increased in temperature until June 4, 1989. Although suppressed in the bloodshed of that day, it probably continues to burn under the surface of Chinese society. Its final public throes came with the fabrication of the statue of the Goddess of Freedom and Democracy as a symbol of the protest movement. The statue was a unique blend of Chinese and Western symbols: In appearance it recalled both the Statue of Liberty and Chinese folk goddesses. In this respect, it was characteristic of the entire culture fever of the 1980s. Though obviously influenced by the accessibility of Western, especially American, ideas, the culture fever was primarily focused on questions of indigenous culture, an ambivalent, conflicted search for a Chinese identity in an interdependent world of global communication and commerce.

Intellectuals were the primary carriers of the culture fever, but, as we shall see, millions of people outside the intelligentsia were exposed to their debates. In the end, culture fever extended far beyond circles of intellectuals. It was an attempt to come to grips with why the Chinese government's political and economic reforms had failed to fulfill their promise and to find a morally adequate vision for the future.

The first stages of economic reform benefited almost everybody in China. Decollectivization of agriculture increased productivity, and the partial introduction of market forces moved light industry and commerce out of the stagnation of the Cultural Revolution era, leading to widespread increases in standards of living. Under a policy allowing "some people to get rich first," some entrepreneurs spurted ahead. But even though Party journals worried about the dangers of envy, "the red-eyed disease," there was a generalized enough improvement in living standards to alleviate its most severe effects. By the mid-1980s, though, the economic reforms were producing losers as well as winners. Increasingly, severe inflation began to erode the incomes of many urban Chinese, especially intellectuals and workers in state-controlled factories. As the expectations of these people were being disappointed, two other groups continued to move ahead: private entrepreneurs, especially in the coastal regions, and high-level Party officials.[3] These trends have continued and even intensified in the 1990s.

From the point of view of the losers in the reform process, the success of the winners was morally problematic. As one oft-repeated phrase put it, "a barber's razor is worth more than a surgeon's scalpel." There may have been some truth in this. In Guangdong province, private entrepreneurs were launching upscale hair-cutting parlors (after the style of those in Taiwan and Hong Kong) that catered especially to nouveau riche merchants, and some of these barbers probably *could* make more than physicians in state hospitals. For those mired in an economically stagnant state sector, the barbers symbolized a morally dubious world of frivolous luxury and, often enough, shady business practices. For intellectuals, it was especially galling that uneducated people could be making more money than those with good educations.

Even more problematic was the success of high Party officials, who prospered through corrupt practices. Two forms of corruption were especially prevalent: accepting bribes from foreign investors wanting to do business with China, and appropriating goods over which they had stewardship in the public sector and selling them at a big profit in the private sector. In the estimation of many intellectuals, these same Party leaders were incompetent in modern economic management and thus responsible for the inflation that was making the lives of so many miserable.

In the thinking of many Chinese intellectuals in the late 1980s, these economic problems raised disturbing questions about the moral basis of Chinese culture. Why were undeserving people getting rich? Why were top Party officials so corrupt? What principles should be followed to make the society not only more prosperous but also more just?[4]

For the most part, Western economists and political scientists did not see this moral debate as important. In their view, economic reform was mainly a technical matter: The Chinese government should allow the prices of land, labor, and capital to conform to the laws of supply and demand, and scientifically based principles of management should be used to reform rigid bureaucracies.[5] If this were done, temporary economic dislocations would in due time give way to general prosperity. Many younger Chinese intellectuals enthusiastically accepted the theories of Western economists and management experts—in 1988, the Great Hall of the People in Beijing was jammed with such intellectuals eager to listen to a lecture by Milton Friedman. But many were deeply upset by how the dislocations were affecting them in practical terms. Their anguish led them to question the capacity of their culture to sustain market reforms in a way that would produce a just society—or at least a society that would adequately reward people with moral integrity and technical skill.

Political as well as economic problems fueled the sense of crisis. The leaders of the Party refused to hold themselves accountable to popular opinion. In 1983 and 1987, they cracked down on intellectuals expressing unorthodox ideas. Yet even as the Party was unwilling in principle to tolerate dissenting voices, it was becoming less able to control the expression of dissent. The Party had lost its ideological legitimacy by introducing market reforms that contradicted its Marxist dogmas; it had lost most of its moral legitimacy because of the perceived incompetence, corruption, and cynicism of its leaders; and its rule was weakened by factional fighting, as different groups with different approaches to reform vied for control of the Party's future. Meanwhile, an expanding market economy and ties with the West were creating opportunities for many Chinese intellectuals to seek financial and moral support from sources not controlled by the Party. Thus, after the crackdown against dissent in 1983 and 1987, intellectuals were not cowed into submission but soon reemerged, more vehemently critical than ever—and a main target was the Chinese proclivity to accept despotic government.

Deathsong of the River

This was the context that led to the creation of *Deathsong of the River,* the most complex, rhetorically powerful product of the culture fever. Created by a group of young intellectuals and broadcast first in June 1988 and again in August, the series was viewed by millions, perhaps hundreds of millions. Its script, published as a book, sold 700,000 copies in 1988 alone. Hundreds of critical essays about *Deathsong* were published, not only in the People's Republic but also in Hong Kong and Taiwan and in Chinese-language newspapers and magazines around the world.[6]

The basic theme of the series was that Chinese culture was not adequate to the challenge of pursuing national glory in the modern world. The "river" in the title was the Yellow River, whose basin was the cradle of Chinese civilization but whose murkiness and unruliness symbolized a mentality and culture unsuited to the demands of modernity. Rhetorically, *Deathsong* expressed its spirit of sorrow and worry by juxtaposing representations of traditional concern with representations of modern aspiration. The result was a tension-packed array of symbols that was riddled with contradictions yet somehow mirrored the psychological tensions of contemporary Chinese society.

Deathsong developed its argument by reinterpreting central symbols in Chinese culture. The Yellow River is a rich metaphor for Chinese history and destiny. "It just so happened that this yellow river bred a yellow-skinned people; and this people just happened to call their first ancestor the Yellow Emperor. . . . Yellow water, yellow soil, yellow people: what a mysterious yet natural connection this is. It would appear as if the skin of this yellow people were dyed by the Yellow River." The river is mighty and awe-inspiring but also turgid and dangerous. "For without doubt, the Yellow River is the most brutal and unrestrained river in the world." [7]

For the Yellow River to find its destiny, it has to empty itself in the blue sea; for the Chinese people to find their destiny, they have to turn away from the yellow soil of their ancient continent and enter the interdependent modern world, symbolized by the blueness of the ocean. "[W]hat the Yellow River could give us has already been given to our ancestors. The Yellow River cannot bring forth again the civilization that our ancestors once created. What we need to create is a brand-new civilization. It cannot emerge from the Yellow River again. The dregs of the old civilization are like the sand and mud accumulated in the Yellow River; they have built up in the blood vessels of our people. We need a great tidal wave to flush them away. This great tidal wave has already arrived. It is industrial civilization. It is summoning us!" [8] The series ended with an image of the earth as seen from the Apollo spacecraft — a blue planet.

Similarly, *Deathsong* argued with the significance of the dragon and the Great Wall. The Chinese are the "descendants of the dragon," and 1988 was the Year of the Dragon (pictures of dragons were emblazoned throughout the big cities in an effort to attract tourists). Yet the dragon is really an emblem of despotism: "The dragon is the tyrant of the natural world while the emperor is the tyrant of the human world." The Chinese people "love the dragon yet hate it, praise it yet also curse it. What a complex emotion this is, as complex as the image of the dragon itself." Another key symbol of Chinese civilization is the Great Wall,

the object of incomparable reverence. . . . People even wish to use it as a symbol of China's strength. And yet, if the Great Wall could speak, it would very frankly tell its Chinese grandchildren that it is a great and tragic gravestone forged by historical destiny. It can by no means represent strength, initiative, and glory; it can only represent an isolationist, conservative and incompetent defence and a cowardly lack of aggression. Because of its great size and long history, it has deeply imprinted its arrogance and self-delusion in the souls of our people. Alas, O Great Wall, why do we still want to praise you?[9]

Having turned key symbols of China's glorious past into symbols of its modern backwardness, *Deathsong* used images of the West, especially the United States, as symbols of the "new industrial civilization" that is summoning China. Often, the series achieved a dramatic effect by juxtaposing grainy, black-and-white footage of China's travails earlier in this century with vividly colored film of American rocket launches, skyscrapers, the neon lights of Las Vegas, sailboats in a blue harbor, fashion shows, department store displays, and so on. *Deathsong* showed no scenes of poverty, drug abuse, or racial conflict in the United States. Some of its images were lifted directly from advertisements. Most of them had the slickly attractive superficiality of modern American advertising — what the sociologist Michael Schudson calls "capitalist realism."[10]

Deathsong's Message

The "deathsong" was at once a lamentation for the travails of Chinese culture, a cry of anger against those responsible for China's problems, and a hymn of hope that the Chinese people could find a way out of their predicament. Although ostensibly about history, it was, as everyone recognized, really about the present; and though explicitly and directly concerned with culture, it was indirectly aimed against the conservative, authoritarian leaders within the Communist Party. Given the scope of its critical intentions, it was embroiled in controversy from the beginning. Many of the political reformers associated with Party General Secretary Zhao Ziyang were sympathetic to it, and Zhao defended it against attacks in the summer of 1988. But as Zhao's faction within the Communist Party began to wane in the fall of 1988, his critics began to direct attacks against *Deathsong*.[11] Most of the creators of the series emerged as prominent supporters of the demonstrations during the 1989 Beijing Spring. After the bloody crackdown on June 4, the government put them on its "most wanted" lists. Several were imprisoned, and the others escaped into exile. In the wake of the crackdown, the government launched a propaganda campaign against

Deathsong, claiming, among other things, that it was a dangerous example of "spiritual pollution" that advocated "all-out Westernization."

In effect, conservatives in the Communist Party condemned *Deathsong* for uncritically advocating that the Chinese people embrace the American Dream. Ironically, some mainstream American academics attacked it for much the same thing, albeit for different reasons. At a symposium held with some of the creators of the series in September 1988, American academics cited the sloppiness of *Deathsong*'s scholarship; they demurred at its broad generalizations, and they scoffed at the way it cited passé authorities such as historian Arnold Toynbee. More pointedly, they found fault with the series' one-sidedly glamorous portrait of the United States and its use of advertising images to represent the American Dream in terms of a superficial consumer culture. Finally, in the name of a relativistic multiculturalism, they criticized it for being too iconoclastic about Chinese culture: You Chinese should not totally reject your traditional values, some of them said — all cultures, after all, have equal dignity. One of *Deathsong*'s authors retorted that such a position was hypocritical: You Westerners, he said, have taken advantage of the weakness of our cultural traditions to exploit us; we want the secret of your power![12]

Deathsong, though, represented an extraordinarily ambivalent interaction of Chinese concerns with Western ideas and values, something that neither critics within the conservative factions of the Chinese Communist Party nor mainstream China specialists from the West fully appreciated, at least at first. Though profoundly troubled by the economic, political, and moral confusion and the loss of self-confidence they saw around them, *Deathsong*'s creators would not yield to despair. They would help China explore a new path to national greatness. To find their dream, the Chinese people needed to reinvigorate themselves by acquiring the spirit of science and democracy, the secret of the West's success. To visualize that success, the film utilized images of Western (especially American) wealth and technological prowess and contrasted these with images of the poverty and weakness of China. But its attitude was by no means one of praise for the West. It portrayed the West as an aggressive, hostile power that had attacked, exploited, and humiliated China. The challenge for China was to revitalize itself to compete with the West. In the end, the mood of the series was assertively nationalistic. It embraced the sentiment expressed by a remark I overheard from a young scholar: "I want to learn English so that I can help create a society in which my children will not have to learn that language."

The authors of *Deathsong of the River* and the millions of (especially) young people who were inspired by it did indeed learn important things from Americans and other Westerners about how to search for a dream that would lead them out of their cultural crisis, but they learned in their own way; they did not accept the lessons that many Americans wanted to teach them. So far, the path they have explored has led to tragedy. But eventually, I think, others like them will explore similar paths, with perhaps happier results. The rise of the vision represented by *Deathsong of the River* demonstrates to Americans not just the power of their ideas about rationality and freedom, science and democracy, but also the limits of their power over such ideas. If Asians adopt these beliefs, they will not borrow them — they will steal them. They will, as they should, interpret them and use them in their own way, in a manner that may not accord with American political and economic interests.

Authors and Audience

Deathsong represented a new language of critical discourse, a dynamic blend of Chinese and Western motifs that sprang from a world outside that defined by the established institutions for academic dialogue between China and the United States. To more fully delineate the social geography and cultural significance of this world, let us first consider the resources drawn upon by the principal creators of *Deathsong*.

"Jin Guantao has no connections," one well-informed Chinese scholar working toward a Ph.D. in political science at an American university told me. Jin Guantao was a philosopher who, together with his wife, Liu Qingfeng, had written a series of seminal, controversial books that provided some of the key intellectual underpinnings of *Deathsong*. His writings, a grand mix of neo-Hegelian philosophy and cybernetic systems theory, had attracted a large following, especially among China's younger generation.[13] But, as my interviewee intimated with an air of disapproval, Jin Guantao stood outside the circles of established scholars in the Academy of Social Sciences and their patrons among high-ranking officials. Besides lacking the proper personal connections, Jin lacked, some said, the professional discipline to be taken seriously. With its jargon, breathtaking scope, and conceptual complexity, his work seemed extremely learned, but more conventional scholars criticized it as superficial. "He is broadly interdisciplinary," said one very prominent intellectual in the academy, "but he is not solidly trained." Some scholars also noted that, although Jin had spent a year in the United States, his spoken English was not good and he did not qualify as an expert on Western culture.

Jin Guantao was in his early forties at the time *Deathsong* was broadcast—which made him one of the oldest of the group who created the series. Su Xiaokang, the principal writer, was thirty-nine. Wang Luxiang, the other major writer, was thirty-two, and Xia Jun, the director, who "really initiated the project" and whose use of images gave the film much of its rhetorical power, was only twenty-seven.[14] At the time, none had traveled outside of China.

The older members of the *Deathsong* group had been swept up in the Cultural Revolution and from that experience had gained a sense of moral earnestness and of tragedy. Some people their age had emerged from this era with a deepened sense of caution, expressed in a concern to find and maintain a secure, stable niche in life. Scholars could do so by cultivating the political connections and developing the reputation for responsibility, loyalty, and competence needed to enter the academic or policy-formulating establishments. One could join either mainline institutes such as the Chinese Academy of Social Sciences or the new think tanks established by reformist leaders such as Zhao Ziyang. Sometimes the latter were called "helicopter institutes" because they enabled ambitious young scholars to rise quickly to the top, unlike the mainline institutes, where junior members had to work their way through the seniority system.

Another way for scholars to find security was to develop the technical expertise to gain an academic career abroad. But some intellectuals in their thirties or forties had not been willing or able to follow these cautious paths out of the chaos of the Cultural Revolution. They retained a grand sense of mission and sometimes pursued it with reckless abandon. Su Xiaokang described himself as belonging to a generation "which dares not refuse to be concerned and whose worries moreover have reached the degree that philosophers call 'ultimate concerns.' In my view, this is the legacy that they have inherited, willing or not, from those past days of folly; it is the result of the fact that they must take the present seriously. . . . We must redeem ourselves."[15]

Infused with what Su Xiaokang called a "sense of mission," such intellectuals engaged themselves not with their elders but with an even younger generation, those in their twenties who had hardly experienced

the Cultural Revolution but grew up in the atmosphere of disillusionment and cynicism that followed it. Wang Luxiang described the members of this generation — his and Xia Jun's generation — as "historical
drifters."

We have no slot to fit into, we have lost any sense of a "generation" to belong
to, we have become drifters unable to find a fixed place in history on this continent. . . . Perhaps it is precisely the deep-rooted fear created by this sense of the
loss of a historical home to belong to that has made us so active in this critical
age. To lack a sense of belonging is to lack anything to rely on or to hold on to.
Perhaps we were born to be critics, because we don't fit in, because we are
transitional figures between generations, because History has not set aside a
time for us to be builders.[16]

Combined with a sense of mission and a confrontation with "ultimate concern," this feeling of being adrift gave shape to the peculiar
spirit of sorrow and worry *Deathsong* evoked as it led its viewers "in
search of a dream." *Youhuan yishi* — "spirit of sorrow and worry" — is a
term deriving from classics of the Chinese tradition. It refers to the example of the sages, who, as a Song dynasty author put it, "neither delighted in the things of the world nor were saddened on account of their
own individual fate. When in high position at court, they worried for
the people; when in exile or in the country, they worried for their ruler;
then whether in or out of office they felt equally worried."[17]

The authors of *Deathsong*, however, added a new note to the classic
virtues embodied for intellectuals in the spirit of sorrow and worry — a
modern note of radical critique. Traditionally, intellectuals expressed
their social sorrow and worry either by loyally serving an upright ruler
or loyally remonstrating with a misguided ruler. But beginning with the
May Fourth Movement of the early twentieth century, leading Chinese
intellectuals have taken an iconoclastic turn: National salvation, they
claim, requires not traditional forms of loyalty but a fundamental transformation of China's economic, political, and cultural systems. *Deathsong*'s authors explicitly invoked the iconoclastic legacy of the May
Fourth Movement (the seventieth anniversary of which was to occur in
1989). As Su Xiaokang put it:

My own feeling is that the reason for the seriousness of this sense of sorrow and
worry in this generation is perhaps due to a very strange motive: they must find
a rational explanation for the days of their youth that they had muddled through
unconsciously — for that life made abnormal by fanaticism, by passion, naivete,
blindness, frankness, and even dedication. . . . We must settle accounts with
ourselves. But, you must excuse us, this settling of accounts cannot help but

touch all those who came through these days, including even our ancestors. In my view, this is where our "spirit of sorrow and worry" and where our "ultimate concerns" lie.[18]

In an ironic way, the capitalist realism used by *Deathsong* to represent the United States paralleled the socialist realism used by the American new left of the 1960s to represent Maoist China. Then as now, the unblemished attractiveness of the Other was used as a means to express the sense of "sorrow and worry" felt about one's own society. Both Chinese dissidents of the 1980s and American dissidents of the 1960s were interested not so much in becoming like the Other as in coming to terms with their own culture. The superficiality of their knowledge of the Other was less important than the profundity of their insight into their own society's problems. As iconoclastic as they sounded, the creators of *Deathsong* were deeply rooted in their own traditions. Far from embracing the cozy pleasures promised by advertisers of consumer capitalism, they were risking their lives out of an ultimate concern to make their own country better. Unlike those individualistic Americans of whom de Tocqueville said that "the woof of time is ever being broken and the track of past generations lost," the Chinese creators of *Deathsong* were engaged in a powerful argument with their ancestors. They were using old images and invoking old values to criticize the way the Communist Party had interpreted the legacy of those forebears.

Official and Unofficial China

The authors of *Deathsong* thus spoke for and to what one might call "unofficial China." By this I mean that part of Chinese society not firmly connected to government systems of control but nonetheless in touch with the language and aspirations of a great many Chinese. In ordinary Chinese speech, "unofficial" is rather closely associated with "unorthodox," even "deviant," underscoring a political system that denies the legitimacy of any forms of association not under the supervision of the Party. In the 1980s, the realm of the unofficial began to expand, as economic reforms and increased contact with the outside world weakened the Party's mechanisms of social control. Works such as *Deathsong* helped give this unofficial world a cultural identity and a voice. To understand how and with what consequences it did this, let us consider how official and unofficial audiences reacted to *Deathsong*.[19]

In Chinese society, the official and unofficial are not neatly separated. Almost everyone is tied to some official controlling agency. Under some circumstances, almost everyone publicly voices the ideology of those agencies. Increasingly, however, even people tied to official control structures are able and willing to voice unofficial ideas and engage in unofficial actions. Official and unofficial form a social and psychological continuum.

The most official of reactions to *Deathsong* came from conservatives within the Communist Party, who denounced it and eventually ordered its authors arrested for denigrating Chinese culture, advocating "all-out Westernization," and thus sowing the seeds for an antisocialist rebellion. Establishment intellectuals, scholars who aspired to be loyal spokespersons for government officials,[20] expressed strong reservations about *Deathsong,* although before the Party officially condemned it many of them were willing to defend its right to be broadcast. *Deathsong*'s message, said one such scholar, was like "saying to a sick person, 'You have no hope.'" In his view, the series did not hold out hope that Chinese society and politics could be reformed in a way that kept basic government structures intact (which was the goal of Zhao Ziyang, the leader most establishment intellectuals supported); also, *Deathsong* encouraged "blind worship" of the United States, which might lead to a loss of Chinese "cultural identity." Though such establishment intellectuals supported the official position in the name of political "responsibility," they were able to adopt a partially independent stance because, before Tiananmen, the official position itself was ambiguous. Furthermore, through their contacts with the West, many learned to think and talk in ways that deviated from official orthodoxy and acquired the practical and moral resources to stand up against its enforcers. Thus, they could concede that some of the iconoclastic points of *Deathsong* rang true and provided Chinese society with an important impetus for critical reflection. *Deathsong* helped give voice to an unofficial side of their consciousness.

But within government universities and research institutes, there were also intellectuals deeply alienated from official orthodoxy. As the biographies of *Deathsong*'s creators suggest, often the factors causing this alienation were generational. Older scholars had little chance to leave their jobs and start new careers, say, by getting accepted into an American graduate school. Resigned to working within the official establishment, they cited traditional notions about the responsibility of scholars to be loyal to authority, resorting to the weary wisdom that comes from a long, hard life. "People in my generation," said a scholar in his sixties, "fought for a perfect ideal. But for my generation, the outcomes of this were less than perfect. You have to settle for the lesser of evils."

Younger scholars had not yet been so worn down by history. Although often extremely cynical and pessimistic about the present, they were thrilled by the existence of opportunities to escape their situation by studying abroad. Even though these opportunities were scarce, there were enough of them to fire the yearning of young scholars for a different future — and to make them more acutely aware of how frustrated they were in their own society. For such young scholars, the attraction of images from American advertising and popular culture was the attraction of forbidden but just possibly attainable fruit. Although they dutifully went through the motions of their assigned jobs in official China, their hearts belonged to unofficial China. They embraced *Deathsong*'s message as giving voice to their truest aspirations.

Cultural exchange programs promoted by academic missionaries of the American Dream bore a complex relationship to official and unofficial China. The largest and best-funded of them, such as the Ford Foundation, took what I have called an essentially "churchlike" approach to their work. They channeled their dollars through the senior establishment intellectuals who ran the major academic research programs in China. In turn, these leaders distributed money and opportunities to go abroad to people who complied with official positions and were politically well connected.

People thus picked were trained by American establishment scholars to take a methodical, technical, specialized approach to solving China's problems. Chinese students who entered graduate programs in the United States were likely to be strongest not in humanistic interpretation — because that would require an outstanding facility in English, which most of them did not possess — but in specialized quantitative analysis. Often, the substance of the ideas they gained from their American training was not so much subversive as irrelevant. For instance, what some Chinese called the "new three theories" of cybernetics, systems theory, and econometrics were replacing the old three theories of materialism, contradictions, and dialectics — and the new theories derived from American social science were just as dogmatic, abstract, and irrelevant as the old. Often scholars returning with American Ph.D.s spoke a conceptual language incomprehensible not only to ordinary Chinese but also to fellow intellectuals outside of their specialities. As long as Chinese intellectuals remained on such levels of irrelevant abstraction, they posed no fundamental challenge to official China.

But insofar as they were confused and disoriented and angry at everything around them, they were attracted to passionate calls to criticism and renewal such as *Deathsong*. They were pulled away from both the political control of Party ideologues and the professional control of technocratic social science toward an agenda of the heart, a call to pursue ultimate concerns with others who constituted unofficial China. *Deathsong* helped give them a resonant rhetoric for the public expression of their discontents.

I saw this process at work when I attended the inaugural meeting of the Chinese Association for American Studies in December 1988. The keynote speeches that set the official tone for the conference — by Winston Lord, at the time the U.S. ambassador to China, and Zi Zhongyun,[21] the director of the Institute of American Studies in the Chinese Academy of Social Sciences — consisted of measured diplomatic generalizations, sidestepping the vital issues that were on the minds of most of the Chinese participants.

The papers presented during the conference approximated the standards of American social science. They strove to be factually accurate, analytically precise, and substantively balanced. In style and tone, they were impersonal, dispassionate, and carefully qualified. However, the discussion sessions that followed the paper presentations were a different matter entirely. Unlike such sessions at most American academic conferences, these quickly strayed away from the content of the papers, focusing instead on the current problems of Chinese society. The participants were little concerned with how adequately the papers had analyzed American society but passionately hoped to find in the papers some lessons that might be applied to China.

For instance, one of the liveliest discussions was touched off by a paper on American neoconservative theories about the hegemony of a "new class" of professionals in American society. Ignoring the fact that American neoconservatives saw this development as a bad thing, the Chinese scholars pounced on it as an example of the Communist Party's lack of respect for intellectuals. This discussion inspired some returned students to vent their grievances about their troubles. His conversation sprinkled with English phrases, a return Ph.D. recalled how isolated he felt when he came back to China: "You have to cut yourself off from all the friends who supported you" in graduate school, he complained.

Even if they returned to try to serve their country, young intellectuals found themselves *in* official China but not *of* it. The way their academic discussions shifted from the matter at hand was reminiscent of how, during the late 1960s, scholars in the CCAS often turned conferences on China into discussions of the United States' role in the world. In 1988 such discussions moved intellectuals into the uncharted territory explored by the authors of *Deathsong*.

Deathsong and works like it, then, helped to establish a new cultural conversation, a language for the lost that helped members of unofficial China find each other and locate themselves in relation to complex, multilayered, contradictory Chinese traditions. It was a language that recognized the fascination of unofficial China with modern consumer culture and that at times utilized some of the pretentious jargon of Western social science. But it creatively tried—albeit with debatable success—to anchor these languages in a "spirit of sorrow and worry" that drew on reinterpreted moral traditions.

Contradictory, inconsistent, exaggerated, sometimes inaccurate, *Deathsong of the River* gave voice to the feelings of confusion, ambivalence, fear, and hope of China's younger generation better than any wellbalanced, analytic academic study ever could. Calling upon an emotionally resonant combination of modern images and traditional symbolism, it cried out for fundamental change.

Renewing Chinese Culture: The Periphery as Home

Deathsong set off an extraordinary debate within the Chinese community throughout the world. Most American China scholars and media outlets ignored *Deathsong* until after June 4, 1989, when the Chinese government began to claim that it was responsible for the democracy movement. But soon after its initial broadcast, it was being viewed and read and ardently debated in Hong Kong, Taiwan, Singapore, and overseas Chinese communities around the world.[22] If a living culture is not a static structure of values but an evolving web of mutual understandings formed through an ongoing conversation about the meaning of venerable but ambiguous symbols, the debate about *Deathsong* was one of the main events that gave life to Chinese culture in the 1980s. It forced Chinese around the world once again to confront what it meant to be Chinese in a global "industrial civilization" represented by the glittering images of American advertising. Chinese in different situations answered the challenges posed by *Deathsong* in different ways. Alienated young people on the mainland radically criticized the traditional values embodied in the "feudal despotism" of hard-line Party elders; conversely, searching for their roots, Chinese in Hong Kong, Taiwan, and the United States defended traditional Chinese values against the alienating acids of modernity.[23]

The rhetoric of *Deathsong* and the debate it inspired represent a new phase in the relationship between the United States and China. In the preceding phase, American ideas and values were conveyed to China primarily by cultural and political elites on behalf of established institutions; Chinese cultural and political elites scrutinized and debated American ideas and values on behalf of the corresponding institutions of official China. But now the interaction between American and Chinese symbols has escaped the control of established elites and institutions on both sides of the Pacific. Now young, uncredentialed, often somewhat alienated Chinese cultural innovators driven by a "sense of mission" are initiating powerful new debates about the nature of Chinese identity in the modern world. What is at issue is not the value of modern Western versus traditional Chinese culture as such but rather the value of those mixtures of traditional and modern impulses achieved by "descendants of the dragon" in Hong Kong versus those in Beijing, those in San Francisco versus those in Taiwan, those in Singapore versus those in Canton.[24]

Insofar as the social movements of 1989 were inspired by a moral and intellectual vision, the rhetoric of *Deathsong of the River* made a more direct contribution to that vision than the ideas contributed through formal cultural exchanges between the United States and China. Insofar as student leaders had any idea of what reforms they wanted, their reference points seemed to be Taiwan or Hong Kong rather than the United States. During the Beijing Spring of 1989, Chinese protesters were not, as the American media suggested, trying to "become like us"; they were trying to make their own history. The movements of 1989 were not an attempt to realize "our" Western values but to develop a new sense of Chinese cultural community, a sense that finds its spiritual center, its creative home, its models for blending moral authority and free enterprise, in the dynamic Chinese communities on the periphery of the mainland, connecting the land of the Yellow River with the blue sea of Asia Pacific.

This perspective helps explain the confused mixture of excitement and consternation the Beijing Spring of 1989 evoked in Americans. The protest movements appealed to the American celebration of popular creativity, but they threatened American understandings of how popular creativity gets connected to political order. From the point of view of the U.S. foreign policy establishment, the protests were both inspiring and inconvenient, because they destabilized China and discredited leaders such as Deng Xiaoping, with whose regime the U.S. government and major American corporations had a good working relationship.

As one Chinese intellectual put it to me in the winter of 1989, as political storm clouds were already gathering over Beijing: "[T]here was a saying at the end of the Qing dynasty that is applicable today — 'Ordinary people fear the officials. The officials fear the foreigners. The foreigners fear the ordinary people.'" Throughout the world, ordinary people are drawing on traditional and modern cultural resources to forge new identities in ways unforeseen and certainly uncontrolled by Americans. These movements threaten the perceived self-interests of many Americans, especially political and cultural elites; they will have to rethink their identities and interests in the light of these popular movements. The convulsions of China in the spring of 1989 dramatically brought the need for such rethinking to Americans' attention. Subsequent events in Eastern Europe and the former Soviet Union have only made this process all the more urgent.

CONCLUSION

An East-West Dialogue
for the Next Century

New Myths for a New World

In his book on the past two decades of U.S.-China relations, Harry Harding refers to the "deeper and more penetrative relationship between the two countries that had emerged in the 1980s,
through which the United States was beginning to influence — sometimes intentionally, sometimes unwittingly — the political values and attitudes of Chinese citizens, especially younger people in urban areas."[1]
The "penetration" metaphor has come frequently and naturally to the
pens of mainstream American social scientists when they describe the
cultural consequences of the changing relationship between the United
States and China.[2] It also fits the thinking of those Chinese who have
been concerned with the invasion or even "pollution" of Chinese culture
by foreign ideas. A primary implication of the preceding chapters, however, is that "penetration" is not a good metaphor to describe the dramatic events that followed the U.S.-China encounter.

In the story that I have told, both Americans and Chinese have been
actively engaged in building mutual relationships. In the long run, there
is no distinction between an active and passive partner in the relationship — no "traumatized feminized Other," as Judith Farquhar and James
Hevia put it in a recent article.[3] There have, of course, been traumas —
societal consequences unintended and unwelcomed by various actors in
the drama of U.S.-China history — but they have been mutually experienced traumas. The metaphor of penetration simply does not capture
this shared aspect.

The metaphor of penetration also blinds us to the complexities and inconsistencies of the Chinese and American cultures and the concomitant complications in their relationship. In the story I have told, there is no such thing as a unitary American culture capable of influencing Chinese culture, although there have been many missionaries of the American Dream who have thought so. I have told the story of U.S.-China relations as a tale of the great debates within the United States about the meaning of ideas such as freedom and democracy in light of the challenge posed by China; within China, it is a story of debates about the meaning and value of Chinese tradition in light of the challenge posed by "industrial civilization." There is no unitary culture to be penetrated and no unitary culture to do the penetrating.

The metaphors used in social science gain their power from their ability concisely to convey the conclusions of more elaborate social theories. When I suggest that certain metaphors for understanding the cultural dimension of U.S.-China relationships are inadequate, I am arguing that the theories behind such metaphors are inadequate, at least for the new kinds of relations being forged at the end of this century. The story I have told challenges us to develop new theories about culture and change, theories better able to describe and understand the confusing transformations occurring among Chinese and Americans as a result of their evolving relationship with one another in a world tied together more intimately than ever by interdependent relations of communication and commerce. Elements of such a theory have been scattered and embedded in the preceding narrative; I now wish to synthesize them and make them explicit.

Culture as Conversation

As I have characterized it, a culture is not a system of fixed ideas. It is an ongoing conversation about the meaning and value of things members of a society share.[4] It is not a complete consensus about ideas and values, merely the capacity and the necessity to argue over issues faced in common. Such a capacity entails a common language and at least some common assumptions about what are the important issues for debate. These assumptions include what Charles Taylor calls common reference points or common meanings.

We could . . . say that common meanings are quite other than consensus, for they can subsist with a high degree of cleavage; this is what happens when a common meaning comes to be lived and understood differently by different groups in a society. It remains a common meaning, because there is the reference point which is the common purpose, aspiration, celebration. Such is, for example, the American Way, or freedom as understood in the U.S.A. But this common meaning is differently articulated by different groups. This is the basis of the bitterest fights in a society, and this we are also seeing in the U.S. today. Perhaps one might say that a common meaning is very often the cause of the most bitter lack of consensus. It thus must not be confused with convergence of opinion, value, attitude.[5]

One sign that what Bennett Berger calls "a piece of culture"[6] — for instance, an idea such as "Freedom" or a symbol such as the American flag — has died, has ceased to be part of a community's common reference points, is that nobody cares enough about it to argue about it anymore. However, sharing a democratic political culture requires more than simply the capacity to argue — it requires the hope that the argument could be mutually educative and that parties to the debate might rationally reach tentative agreement about how to work together for the common good. Such hope is based on a core of agreement about how the debates should be carried out.

For Americans, China — an image of China, an experience of China, a looming, dimly perceived reality of China — is not nearly as central, important, or enduring a common reference point as, say, the idea of freedom. China is what one might call a secondary reference point, the focus of important discussions that contribute to debates about central common meanings. For instance, during the height of the cold war, China was important in addressing questions about the viability and universal applicability of American forms of liberal democracy in a world inhabited by powerful communist rivals. If a rival like China was deemed too incorrigible, too powerful, and too threatening, Americans might have to mobilize their society into a militant, authoritarian national security state in danger of suppressing domestic freedom in the name of saving it. If, conversely, China was destined to "modernize" into a society dominated by pragmatic technocrats — and if, as it seemed to many Americans, such modernization was naturally connected with democratic freedom — then Americans might not have to take such drastic measures; they could preserve their freedom by entering into better communication with China, hastening its transformation into a modern, pragmatic society.

"Facts" about China were collected and organized according to such questions. The struggle to understand China became part of a struggle by Americans to understand themselves as a national community of democratic citizens committed to the universal good of freedom, which was seen as inextricably tied up with the political economy of capitalism and based on scientific reason. What I have called the liberal myth about China contributed a set of common assumptions about the purposes of American involvement with China and a common framework for arguing over how to implement those purposes. This allowed the debates to gravitate toward a moral center. With the establishment of the liberal myth, Americans could hope that public debates over China could be enlightening and productive, leading to workable agreements about how American institutions should respond to China.

In this book I have attempted to illuminate the part played by "secondary common reference points" in structuring debates over the primary common reference points that constitute the central public issues of a culture. Since the establishment of the republic, Americans have been locked in arguments about how to understand, protect, and foster democratic freedom, economic progress, and scientific enlightenment. For most of U.S. history, debate about China has not formed an important part of this ongoing national argument, but it has in the last half of the twentieth century. I have tried to show how and why China became an important, albeit secondary reference point for national public debate over the past three decades. I have, moreover, tried to document the different roles China played under different circumstances in this American cultural debate, and I have tried to show how and why the roles changed over time. In a complementary way, I have tried to show the role the United States played in Chinese debates about central issues in their culture.

As Charles Taylor puts it, the common reference points of a community's culture consist in "common purpose, aspiration, celebration." These are expressed not simply through abstract ideas but through powerfully evocative narratives — what I have called "myths" — which become fraught with significance through being publicly reaffirmed in sacred rituals. Public discussion of China, I have suggested, became associated with discussion of central American myths, which meant that the "China question" became suffused with urgency and passion. How did this happen? I have suggested that this urgency was not simply a consequence of China's political or strategic importance. Rather, talk about China had acquired a measure of sacred significance, being carried out not simply in bureaucratic discussions and academic seminars but also in countless sermons in churches involved with China through the American missionary movement. Because of their connection with central American myths, debates about China could not simply evolve incrementally through logical analysis or empirical investigation. They lurched forward and backward in quantum leaps stimulated by public rituals or public spectacles.

The public debates about a society's central myths are carried out through action as well as through talk. A society's central myths justify the moral norms that form the basis of a society's institutions. For instance, the stories we tell ourselves about the meaning of democratic freedom and progress help justify the institutions of our free market consumer economy, as well as the institutions of our democratic polity and, for that matter, the institutions of our religious life and family life. Those who give new interpretations of our central myths — for instance, by calling into question whether freedom is to be understood simply in terms of maximum individual independence from all social responsibility — can thereby threaten to undermine the moral justification for central institutions — for instance, the market economy. By the same token, one of the most powerful ways to challenge a society's central myths is to dare to take action that contradicts the norms justified by dominant interpretations of the myths.

Debate about a society's central meanings therefore almost always entails not just intellectual struggle but political struggle. Powerful vested interests have a stake in maintaining certain institutional norms and justifying them with reference to the society's central myths. As John Courtney Murray once put it, "We are not really a group of men singly engaged in the search for truth, relying solely on the means of persuasion, entering into dignified communication with each other, content politely to correct opinions with which we do not agree. As a matter of fact, the variant ideas and allegiances among us are entrenched as social powers; they occupy ground; they have developed interests; and they possess the means to fight for them. The real issues of truth that arise are complicated by secondary issues of power and prestige, which not seldom become primary."[7] Among other things, debates in the United States about China entailed struggles for power and prestige between senior and junior scholars in universities, between executive and legislative branches of government, and between liberal and conservative churches. Debates in China about America entailed analogous power struggles.

Horizons and Cultural Change

But knowledge is not always a reliable instrument for the maintenance of power. In the history of U.S.-China relations recounted here, interpretations of the central myths of both Chinese and American culture changed in ways that were unanticipated and unwanted by powerful interests in both societies.

Such changes can be characterized as changes in the horizons of Chinese and American culture. Besides its common reference points, which are the focus of its principal public debates, a culture is given coherence by unquestioned assumptions that seem so "natural" that they are not subject to debate. These unexamined assumptions constitute the culture's horizon; they define the limits of what can be seriously discussed within the culture and often provide the hidden shared rules for dialogue that enable disputants to reach agreements. The assumptions that constitute a horizon are unexaminable because under certain historical circumstances there exist linguistic, technological, or political barriers to communication with societies that would contradict such assumptions. Horizons expand when such barriers fall. When horizons expand, people within a culture start to think what before was unthinkable. Debates about old common reference points start to lost their relevance, and a new structure of debate gradually emerges. But throughout this process there is usually widespread confusion, the inability to reach any significant public agreements at all, and often social turmoil.[8]

Because the assumptions that constitute a horizon are by definition unexaminable, powerful interests cannot anticipate what will happen when a horizon expands. Often, they react with the sense of consternation and desperation that comes with a sense of loss of control. By the same token, once horizons expand, formerly subordinate groups become emboldened, as they sense possibilities for developing new rules of a game at which they can win. When horizons expand suddenly, though, this exhilaration is often for a time unfocused, a matter of inchoate hope rather than a practical program.

After normalization of U.S.-China diplomatic relations, the horizons of both societies expanded with explosive speed. Suddenly, there was a vast increase in the extent of contacts between the two societies. Increasing numbers of people on both sides of the Pacific learned to speak one another's languages — although vastly more (ten thousand times more) Chinese tried to learn English than the reverse. News about each other dramatically increased, aided by a technological revolution in global telecommunications. This expansion of horizons forced both Chinese and Americans to reexamine previously taken-for-granted assumptions about their places in the world. In ways that could not have been anticipated within the confines of their old horizons, this questioning of assumptions enabled and indeed forced people in both societies to lose confidence in the myths that gave direction to their endeavors and focus to their debates.

The consequences confused, surprised, and disconcerted powerful people in both societies, threatening their interests. Great numbers of Chinese were now suddenly forced to question the moral superiority of their familistic particularism, their respect for authority, their concern for social order, their quest even for a politically unified national society. The depth and intensity of this feverish questioning transformed the rules of the political game in China, leading to the convulsions of 1989. In the United States, the Tiananmen massacre called into question the assumption that there is an intimate and inevitable connection between market reforms and the creation of democratic institutions. Americans might even have to reexamine common assumptions about the universal applicability of their form of democracy. The debates swirling around the meanings of freedom and progress would then take on a new shape; new social actors might be emboldened to participate in those debates; and the moral foundations of economic, political, and cultural institutions might shift.

The outcomes of all of this change are impossible to predict as long as we are still trapped at least partially within the assumptions of our old horizons. An astute social scientist might be able to predict short-term outcomes of the debates through which a society agonizes over its common reference points. But the outcomes of a change in horizons can only be known ex post facto — the owl of Minerva takes wing when the shades of dusk have fallen.

The Shape of a New World

In the few years since the Tiananmen massacre, the collapse of communist regimes in Eastern Europe, and the disintegration of the Soviet Union, our horizons have expanded enough for us to see, through a glass, darkly, the shape of the new world in which Americans and Chinese will struggle to find their places. In this new world, both Americans and Chinese are finding their societies—indeed, their individual psyches—pulled apart by powerful global trends that transcend the control of any single nation-state.[9]

During the height of the cold war, the United States and China confronted each other not just as two political regimes but as two unified and contrasting sociocultural systems. When they looked at their own domestic situations, members of each society could see plenty of fissures (between McCarthyites and liberals and new leftists; between Maoists and revisionists, for instance). But when they took a global perspective, they saw themselves as belonging to contrasting wholes, enfolded by distinctive patterns of economic, political, social, and cultural life. When they look at their domestic circumstances today, they still see an abundance of tensions and conflicts, although these take different forms than before. But taking a global perspective gives little relief from this picture of fragmentation. For better or worse, members of both societies are now fatefully becoming engaged with vast, divergent global politico-economic trends that benefit some, disadvantage others, and confuse almost all.

The first of these trends is the internationalization of capital. Americans used to think of themselves, for better or worse, as leaders of the capitalist world; Chinese used to think of themselves, for better or worse, as leaders of the socialist world. Now both Americans and Chinese have to see themselves as parts of a global capitalist market economy that is far bigger than both of them and subjects them all to an often painful common discipline. American capitalism did not defeat Chinese socialism. The pressures of a world capitalist economy forced reform on the Chinese economy, and it is forcing unpopular reforms on the American economy as well. The most dynamic sector of the world capitalist economy, indeed, is no longer the United States but the newly industrializing countries, especially the "little dragons" of the Asia-Pacific region, including the coastal regions of China. In many respects, the authoritarian governments of East Asia are better able than liberal democratic welfare states to keep their workers in line while exposing them to the insecurities attendant on a competitive market economy. Seen from this perspective, American capitalism did not defeat Chinese socialism; but, ironically, Chinese capitalism, as exercised in Taiwan, Hong Kong, Singapore, and now in Guangzhou, Xiamen, Shanghai, and Tianjin, may be contributing to a weakening of the American welfare state.[10]

A second global trend that confronts Americans and Chinese alike is the professionalization of management. By this, I mean the systematic application of behavioral science to the design and management of organizations able to coordinate and control people efficiently. In an older usage in the West, "professional" referred to a combination of moral cultivation and technical expertise for the sake of public service. A residue of this older sense is still carried in the phrase "dedicated professional." But in its more modern usage, "professional" increasingly denotes an amoral technical expertise, the ability systematically to develop effective means without reference to the ends for which the means are used.[11]

Tied to constantly evolving behavioral sciences, the professionalization of management leads dynamically to new ways of utilizing "human resources." The bureaucrat in older sociological literature was a narrowly focused expert unimaginatively administering an office in a cumbersome hierarchical organization and assuring compliance through the manipulation of material incentives. Today, armed with modern psychological as well as economic research, the professional manager claims to be able to improve organizations by experimenting with forms of cooperation more effective than the old-fashioned hierarchies and by playing on workers' psychic needs for self-esteem as well as their desires for more money. The result is the evolution of more supple forms of organization, which private and public organizations throughout the world have to adopt if they are to remain competitive.[12]

The cumbersome organizations of state socialism have proven absolutely no match for the organizations developed by modern professional management. This imbalance has led to the collapse of most state socialist regimes and has forced China, even after the Tiananmen massacre, to continue to engage in far-reaching economic reforms. In China these reforms, for the time being, entail a compromise: a core of older-style state enterprises, with more and more sectors of the country reorganized according to the specifications of multinational corporations. In the long run this compromise will probably not be sustainable, and the central institutions of state socialism will have to yield to the demands of more professionally managed global organizations.

But even this does not amount to a victory for the United States over China. It is the victory of a global process, which runs contrary to some important social interests not only in China but in the United States as well. The application of management science and the professionalization of management may have been pioneered in the United States, but it has now become completely cosmopolitan and is used in many cases more effectively by multinational corporations and by foreign corporations and governments than by organizations primarily committed to serving the interests of American citizens.

A third global trend that affects both China and the United States is partly a consequence of the first two trends and partly a consequence of the development of new global communications media. This is a global trend toward particularism — a search for particular communities that give people an identity and a home in the midst of a vast, bewildering, impersonal, and competitive world.

When the Cantonese scholar quoted in Chapter 7 said, "We are finding ourselves for the first time," he was discovering not a Chinese identity but a Cantonese one. He and others in his region were rejoicing in renewed hegemony for the Cantonese language, a renewed connection with Cantonese history, and a renewed identification with regional Cantonese interests. A similar sense of regional identity is gaining strength in other parts of China. New forms of ethnic identity are also blooming; for instance, some Chinese Muslims see themselves as more Muslim than Chinese. China seems to be beginning to decompose, at least spiritually if not politically, into many Chinas. Even fiercer forms of decomposition are occurring in the former Soviet Union, of course. But this is not just a trend affecting former state socialist societies. The United States, too, has begun to split up into many different "Americas," each with its own versions of history, its special collective commitments, and its particular sense of place. It now makes less sense to speak of "U.S.-China relations" than to talk of how one part of the United States (for instance, Chinese Americans, southern black textile workers, or directors of multinational corporations) relates to one part of China (for instance, Beijing intellectuals, Guangdong entrepreneurs, or central government officials).

Cultural Discordances

Each of the three global politicoeconomic trends I have sketched above is implicated with a characteristic, emergent culture; each sustains its own ongoing global conversation through distinctive symbols, centered on different common reference points. Most people participate to some degree in each of the three conversations; but each of these cultures has its distinctive elites, its particular conservators and innovators, its priests and prophets. Each, too, has its own logic of development. Under certain circumstances in the past, these three global conversations might have resonated with one another. At present, though, they are in discord, and their discordance defines the characteristic patterns of confusion and ambivalence of this age of transition.

The global conversation associated with the internationalization of capital is carried on through a moral language of competition and consumption. Though intimately linked to the world market system, this cultural conversation can be analytically distinguished from it. It provides the common understandings that enable people to identify themselves as market actors and motivates them to participate energetically in the market system. During the 1980s, many people in China began to think of themselves as market actors and began wanting to live as such, even though they were still enmeshed in a socialist economy. The scholar quoted in Chapter 7 who learned the lesson of "competition, competition, competition" from his stay in the United States and who marveled at how "even the beggars in Berkeley were competitive" was at the time I interviewed him still working for a state-run research institute in China. His and his colleagues' salaries bore no relation to their productivity as commodity producers; their housing and much of their food was allocated by the state rather than through the market. But now they thought of themselves as subjects of the regime of the global market — as some of them described it, the ability to think this way came with the force of a revelation. In their social being, they may have remained socialist, but in their consciousness they were capitalist.

They had learned the key elements of a vocabulary that enabled them to identify themselves as individuals locked in a race for success, defined in terms of status symbols available as commodities on the world market. "Capitalism concentrated in a bottle" was how the *People's Daily* described Coca-Cola in 1983 as the soft drink, reintroduced to China in 1978, soared in popularity during the early 1980s.[13] There was some small truth in the *People's Daily* allegation. As China's exchanges with the West expanded, people in many walks of life — notably urban elites but also peasants in regions such as Guangdong with access to international popular culture through Hong Kong television — began to talk of the good life in terms of a global world of consumer goods. They began to recognize that in the world of global commerce, Coca-Cola was far more important than, say, ginseng tea. And although on their initial encounters they often thought Coke tasted strange, they soon learned to perceive that it did indeed taste better than Chinese beverages. They began to think of the capacity to purchase Coke (which in the early 1980s cost far more than local soft drinks) as a mark of success in reaching world standards of consumption. They were driven to strive to earn the money necessary to purchase such symbols of success, which would eventually include everything from Coca-Cola to Reebok running shoes to Mercedes Benz automobiles.

The priests and prophets of the culture of competition and consumption — those who develop its language and rhetoric and spread it around the world — are marketers, advertisers, and creators of popular culture (commercial movies, TV programs, pop music, and pulp fiction). The global reach of modern media extends these works around the world, creating universal languages of human aspiration and directing conversation toward common reference points: Which commodities are the best symbols of success, and which opportunities promise the economic growth necessary to bring these commodities within reach?

As we saw in the case of China, sudden induction into this universe of discourse is both thrilling and disorienting. Among many Chinese youth, especially, it inspired both great excitement and a debilitating sense of inferiority, as would-be consumers found that they did not (and probably for a long time would not) have enough money to get very far up the international ladder of consumer success. For the industrialized nations of the West, of course, induction into this universe of discourse takes place gradually, from earliest childhood, and its disorienting effects are not as dramatically spectacular as in the case of the 1980s generation of Chinese. But a disorienting loss of meaning occurs nonetheless, as manifested through the widespread cynicism afflicting American society, and the sense of confusion and meaninglessness becomes exacerbated when a contracting economy makes it more difficult for many people to achieve the good life as the culture of competition and consumption defines it.

Both in China and to a somewhat different degree in the United States, this culture has become discordant with the cultural conversation associated with the second global trend I have identified, the trend toward professionalization of management — what one might call the "culture of organization and control." This is a conversation carried on through a universal language derived from the social sciences for measuring efficiency and discussing the marginal utility of different incentive structures.

The culture of organization and control has become global in the sense that there are now universal standards for determining whether an organization is operating efficiently. These standards are compelling even to people in societies that, like China or Eastern Europe, are forced to admit in shame that their organizations do not measure up.[14] Since the end of the cold war, these common standards of organizational efficiency and ways of talking about how to achieve it have spread via exchanges of professional experts and the globalization of the Western social science professions.

In China during the 1980s, a host of visiting delegations of experts in economics, political science, and sociology purveyed advice on how their Chinese counterparts should reform their political, economic, and social organizations, and a host of academic programs provided opportunities for Chinese students to go abroad, especially to the United States, to receive training in the social sciences. Increasingly, scholars in Chinese research institutes and think tanks — even scholars who did not go abroad — came to accept the analytical and methodological standards of the international social science professions (together with the ideals of professional autonomy that those standards were meant to preserve) and to aspire to produce work that met those standards.

There were, to be sure, tensions between, on the one hand, younger scholars who went abroad and returned full of the most abstract, technical jargon of cybernetics, systems theory, and econometrics and, on the other, a middle generation of reformers concerned with finding solutions that were practical in a Chinese context — just as there are tensions between management school experts and practically seasoned executives in American corporations. But increasingly in China during the 1980s — as in the United States and indeed around the world — this tension between scientifically trained experts and practical managers defined the poles of a cultural conversation focused on a shared purpose: how to control the behavior of large numbers of individuals so that they would work with maximum efficiency and reliability for common goals.

This set of common reference points is ultimately at odds with the culture of competition and consumption. The culture of organization and control is concerned with cooperation, collective goal attainment, and getting the maximum productivity out of workers for the minimum reward. Its priests and prophets are not reckless entrepreneurs, slick advertisers, or flamboyant popular artists but earnest social scientists given to measured advice backed up by carefully controlled methodologies and sober administrators concerned with preserving a stable, predictable environment for their organizations. Although the quest for self-gratification celebrated by the prophets of consumption makes people want to be served by efficient organizations, it does not especially incline them to contribute to organizational effectiveness, and it sometimes leaves them hungering for a sense of excitement and personal and social renewal that does not well accord with the manager's desires for order and efficiency.

The culture of competition and consumption and the culture of organization and control are both examples of what we might call Weberian processes. They represent different phases of a larger process of individuation and rationalization — the extrication of individuals from organic social ties and their reintegration into universal systems of classification and control legitimated through instrumental rationality. However, the culture connected with the third global trend, the universal trend toward particularism, represents a logic that might be called Hegelian. For it was Hegel who stressed the need for modern societies to provide for their members differentiated ethical communities, particular bounded social wholes that could provide individuals with identity, continuity with a historical past, and a moral purpose toward the future, at the same time allowing them to see these partial communities as elements in a larger whole.[15]

We might call the cultural conversations that create such communities examples of a "culture of interpretation." Each entails a nonuniversalizable language, a particular configuration of metaphors, historical references, imaginative allusions to historical destiny and moral purpose — a language densely textured enough that no one who has not participated deeply in the life of the community can fully understand it.

The priests and prophets of this culture of interpretation are intellectuals and charismatic leaders. By intellectuals I refer here not to technocratic scholars but to the imaginative interpreters of the common symbols of a community's heritage. In this sense, an intellectual is a generalist able to provide a community with a vision of itself as a whole. The late twentieth century has not been kind to such intellectuals. In China the Party hates them, in the United States the political establishment distrusts them, and in both societies the commercial and bureaucratic sectors have little use for them. In the United States universities used to provide a home for such intellectuals, but this is increasingly less so today, as universities have become dominated by a spirit of professional expertise.[16] In China today, such intellectuals are not only harassed by Party functionaries, but they are looked down upon by technically trained scholars who know how to make money in the new economic climate. In both China and the United States — and in most of the rest of the world as well — intellectuals of this type are mostly to be found on the fringes of established cultural institutions: on the fringes of universities, perhaps on the fringes of some churches, and among circles of artists on the fringes of commercial and political respectability. Now, however, for the brief wrinkles in time caused by shifting cultural horizons, as people seek larger frameworks of meaning than can be provided by narrowly technical expertise, such intellectuals can have dramatic effects on their societies. In China, a case in point was the creation of the *Deathsong of the River*.

Another source of community formation comes from charismatic political leaders — not infrequently drawn from the ranks of intellectuals — who successfully formulate populist appeals to widespread feelings of resentment. Such perhaps were the leaders of the student movement of 1989 in China. But throughout the world today the appeal of such charisma is proving to be as dangerous as it is seductive. As illustrated most tragically in the case of Bosnia, in the 1990s the inspirational populism of charismatic leaders is as likely to bring chaos and civil war as it is to bring a larger vision of social healing and renewal.[17] Many ordinary Chinese were right to fear the chaos that might have come if the leaders of the 1989 movement had triumphed. This is a fact that many Americans, inspired from afar by the movement, have difficulty accepting.

A New East-West Dialogue in a New World

There are many new facts that Americans, Chinese, and people around the world are going to have a difficult time accepting. From the point of view of both Americans and Chinese, the moral history of U.S.-China relations recounted in this book reflects the transformation of an antagonistic relationship into, first, an incipient cooperative relationship in which each side hoped to benefit from the other and, then, an ambiguous relationship in which the very boundaries between sides become blurred and all participants find themselves confronted with unresolvable dilemmas. It is a relationship typical of contemporary social and political life, which increasingly forces us to choose not between right and wrong but between incompatible goods attached to unacceptable evils — a situation I have described in terms of the discordance among three different global cultures.

Perhaps the three cultures have always represented tendencies fundamentally at odds with one another. But in the early years of the cold war, within both the United States and China — in fact, within most of the "free world" and most of the "socialist camp" — the three cultures resonated enough that they seemed to form integrated social systems. From the point of view of many Americans, for instance, the culture of competition and consumption seemed quite consistent with the culture of efficient organization and control — and together these could sustain a life that satisfied the modern longing for "freedom" in a way consistent with voluntarily accepted responsibility for the community good. But this apparent conjunction was a product of transient historical circumstances: strong economic growth offering generalized opportunities for individual accomplishment; a commonly felt need to create strong, efficient, yet flexible instruments of social control to combat the (presumed) threat of international communism; and the persistence of a widespread sense of self-discipline and social responsibility carried over from American religious traditions. Now we face the consequences of limits to economic growth exacerbated by worldwide market competition, the lack of a plausible common enemy, and the erosion of common moral assumptions. In this new world, measures pursued to increase economic growth tend to clash with those taken to assure predictable organizational environments and those taken to give people a sense of community.[18]

Analogously, in early 1950s China, the victory of the Communists brought a long-yearned-for stability and hope for an improving standard of consumption; the cold war justified a strong, controlling government; and a seemingly triumphant communist ideology made meaningful a measure of personal sacrifice for the collective good. But the state socialist method of improving standards of consumption turned out to be a failure; the cold war ended; and communist ideology lost its credibility. Now China has rapid economic growth — much more rapid than the United States' — but the growth is uneven and psychologically unsettling, fueling quests for partial community and tensions that undercut the social control necessary to maintain a stable business environment.

For both Americans and Chinese, therefore, the new world appearing on the horizon after the end of the cold war is a world where, once again, things fall apart. As the Chinese intellectual quoted in Chapter 7 said, "[O]ur problem is not that we lack ideas — everybody has plenty of ideas. But nobody has the same ideas." What he said of China is increasingly true of the United States. People talk past each other. Public discourse is filled with debates that seem unresolvable because the participants no longer share a common symbolic language, no longer seek common goals, no longer share common reference points. In the name of "multiculturalism," some American scholars even celebrate the inability of people ever to reach rational agreement on a truth that transcends even tentatively the limitations of ethnicity, gender, and class.

The confusions and anxieties of these times are thus best described in terms of a discordance among global cultures. It is perhaps less difficult for Chinese to reach common moral understandings with Americans than it is for consumerist advertisers (whether Chinese or American) to reach common moral understandings with managerial professionals or with fervent ethnic nationalists. Coca-Cola is committed to the notion that a common taste for Coke will, as their advertisement broadcast during the 1992 Olympic games put it, "make the whole world one." The company will resist the idea that a common taste for Coke may just as well divide societies between those who can regularly afford to buy the soft drink and those who cannot (not to mention between manufacturers of local beverages and agents of the multinational Coca-Cola empire). Indeed, such division partly developed when Coca-Cola — capitalism concentrated in a bottle — was reintroduced into China.

Likewise, the "responsible" social scientists who expertly advise corporations how to become more efficient often fail to comprehend how the products marketed by such corporations can stimulate a quest for self-fulfillment that undermines organizational discipline.[19] The U.S. government officials and mainstream scholars who advised the Chinese government to reform itself envisioned an orderly process of reform, effected from the top down by enlightened managers, leading to a steady increase in organizational flexibility and efficiency. They were surprised when the processes of reform stimulated rapidly escalating popular demands for self-expression that could not be contained or directed from above.

Finally, the prophets of community — such as those intellectuals who contributed to China's "cultural fever" of the 1980s and in the process helped greatly to create the ferment that led to the Tiananmen upheavals — like to assume that commitments to community will be compatible both with the organizational regularity and the entrepreneurial energies required to generate affluence in the modern world. They think they can have community, individual autonomy, and affluence as well. Often enough, they don't know what to do when they are disappointed.

A casualty of this moral and intellectual fragmentation is the idea and practice of democracy. In 1989, the Tiananmen demonstrations and subsequent uprisings throughout Eastern Europe illustrated how widespread the quest for democracy has become. But the Tiananmen demonstrations also illustrated the illusiveness of the democratic ideal. As Orville Schell reported, "when pressed to be more precise about their vision of reform or their precise notions of how democracy might work in China, [student demonstrators on Tiananmen] tended to become vague and even flustered. . . . As one student only half-facetiously said, 'I don't know exactly what we want, but we want more of it.'"[20] Such confusion, though, is not limited to changing socialist societies such as China. Many Americans might become just as vague and flustered as the Chinese student if pressed to define exactly how to protect individual rights and give a voice to all the diverse citizens of the United States or how to achieve economic growth while ensuring a modicum of security and justice for all Americans. Democracy is not simply about freedom; it is about voluntarily accepted discipline, enforced by legitimate institutions, based on some degree of public agreement arrived at rationally through vigorous debate. Because of the moral and intellectual fragmentation of the modern world, it is getting difficult to see how public debate can lead to the common agreements necessary to sustain democratic institutions, not only in China but in the United States as well.[21]

After the Los Angeles riots of 1992, a Chinese friend — an intellectual who had camped out with the students on Tiananmen in 1989 — wrote to me expressing concern that I might have been harmed in the "black people's riot." The word she used for "riot" (*baoluan*) was the same one the Chinese government used to describe the Tiananmen democracy movement and to justify suppressing it. The letter reminded me of the difficulty of assigning a common moral meaning to political events that bring together people with widely different interests in a complex society. It reminded me also that the United States is not a paragon of democracy that could be an unambiguous model for reformers in China or anywhere else in the world. Although the democratic tradition is more deeply embedded and more fully realized in the United States than in China, Americans have cause to be humble when speaking to the rest of the world about democracy. I mean humility in the sense that Reinhold Niebuhr used the word — as an active virtue that impels people forward to seek high ideals even as they grasp in faith a transcendent dimension in their culture "from the standpoint of which the element of vanity in all human ambitions and achievements is discerned."[22] Such an active humility is no excuse, say, for ignoring human rights violations in the name of cultural relativism. It is motive for continuing to pursue the cause of basic human decency around the world while realizing that this can never be accomplished unless one also reforms oneself. Americans, as well as Chinese, need to search out anew what democracy would practically mean in their own contexts. What is required is not so much for the United States to teach China about democracy as for people in both societies to help each other search for democracy amid the confusing contradictions of the modern world.

One important step in preparing for a fuller realization of democracy is to find new integrative visions that can help people reconcile and balance the ambitions unleashed by the market, the necessities recognized by the social science professions, and the yearnings activated in the quest for community. Such new visions would take the form not of arid, abstract theories but of powerful new master narratives, new American and Chinese dreams, drawing sacred power from the most resonant aspirations of their cultural traditions. These new moral visions would enable Americans, Chinese, and the other peoples of the world to recognize the limitations as well as the strengths and insights of their various traditions; they would encourage them not only to tolerate but also to learn from each other and give them a realistic hope that they could see a new way forward to a just and prosperous world community. In the words of Vaclav Havel, the intellectual on the world stage who has come the closest to evoking such a new narrative: "[T]he end of Communism has brought a major era in human history to an end. It has brought an end not just to the 19th and 20th centuries, but to the modern age as a whole. . . . Sooner or later politics must find a post modern face."[23]

As I have argued in this book, the moral drama of U.S.-China relations helped the last several generations of Americans sustain a liberal master narrative that focused the debates and directed the hopes of a great fractious variety of Americans toward a moral center. Another word for such a narrative is "myth." As I have used the term in this book, a myth is not simply a scientifically inaccurate history; it is, as Aristotle put it, made up of things to wonder at.[24] It guides the imagination to search for a viable connection between moral ideals carried on from a society's past and realistic aspirations for the future. For Americans from the late 1960s to the early 1980s, the liberal myth about U.S.-China relations provided an account of history that was not empirically verifiable but was, in the context of its times, morally helpful. That context has now passed. Americans and Chinese now need more morally adequate myths, postmodern master narratives to beckon the way toward a humane postmodern global politics.

In the twenty-first century, perhaps the drama of U.S.-China relations will once again stimulate Americans and Chinese to develop such master narratives for a new world, new visions allowing a new politics to show its postmodern face. This time, probably, the primary dialogue creating such visions will be not between Beijing and Washington — two capitals that seem singularly devoid of vision these days — but between a multitude of diverse Chinese and Americans interacting within the fertile spaces on the edges of both societies: in Hong Kong, Taiwan, and multiethnic metropolises such as San Francisco and Los Angeles. Within such places are occurring new conversations about the deepest meaning of Asian and Western cultural traditions, fruitful comparisons between American and Chinese assumptions about the relation between self and society, about the legitimate bases of authority, about the proper bond between political and economic life in the rapidly changing conditions of the Pacific Rim.[25] Amid the anxieties and uncertainties of this transitional time, this cultural ferment offers some hope for the creation of humane new visions about how Chinese and Americans might create a common home in the intricately interdependent world of the twenty-first century.

Notes

Preface

1. Harry Harding, *A Fragile Relationship: The United States and China since 1972* (Washington, D.C.: The Brookings Institution, 1992). For an excellent study of the development of business relations with China, see Randall E. Stross, *Bulls in the China Shop and other Sino-American Business Encounters* (New York: Pantheon Books, 1990). See also Michael Yahuda, *Towards the End of Isolationism: China's Foreign Policy after Mao* (New York: St. Martin's Press, 1983); Samuel Kim, ed., *China and the World: Chinese Foreign Policy in the Post-Mao Era* (Boulder, Colo.: Westview Press, 1984); and Richard H. Solomon, ed., *The China Factor: Sino-American Relations and the Global Scene* (Englewood Cliffs, N.J.: Prentice Hall, 1981).

I have also taken into account the literature about the history of U.S.-China relations earlier in this century. Representative works are Warren I. Cohen, *America's Response to China: A History of Sino-American Relations,* 3rd edition (New York: Columbia University Press, 1990); Akira Iriye, *Across the Pacific: An Inner History of American–East Asian Relations* (New York: Harcourt, Brace, and World, 1967); Akira Iriye, *After Imperialism: The Search for a New Order in the Far East, 1921–31* (Cambridge, Mass.: Harvard University Press, 1965); Michael H. Hunt, *The Making of a Special Relationship: The United States and China to 1914* (New York: Columbia University Press, 1983).

2. David Shambaugh, *Beautiful Imperialist: China Perceives America, 1972–1990* (Princeton, N.J.: Princeton University Press, 1991).

3. Richard Madsen, *Morality and Power in a Chinese Village* (Berkeley: University of California Press, 1984). See also Anita Chan, Richard Madsen, and

Jonathan Unger, *Chen Village under Mao and Deng* (Berkeley: University of California Press, 1992).

4. Robert N. Bellah, Richard Madsen, William M. Sullivan, Ann Swidler, and Steven M. Tipton, *Habits of the Heart: Individualism and Commitment in American Life* (Berkeley: University of California Press, 1985), and *The Good Society* (New York: Knopf, 1991).

5. For a good general introduction to this approach, see Paul Rabinow and William M. Sullivan, eds., *Interpretive Social Science: A Reader* (Berkeley: University of California Press, 1979). I have also benefited from reading Edward W. Said's *Orientalism* (New York: Pantheon Books, 1978). However, although I agree with Said that Western scholarship about the "Orient" — as is true of scholarship about anything else — is never purely objective but has been shaped by relationships of power, I insist that power is only one important factor in the way we understand the "Other." I will argue that the particular cultural resources available to Americans have importantly shaped their thinking about how to exercise their power and that the cultural resources available to people in China have shaped their thinking about how to respond to their relative lack of power. I will also suggest that in spite of the ways power relationships shape our knowledge, we can sometimes learn from each other truths that transcend our power interests and enable us to criticize the way we have exercised power. See Benjamin I. Schwartz, "Area Studies as a Critical Discipline," *Journal of Asian Studies*, Vol. 40, No. 1 (November 1980).

6. Bellah et al., *Habits of the Heart*, 297–307; *The Good Society*, 287–306.

7. This understanding of institutions is more fully elaborated in Bellah et al., *The Good Society*. See especially 10–12, 287–293.

Chapter One

1. There have been wide discrepancies in the number of dead reported, ranging from a figure of several hundred reported by the Chinese government to several thousand reported by some Chinese dissidents. One of the most careful, comprehensive siftings of the evidence about numbers of casualties is in the *Amnesty International Report 1990*, which estimates the figure to be around one thousand (New York: Amnesty International Publications, 1990).

2. Those executed were people accused not simply of protesting but of damaging state property or inflicting bodily harm. The most widely publicized executions were those of three young workers in Shanghai accused of burning a train after the locomotive had run over six demonstrators who had been blocking a railway.

3. There is by now a very large body of literature on the 1989 democracy movement and the June 4 crackdown. Some representative books in English include Roger Des Forges, Luo Ning, and Wu Yen-bo, eds., *China, the Crisis of 1989: Origins and Implications* (Buffalo, N.Y.: Council on International Studies and Programs, State University of New York at Buffalo, 1990); Michael S.

Duke, *The Iron Horse: A Memoir of the Chinese Democracy Movement and the Tiananmen Massacre* (Layton, Utah: Peregrine Smith Books, 1990); Lee Feigon, *China Rising: The Meaning of Tiananmen* (Chicago: Ivan Dee, 1990); Han Minzhu, ed., *Cries for Democracy: Writing and Speeches from the 1989 Chinese Democracy Movement* (Princeton: Princeton University Press, 1990); George Hicks, ed., *The Broken Mirror: China after Tiananmen* (Chicago: St. James Press, 1990); Peter Li and Marjorie Li, *Politics of Conflict in China: Confrontation at Tiananmen Square, Essays and Documents* (New Brunswick, N.J.: Transaction Books, 1990); Nan Lin, *The Struggle for Tiananmen: Anatomy of the 1989 Mass Movement* (Westport, Conn.: Praeger, 1992); Liu Binyan, Ruan Ming, and Xu Gang, *"Tell the World": What Happened in China and Why,* trans. Henry Epstein (New York: Pantheon Books, 1989); Suzanne Ogden, Kathleen Hartford, Lawrence Sullivan, and David Zweig, eds., *China's Search for Democracy: The Student and the Mass Movement of 1989* (Armonk, N.Y.: M. E. Sharpe, 1991); Michel Oksenberg and Marc Lambert, eds., *Beijing Spring 1989: Confrontation and Conflict, the Basic Documents* (Armonk, N.Y.: M. E. Sharpe, 1990); Tony Saich, ed., *The Chinese People's Movement: Perspectives on Spring 1989* (Armonk, N.Y.: M. E. Sharpe, 1990); Scott Simmie and Bob Nixon, *Tiananmen Square* (Seattle: University of Washington Press, 1989); Yi Mu and Mark Thompson, *Crisis at Tiananmen: Reform and Reality in Modern China* (San Francisco: China Books, 1989); and Shen Tong, *Almost a Revolution* (Boston: Houghton Mifflin, 1990).

4. These events are conveniently summarized in *China Update,* No. 1 (1989). For further analysis, see Alexander Lukin, "The Initial Soviet Reaction to the Events in China in 1989 and the Prospects for Sino-Soviet Relations," *The China Quarterly,* No. 125 (March 1991): 119–136; and David Shambaugh, "Peking's Foreign Policy Conundrum since Tiananmen: Peaceful Coexistence vs. Peaceful Evolution," *Issues and Studies* Vol. 28, No. 11 (November 1992): 65–85.

5. Quoted in Mark Hertsgaard, "China Coverage Strong on What, Weak on Why," *Rolling Stone,* September 21, 1989, 37.

6. Gallup Poll cited in Harry Harding, *A Fragile Relationship: The United States and China since 1972* (Washington, D.C.: The Brookings Institution, 1992), 372.

7. Summarized in ibid., 247–296; and in David Shambaugh, "Patterns of Interaction in Sino-American Relations," in Thomas W. Robinson and David Shambaugh, eds., *Chinese Foreign Policy: Theory and Practice* (New York: Oxford University Press, 1993), 208–209.

8. See, for instance, Craig Calhoun, "Tiananmen, Television, and the Public Sphere: Internationalization of Culture and the Beijing Spring of 1989," *Public Culture* Vol. 2, No. 1 (Fall 1989): 54–70.

9. CBS News and *New York Times* poll, cited in Sanford J. Unger, ed., *Estrangement: America and the World* (New York: Oxford University Press, 1985), 19.

10. For figures on landlord casualties and famine victims, see Richard Madsen, "The Countryside under Communism," in *The Cambridge History of Modern China, Volume 15* (Cambridge: Cambridge University Press, 1991), chap.

9, 625 and 642. For figures on victims of the anti-rightist campaign, see Merle Goldman, "The Party and the Intellectuals," in *The Cambridge History of Modern China, Volume 14*, chap. 5, 257. For figures on victims of the Cultural Revolution, see Harry Harding, "The Chinese State in Crisis," in *The Cambridge History of Modern China, Volume 15*, chap. 2, 214.

11. It is not fashionable these days for professional social scientists to write history as a form of moral narrative or drama. Dramatic accounts imply goodness and badness, a progress of events directed toward a morally meaningful goal. Most social science aspires to be "value-free." It eschews the notion that history has any moral purpose (or at least leaves that notion to be explored by philosophers and theologians). It explains events in terms of impersonal laws. It speaks not of goodness or badness but of perceptions of goodness and badness by certain actors (and it tries to find psychological or sociological causes for those perceptions). It writes not of triumph or tragedy but of "outcomes." But it requires a certain asceticism to write such disenchanted history, which is not — and I believe should not be — satisfactory to the general public.

12. See Michael Schudson, *Watergate in American Memory: How We Remember, Forget, and Reconstruct the Past* (New York: Basic Books, 1992), especially 103–126; and John MacAloon, ed., *Rite, Drama, Festival, Spectacle: Rehearsals Toward a Theory of Cultural Performance* (Philadelphia: Institute for the Study of Human Issues, 1984). Complex historical processes that do not lend themselves to this kind of dramatic representation tend not to get reported by journalists. In my view, though, it is precisely such processes that most need to be understood in terms of narratives that have moral meaning for the public. How to do this, however, is a difficult challenge for which most writers are not adequately prepared in the academy.

13. A classic example of this writing is Arthur Smith, *Chinese Characteristics* (New York: Fleming H. Revell, 1894).

14. Stephen R. Mackinnon and Oris Friesen, *China Reporting: An Oral History of American Journalism in the 1930s and 1940s* (Berkeley: University of California Press, 1987).

15. Harold R. Isaacs, in his classic *Scratches on Our Minds: American Views of China and India* (New York: John Day Co., 1958; 2d edition, White Plains, N.Y.: M. E. Sharpe, 1980), argues that a result of this legacy has been the accumulation in the American popular consciousness of highly charged images of China — both positive and negative — that undergo sudden shifts in response to the vicissitudes of U.S.-China relations. For a recent extension of Isaacs's pathbreaking work, see Michael Hunt, David Shambaugh, Warren Cohen, and Akira Iriye, *Mutual Images in U.S.-China Relations,* Occasional Paper 32 (Washington, D.C.: The Wilson Center Asia Program, 1988).

16. For an evocation of the worlds of liberal Protestant missionaries in China, see John S. Service, *Golden Inches: The China Memoir of Grace Service* (Berkeley: University of California Press, 1989).

17. The theoretical background to these statements comes from my reading of Hans-Georg Gadamer, *Truth and Method,* ed. Garrett Barden and John Cuming (New York: Seabury, 1975), and "The Problem of Historical Con-

sciousness," in Paul Rabinow and William M. Sullivan, eds., *Interpretive Social Science: A Reader* (Berkeley: University of California Press, 1979), 103–160.

18. Robert N. Bellah, Richard Madsen, William M. Sullivan, Ann Swidler, and Steven M. Tipton, *Habits of the Heart: Individualism and Commitment in American Life* (Berkeley: University of California Press, 1985), 23–25.

19. See Hertsgaard, "China Coverage," 37ff.

20. NSC 68 in Thomas H. Etzold and John Lewis Gaddis, eds., *Containment: Documents on American Policy and Strategy, 1945–1950* (New York: Columbia University Press, 1978), 388.

21. *Time,* January 1, 1979, and January 6, 1986.

22. See Simmie and Nixon, *Tiananmen Square,* 43, 123.

23. See Randall E. Stross, *Bulls in the China Shop and other Sino-American Business Encounters* (New York: Pantheon Books, 1990), 275–288; and Harding, *A Fragile Relationship,* 169–172.

24. For example, Fox Butterfield, *China: Alive in the Bitter Sea* (New York: Times Books, 1982); Richard Bernstein, *From the Center of the Earth: The Search for the Truth about China* (Boston: Little Brown, 1982); Orville Schell, *"Watch Out for the Foreign Guests!" China Encounters the West* (New York: Pantheon, 1980); Orville Schell, *To Get Rich Is Glorious* (New York: Pantheon, 1984); and Orville Schell, *Discos and Democracy: China in the Throes of Reform* (New York: Pantheon, 1988).

25. "Which China Is for Real?" *New York Times,* June 19, 1989.

26. Barry Naughton, *Growing out of the Plan: Chinese Economic Reform, 1978–1993* (New York: Cambridge University Press, 1994).

27. Pat Buchanan, "Caught in the Dragon's Wrath," *Washington Times,* June 7, 1989.

28. This was an early draft of a document that was considerably toned down before being publicly disseminated. I attended the meetings of this group and have copies of the drafts. The early drafts reflect well the sentiments of the group members during their first reaction to the Tiananmen massacre.

29. Richard Nixon, "Keep Repression of Tiananmen Square Protestors in Perspective," *Boston Herald,* June 25, 1989.

30. Henry Kissinger, "The Drama in Beijing," *Washington Post,* June 11, 1989.

31. Henry Kissinger, "The Caricature of Deng as a Tyrant Is Unfair," *Washington Post,* August 1, 1989. In the August 6, 1989, edition of the *Washington Post,* Stephen J. Solarz referred to this stance as "Kissinger's Kowtow."

32. Thelen, Marrin, Johnson and Bridges, *China Business: Current Regulation and Practice,* Fall 1989.

33. John A. Hall, *Liberalism: Politics, Ideology, and the Market* (London: Paladin Grafton Books, 1987). A country can have a high growth rate and still, because of inequality in distribution of incomes, have widespread poverty in the midst of affluence.

34. David R. McCann, foreword to Kim Dae Jung, *Prison Writings* (Berkeley: University of California Press, 1987), x.

35. There is considerable controversy among Western economists about

how to measure China's per capita income. At the official exchange rate, the figure is equivalent to $370 a year. But if per capita income is calculated according to a measure of real purchasing power, estimates range from a per capita income of about $650 per person to about $4,000 per person. China's figures for life expectancy and average calories consumed are similar to those of countries with a gross national product of about $2,000 per capita. By these measures, the per capita income of the United States is about $24,000. This information is summarized from Nicholas D. Kristof, "Incomes Are Low but Even Dog Meat Is Cheap," *New York Times*, February 14, 1993, 6.

36. See Deng Xiaoping's speech of June 9, 1989; and He Xin, *Xifang Guojiade Heping Bianhua Zhanlue* [The West's Peaceful Evolution Strategy] (Beijing: Gaodeng Jiaoyu Chubanshe, 1990).

37. Thomas L. Pangle, *The Spirit of Modern Republicanism: The Moral Vision of the American Founders and the Philosophy of Locke* (Chicago: University of Chicago Press, 1988), 278.

38. Jean Tepperman, *San Francisco Bay Guardian*, July 12, 1989, 17.

39. Orville Schell, "China's Spring," *New York Review of Books*, June 26, 1989, 6.

40. Sarah Lubman, "The Myth of Tiananmen Square," *Washington Post*, June 30, 1989.

41. Ibid.

42. Hertsgaard, "China Coverage," 39. This is a common criticism about journalism, not only in its coverage about China but about political movements around the world.

43. One facet of the story that some reporters inexcusably suppressed was that some of the "hunger strikers" in Tiananmen Square were not really fasting at all. Harding, *A Fragile Relationship*, 241.

44. *Washington Post*, June 5, 1989; *New York Times*, June 6, 1989. These reports were based on an article published in Hong Kong's *Wen Hui Bao*.

45. The Chinese Red Cross figures are cited in Simmie and Nixon, *Tiananmen Square*, 194.

46. A tape recording of Yuan Mu's press conference and other footage from government-controlled television was disseminated to American scholars from Chinese consulates in the United States. I base this description on the tape I viewed at the University of California at Berkeley's Center for Chinese Studies.

47. Hertsgaard, "China Coverage," 37.

48. *New York Times*, June 14, 1989.

49. Ibid.

50. Anita Chan, Richard Madsen, and Jonathan Unger, *Chen Village under Mao and Deng* (Berkeley: University of California Press, 1992), 328. "Chen Village" is a pseudonym.

51. See editors of *Time* magazine, *Massacre in Beijing: China's Struggle for Democracy* (New York: Time Books, 1989), 59.

52. Although many China scholars had begun to develop this understanding of the June 4 massacres within a few months after the events, it was not comprehensively depicted in the press until more than a year later — and then

not in the mainstream press but in *The Nation.* Robin Munro, "The Real Story of the Slaughter in Beijing," *The Nation,* Vol. 250, No. 23 (June 11, 1990): 811–822.

53. These are well summarized in the *Amnesty International Report, 1990.*

54. Henry Rosemont, Jr., "China: The Mourning After," *Z Magazine,* March 1990, 87. See also Henry Rosemont, Jr., *A Chinese Mirror: Moral Reflections on Political Economy and Society* (La Salle, Ill.: Open Court, 1991).

55. *Newsweek,* June 12, 1989.

56. Charles Taylor, *Hegel and Modern Society* (Cambridge: Cambridge University Press, 1979), 154–166.

Chapter Two

1. Such shared perspectives are necessary for any kind of intellectual enterprise. What is true of science is true in its own way of all forms of public discourse. As the physicist Steven Weinberg has said: "Scientific practice is not really in danger from a false consensus. It needs a consensus, in order for us to have something to talk about with each other, in order that our work adds up. Without a consensus, you don't have any way of knowing even if the consensus is wrong." Quoted in Daniel J. Kevles, "The Final Secret of the Universe?" *New York Review of Books,* May 16, 1991, 32.

2. There is by now a large literature on the American missionary movement in China. For a general account of the main people and institutions involved, see Paul A. Varg, *Missionaries, Chinese, and Diplomats: The American Protestant Missionary Movement in China, 1890–1952* (Princeton: Princeton University Press, 1958). For an influential analysis of the role of missionaries in influencing American views of China, see Harold R. Isaacs, *Scratches on Our Minds: American Views of China and India* (Armonk, N.Y.: M. E. Sharpe, 1980; 1st edition, New York: John Day, 1958), especially 124–164.

3. "Hardly a town in our land was without its society to collect funds and clothing for Chinese missions . . . and to hear the missionaries' inspiring reports. Thus was nourished the love portion of the love-hate complex that was to infuse so much emotion into our later China policy." Dean Acheson, *Present at the Creation* (New York: W. W. Norton, 1969), 8.

4. Robert W. Greene, *Calvary in China* (New York: G. P. Putnam's Sons, 1953).

5. E. J. Kahn, Jr., *The China Hands: America's Foreign Service Officers and What Befell Them* (New York: Viking Press, 1975); and Gary May, *China Scapegoat: The Diplomatic Ordeal of John Carter Vincent* (Washington, D.C.: New Republic Books, 1979).

6. Ross Y. Koen, *The China Lobby in American Politics* (New York: Harper and Row, 1974). This book was first published by Macmillan in 1960, but under pressure from the China lobby it was withdrawn by the publishers.

7. See the references to the Quakers in Edwin Scott Gaustad, *A Religious History of America* (San Francisco: Harper and Row, 1990).

8. Robert Mang, "Origins of the National Committee on United States–China Relations," unpublished paper in the archives of the National Committee, 8.

9. Ibid.

10. Summarized from ibid., 8–10.

11. *The Economist,* March 12, 1966.

12. See Robert N. Bellah, Richard Madsen, William M. Sullivan, Ann Swidler, and Steven M. Tipton, *The Good Society* (New York: Knopf, 1991), 145–178.

13. Ibid., 179–192.

14. Mang, "Origins," 10–11.

15. Ibid., 11.

16. Cecil Thomas letter, February 28, 1965, National Committee archives.

17. Mang, "Origins," 12.

18. Thomas, February 28, 1965, letter.

19. Mang, "Origins," 12–13.

20. Thomas, February 28, 1965, letter.

21. John Maxwell Hamilton, *Edgar Snow* (Bloomington: Indiana University Press, 1988), especially 216–250.

22. *New Republic,* May 8, 1965.

23. *The Nation,* May 14, 1965.

24. *Milwaukee Journal,* May 1, 1965; *Providence Journal,* May 9, 1965.

25. *Rocky Mountain News,* June 1, 1965.

26. Daniel Tretiak, "China Talk," *Far Eastern Economic Review,* Vol. 49, No. 2 (July 8, 1965); A. T. Steele, *The American People and China* (New York: McGraw-Hill, 1966).

27. As stated on the program of the conference.

28. Mang, "Origins," 15.

29. Thomas, February 28, 1965, letter.

30. *The Nation,* May 14, 1965.

31. William M. Sullivan, *Reconstructing Public Philosophy* (Berkeley: University of California Press, 1982), 24–26.

32. Mang, "Origins," 17.

33. See Akira Iriye, ed., *U.S. Policy toward China: Testimony Taken from the Senate Foreign Relations Committee Hearings — 1966* (Boston: Little, Brown, and Co., 1968). Besides hearing testimony from China experts, the Fulbright Committee also heard testimony from several general experts in international affairs, including Dean Rusk, James Gavin, George Kennan, Maxwell Taylor, and Hans Morgenthau.

34. Ibid., 61.

35. Ibid., 85.

36. Ibid., 130.

37. Ibid., 131–132.

38. Ibid., 105–106.

39. Ibid., 153.

40. Miriam London, "The Romance of Realpolitik," in George Hicks, ed., *The Broken Mirror: China after Tiananmen* (Chicago: St. James Press, 1990), 247–248.

41. Mang, "Origins," 20.

42. National Committee archives.

43. See Robert N. Bellah, Richard Madsen, William M. Sullivan, Ann Swidler, and Steven M. Tipton, *Habits of the Heart: Individualism and Commitment in American Life* (Berkeley: University of California Press, 1985), 200–203.

44. Mang, "Origins," 27.

45. Ibid.

46. Ibid., 28–29.

47. Ibid., 29.

48. Ibid., 31.

49. Ibid., 25.

50. The same would largely hold true for the other two centrist, national organizations set up to lobby and prepare for a resumption of relationships with the People's Republic: the Committee on Scholarly Communication with Mainland China and the National Council on U.S.-China Trade. The main difference is that these other organizations did not claim to be as inclusive as the National Committee. The Committee on Scholarly Communication aimed to bring together a broad variety of scholars, and the National Council was supposed to represent a broad range of businesspeople.

51. Statement of Purpose formulated at the CCAS Conference in Boston, March 28–30, 1969. First reprinted in *Bulletin of Concerned Asian Scholars,* Vol. 2, No. 1 (October 1969): 8.

52. Ibid.

53. John K. Fairbank and Jim Peck, "An Exchange," *Bulletin of Concerned Asian Scholars,* Vol. 2, No. 3 (April–July 1970): 67.

54. *CCAS Newsletter,* No. 1 (May 1968): 1.

55. CCAS Statement of Purpose, 8.

56. An authoritative account of the emergence of the China studies field is provided in John M. Lindbeck, *Understanding China* (New York: Praeger, 1971).

57. "Capitalist roader" is a Cultural Revolution term for a revisionist who has sold out Marxism.

Chapter Three

1. See Alisdair MacIntyre, *After Virtue* (Notre Dame, Ind.: University of Notre Dame Press, 1981), 76–83.

2. My thinking about "mythical facts" has been influenced by Michael Schudson, *Watergate in American Memory* (New York: Basic Books, 1992), 103–126.

3. Richard Nixon, "Keep Repression of Tiananmen Square Protestors in Perspective," *Boston Herald,* June 25, 1989.

4. Henry Kissinger, *The White House Years* (Boston: Little, Brown and Company, 1979), 1475.

5. Ibid., 171–179.

6. Ibid., 180.

7. Ibid., 193.

8. Ibid., 686.

9. See Walter Russell Mead, *Mortal Splendor: The American Empire in Transition* (Boston: Houghton Mifflin, 1987), 48.

10. Dean Rusk, as told to Richard Rusk, *As I Saw It* (New York: W. W. Norton, 1990), 435.

11. E.g., in my view: Kissinger, *White House,* 700, 701.

12. Ibid., 701.

13. Ibid.

14. Ibid., 702.

15. See Harry Harding, *A Fragile Relationship: The United States and China since 1972* (Washington, D.C.: The Brookings Institution, 1992), 55.

16. Kissinger, *White House,* 710.

17. Ibid., 759.

18. Ibid., 755.

19. Ibid., 914–915.

20. Reinhold Niebuhr, *Moral Man and Immoral Society* (New York: Charles Scribner's Sons, 1932), 84. Niebuhr was quoting from Johannes Haller, *Die Aera Bulow.*

21. Kissinger, *White House,* 191.

22. Ibid., 1074.

23. Ibid., 748. Zhang Wenjin, who accompanied Kissinger on his first visit to China, recalled for me that the Chinese in the escort party were amused by the disparity between Kissinger's thick briefing books and Zhou Enlai's single sheet of notes.

24. Don Oberdorfer, "The China TV Show," *Washington Post,* February 20, 1972, B7.

25. Kissinger, *White House,* 734.

26. Ibid., 742.

27. Ibid., 57–58.

28. Richard Nixon, *The Memoirs of Richard Nixon* (New York: Grosset & Dunlap, 1978), 552. But compare with Kissinger, *White House,* 727: "My recollection is not so precise; it was probably too early to make such exalted claims. But the quotation reflects accurately the emotion and the rekindled hope that out of the bitterness and division of a frustrating war we could emerge with a new national confidence in our country's future."

29. Nixon, *Memoirs,* 557–558.

30. Kissinger, *White House,* 1051.

31. Nixon, *Memoirs,* 3.

32. Oberdorfer, "TV Show."

33. Kissinger, *White House,* 1054.

34. Ibid., 674.

35. Ibid., 1078.

36. Ibid, 194.

37. Nixon, *Memoirs*, 35.

38. Kissinger, *White House*, 744–745.

39. See Harold R. Isaacs, *Scratches on Our Minds: American Views of China and India*, 3rd edition (Armonk, N.Y.: M. E. Sharpe, 1980), xxiv–xxvii.

40. Thomas L. Pangle, *The Spirit of Modern Republicanism* (Chicago: University of Chicago Press, 1988), 278.

41. *New York Times*, February 25, 1972. Nixon's remarks were also played on the major networks' news broadcasts on that day.

42. For an excellent summary of the politics of this period, see Roderick MacFarquhar, "The Succession to Mao and the End of Maoism," in Roderick MacFarquhar and John K. Fairbank, eds., *The Cambridge History of Modern China, Volume 15*, 305–401.

43. A good retrospective account of the work of Ladany is provided by Simon Leys, "The Art of Interpreting Non-existent Inscriptions Written in Invisible Ink on a Blank Page," *New York Review of Books*, October 11, 1990, 8–10.

44. Joseph Kraft, "America's China Myths," *Washington Post*, February 20, 1972, B7.

45. Hans Morgenthau, preface to Tsou Tang, *America's Failure in China* (Chicago: University of Chicago Press, 1963).

46. Kraft, "China Myths."

47. *Time*, "Interview: Paying the Price," April 2, 1990, 46.

48. For a text of the Shanghai Communique, see Kissinger, *White House*, 1492.

49. Oriana Fallaci, *Interview with History*, trans. John Shepley (New York: Liveright, 1976), 43.

50. Ibid.

51. Isaacs, *Scratches on Our Minds*, xxxiv–xxxv.

52. For Nixon's account of these events, see *Memoirs*, 531–532.

53. The "plumbers" were organized in July 1971 in response to Daniel Ellsberg's leaking of the "Pentagon Papers." See Nixon, *Memoirs*, 514. At the time, publication of the Pentagon Papers was seen as particularly dangerous because it might have endangered Kissinger's secret diplomacy with China. According to Kissinger, "Our nightmare at that moment was that Beijing (Peking) might conclude our government was too unsteady, too harassed, and too insecure to be a useful partner. The massive hemorrhage of state secrets was bound to raise doubts about reliability in the minds of other governments, friend and foe, and indeed about the stability of our political system." But Kissinger "was not aware of other steps taken later [to plug the leaks], the sordidness, puerility, and ineffectuality of which eventually led to the downfall of the Nixon administration" (*White House*, 730).

Chapter Four

1. Statistics are taken from Harry Harding, *A Fragile Relationship: The United States and China since 1972* (Washington, D.C.: The Brookings Institution, 1992), 64. According to a Harris poll taken just after the Nixon visit, 73 percent approved of the president's trip. Two years later, a Gallup poll commissioned by the Taiwan government showed a plurality of 45 percent in favor. The percentage of those who held "favorable views" of China went from 5 percent in 1967 to 50 percent just after the Nixon visit, but by 1976 the percentage of favorable views had declined to 20 percent.

2. Henry Kissinger, *The White House Years* (Boston: Little, Brown and Company), 194.

3. *Christianity Today,* April 23, 1971, 26.

4. See Randall E. Stross, *Bulls in the China Shop and Other Sino-American Business Encounters* (New York: Pantheon Books, 1990), 3–22.

5. Joyce K. Kallgren, "Public Interest and Private Interest in Sino-American Exchanges: De Tocqueville's 'Associations' in Action," in Joyce K. Kallgren and Denis Fred Simon, eds., *Educational Exchanges: Essays on the Sino-American Experience* (Berkeley: University of California, Institute of East Asian Studies, 1987), 65.

6. William Hinton, *Fanshen: A Documentary of Revolution in a Chinese Village* (New York: Vintage Books, 1966).

7. Miriam London, "The Romance of Realpolitik," in George Hicks, ed., *The Broken Mirror: China after Tiananmen* (Chicago: St. James Press, 1990), 246–256.

8. Steven W. Mosher, *China Misperceived: American Illusions and Chinese Reality* (New York: Basic Books, 1990).

9. Simon Leys, *The Burning Forest: Essays on Chinese Culture and Politics* (New York: Holt, Rinehart and Winston, 1983).

10. Jonathan Mirsky, "The Myth of Mao's China," *New York Review of Books,* May 30, 1991, 19–27.

11. See Robert N. Bellah, Richard Madsen, William M. Sullivan, Ann Swidler, and Steven M. Tipton, *The Good Society* (New York: Knopf, 1991), 287–306.

12. Ibid., 10–12.

13. Mao Zedong, "Combat Liberalism," in *Collected Works of Mao Zedong,* Vol. 2 (Beijing: Foreign Languages Press, 1967), 31–33.

14. My argument here is influenced by Walter Russell Mead, *Mortal Splendor: The American Empire in Transition* (Boston: Houghton Mifflin, 1987), 32–49.

15. This expansion can take different, though often interrelated forms. It can be geographical, as in the case of the nineteenth-century Christian churches that sought to expand their mission to save Chinese as well as American souls. It can be social, as in the case of modern medicine's attempt to subsume problems that were once thought moral or religious (such as drug addiction) into

the realm of therapy. It can be numerical, as in the attempt of higher education to make itself available for and necessary to greater numbers of people. Or it can be political, as in the case of the learned professions' efforts to make their judgments the primary legitimate basis for public policy decisions.

The drive toward expansion often challenges people to rethink the assumptions that undergird an institution's rules and practices. But these rules and practices often have a strong inertia. Thus, people acting within institutions often delude themselves that they are contributing to progress when no such thing is happening. Changes in our basic institutions take place not incrementally but convulsively, as what seems to be a period of successful expansion finally collapses under the shock of the revelation that the success was spurious.

16. Mary Brown Bullock, *An American Transplant: The Rockefeller Foundation and Peking Union Medical College* (Berkeley: University of California Press, 1980).

17. See James Reardon-Anderson, *The Study of Change: Chemistry in China, 1840–1949* (New York: Cambridge University Press, 1991), 365–375. See also Richard P. Suttmeier, "Academic Exchange: Values and Expectations in Science and Engineering," in Kallgren and Simon, *Educational Exchanges,* 214–232.

18. Anne F. Thurston and Jason H. Parker, eds., *Humanistic and Social Science Research in China* (New York: Social Science Research Council, 1980).

19. Committee of Concerned Asian Scholars, *China! Inside the People's Republic* (New York: Bantam Books, 1972).

20. For a left-wing reaction, see David Kolodney, "Et Tu China?" *Ramparts,* Vol. 10, No. 11 (May 1972): 9–12.

21. Such was the argument of James Peck, "The Roots of Rhetoric: The Professional Ideology of America's China Watchers," *Bulletin of Concerned Asian Scholars,* Vol. 2, No. 1 (October 1969): 59–69; and "Revolution versus Modernization and Revisionism: A Two-Front Struggle," in Victor Nee and James Peck, eds., *China's Uninterrupted Revolution* (New York: Pantheon Books, 1973), 57–217.

22. My philosophical argument here is influenced by George Parkin Grant, *English Speaking Justice* (Notre Dame, Ind.: Notre Dame University Press, 1985), 1–12; and Walter Russell Mead, *Mortal Splendor,* 1–83.

23. John K. Fairbank, *Chinabound: A Fifty-Year Memoir* (New York: Harper and Row, 1982), 413–424.

24. John K. Fairbank, "The New China and the American Connection," *Foreign Affairs,* Vol. 51, No. 1 (October 1972): 31–43.

25. Mosher, *China Misperceived,* 134.

26. Paul M. Evans, *John Fairbank and the American Understanding of Modern China* (New York: B. Blackwell, 1988).

27. Columbia University CCAS, "The American Chinese Studies Establishment," *Bulletin of Concerned Asian Scholars,* Vol. 3, No. 3 (Summer–Fall 1971): 92–103; Moss Roberts, "Some Problems concerning the Structure and Direction of Contemporary China Studies—A Reply to Professor Fairbank," ibid., 113–137; and David Horowitz, "Politics and Knowledge: An Unorthodox History of Modern China Studies," ibid., 139–168.

28. Fang Lizhi, *Bringing Down the Great Wall: Writings on Science, Culture, and Democracy in China* (New York: Knopf, 1990), 272.

29. "Protestant missionaries did not arrive in China until after the Treaty of Nanking (1842). Conversions came slowly in the early decades, but by 1949 there were 936,000 baptized members and 2,963 clergy, 68 percent of them Chinese and the rest foreign missionaries." Donald MacInnis, *Religion in China Today: Policy and Practice* (Maryknoll, N.Y.: Orbis Books, 1989), 313.

30. The evolution of attitudes within the North American Protestant churches toward China is briefly summarized in Ray Whitehead, preface to Theresa Chu and Christopher Lind, eds., *A New Beginning: An International Dialogue with the Chinese Church* (Toronto: The Canada China Program of the Canadian Council of Churches, 1983), iii–iv; and Katharine B. Hockin, "From 'Church to the World' to 'Church for the World,'" ibid., 121–127. See also Philip L. Wickeri, *Seeking the Common Ground: Protestant Christianity, the Three-Self Movement, and China's United Front* (Maryknoll, N.Y.: Orbis Books, 1988), 7–14. For an evangelical Protestant perspective, see Arthur F. Glasser, "China Today and the Christian Movement," paper delivered at the China Conversation at the Overseas Ministries Study Center, Ventnor, N.J., April 1980.

31. James Davidson Hunter and John Steadman Rice, "Unlikely Alliances: The Changing Contours of American Religious Faith," in Alan Wolfe, ed., *America at Century's End* (Berkeley: University of California Press, 1991), 318–339. See also James Davidson Hunter, *Culture Wars: The Struggle to Define America* (New York: Basic Books, 1991).

32. *Christianity Today*, April 23, 1971, 26.

33. Joachim Pillai, "Maoist Ethics and Judaeo-Christian Traditions," in *Christian Faith and the Chinese Experience* (Geneva and Brussels: Lutheran World Federation/Pro Mundi Vita, 1974), 82. I participated in this conference under the sponsorship of the National Council of Churches China Program.

34. *Christian Faith and the Chinese Experience*, 21.

35. Raymond Whitehead, *Love and Struggle in Mao's Thought* (Maryknoll, N.Y.: Orbis Books, 1977).

36. *Christian Faith and the Chinese Experience*, 21–22.

37. For statistics on changing patterns of religious affiliation, see Wade Clark Roof and William McKinney, *American Mainline Religion* (New Brunswick, N.J.: Rutgers University Press, 1987), 158–183 and 230–236.

38. David M. Stowe, "Future of the Missionary," *Tripod*, No. 45 (June 1988): 33–43.

39. *The Christian Century*, November 27, 1974, 1128.

40. See Wickeri, *Common Ground*, especially 3–17.

41. Ibid., 154–179.

42. For an example of study materials used in the Presbyterian church at this time, see *Church and Society* (January–February 1975).

43. David Shambaugh, *Beautiful Imperialist: China Perceives America: 1972–1990* (Princeton: Princeton University Press, 1991), 5–16. See also David Shambaugh, "China's America Watchers," *Problems of Communism*, No. 37 (May–August 1988): 71–94.

44. Shambaugh, *Beautiful Imperialist*, 42.

45. Ibid.

46. Ibid. For an account of Chinese journalists' reports on the United States in the early 1970s, see especially 158–161.

47. Zi Zhongyun, "Zhongguode Meiguo Yanjiu," *Meiguo Yanjiu*, No. 1 (Spring 1987): 12–13. The translation used here is from a mimeographed translation done by Zi Zhongyun herself.

Chapter Five

1. An excellent summary of the history of this period is in Harry Harding, *A Fragile Relationship: The United States and China since 1972* (Washington, D.C.: The Brookings Institution, 1992), 47–106. Harding's account summarizes a wide range of secondary literature besides the memoirs of Carter, Brzezinski, and Vance cited in this chapter. Some of the most important secondary literature includes Jew-ling Joanne Chang, *United States–China Normalization: An Evaluation of Foreign Policy Decision Making* (Denver, Colo.: University of Denver, Graduate School of International Studies, Monograph Series in World Affairs, 1986); Yufan Hao, *Solving the Dilemma in China Policy, 1978–1979: A Case Study of Normalization of U.S.-China Relations and the Taiwan Relations Act* (Ph.D. dissertation, Johns Hopkins University, School of Advanced International Studies, 1989); Robert G. Sutter, *The China Quandary: Domestic Determinants of U.S.-China Policy, 1972–1982* (Boulder, Colo.: Westview Press, 1983).

2. See Harding, *A Fragile Relationship*, 68–75.

3. The congressional debate produced the Taiwan Relations Act, which passed by wide margins in both the House and Senate. This act amended White House proposals somewhat in Taiwan's favor. For instance, it allowed the American Institute in Taiwan to perform consular functions and permitted the agency unofficially representing Taiwan's interests in the United States to have as many offices as Taiwan had previously had consulates; it stated more forcefully than the administration had wished that use of force against Taiwan would be of "grave concern" to the United States; and it explicitly provided for the sale of weapons to Taiwan. Carter signed the act (he did not have sufficient support to sustain a veto) "while simultaneously reassuring the Chinese that he had substantial discretion in interpreting and implementing the law, and that he would do so in ways fully consistent with the understandings on normalization that he had reached with Beijing (Peking)." Harding, *A Fragile Relationship*, 86–87. See also Louis W. Koenig, James C. Hsiung, and Kingyuh Chang, eds., *Congress, the Presidency, and the Taiwan Relations Act* (New York: Praeger, 1985); Ramon H. Myers, ed., *A Unique Relationship: The United States and the Republic of China under the Taiwan Relations Act* (Stanford: Hoover Institution Press, 1989); and Lester L. Wolff and David L. Simon, eds., *Legislative History of the Taiwan Relations Act: An Analytic Compila-*

tion with Documents on Subsequent Developments (Jamaica, N.Y.: American Association for Chinese Studies, 1982).

4. Quoted in Harding, *A Fragile Relationship*, 84.

5. John K. Fairbank, "Solving the China Problem," *New York Review of Books*, January 26, 1978, 31.

6. George Bush, "Our Deal with Peking: All Cost and No Benefit," in John Tierney, Jr., ed., *About Face: The China Decision and Its Consequences* (New Rochelle, N.Y.: Arlington House, 1979), 406–410.

7. David Pietruza, "Review of John Tierney Jr., ed., *About Face: The China Decision and its Consequences,*" *Modern Age*, Vol. 24, No. 1 (Winter 1980): 108.

8. In public, however, "Nixon would only say that he would not second-guess Carter's decision." Harding, *A Fragile Relationship*, 84.

9. The quotes are taken from Gaddis Smith, *Morality, Reason, and Power: American Diplomacy in the Carter Years* (New York: Hill and Wang, 1986), 29, 32.

10. Cyrus Vance, *Hard Choices: Critical Years in America's Foreign Policy* (New York: Simon and Schuster, 1983), 75–83, 113–122; Zbigniew Brzezinski, *Power and Principle: Memoirs of the National Security Adviser, 1977–1981* (New York: Farrar, Straus and Giroux, 1983), 415–419; Harding, *A Fragile Relationship*, 73–75.

11. Brzezinski, *Power and Principle*, 196–197.

12. Ibid., 201.

13. Ibid., 209–219.

14. Ibid., 232.

15. Christopher Lasch, *The True and Only Heaven: Progress and Its Critics* (New York: Norton, 1991).

16. See Smith, *Morality, Reason, and Power;* Bruce Cumings, "Chinatown: Foreign Policy and Elite Realignment," in Thomas Ferguson and Joel Rogers, eds., *The Hidden Election: Politics and Economics in the 1980 Presidential Campaign* (New York: Pantheon Books, 1981), 196–231; Robert N. Bellah, Richard Madsen, William M. Sullivan, Ann Swidler, and Steven M. Tipton, *The Good Society* (New York: Knopf, 1991), 34–36.

17. Walter Russell Mead, *Mortal Splendor: The American Empire in Transition* (Boston: Houghton Mifflin, 1987), 96.

18. This sentence about public opinion is paraphrased from Harding, *A Fragile Relationship*, 87.

19. See ibid., 100–103.

20. Jimmy Carter, *Keeping Faith: Memoirs of a President* (New York: Bantam Books, 1982), 202.

21. Brzezinski, *Power and Principle*, 406.

22. Ibid., 407.

23. Carter, *Keeping Faith*, 208.

24. Ibid., 206.

25. Brzezinski, *Power and Principle*, 415. According to Thomas P. Bernstein: "During China's brief war against Vietnam in February 1979, the new relationship with the U.S. may well have restrained the Soviets from retaliating against China." See *The Negotiations to Normalize U.S.-China Relations*

(New York: Columbia University School of International and Public Affairs, 1988), 43.

26. Carter, *Keeping Faith*, 202.

27. Mead, *Mortal Splendor*, 100.

28. Amnesty International, *Political Imprisonment in the People's Republic of China* (London: Amnesty International, 1978).

29. Smith, *Morality, Reason, and Power*, 51–55, 95–103.

30. Carter, *Keeping Faith*, 201–202; Brzezinski, *Power and Principle*, 416–419; Harding, *A Fragile Relationship*, 95–98. Quotes are taken from the *Congressional Record*, January 24, 1980.

31. Brzezinski, *Power and Principle*, 226.

32. Ibid.

33. Denis Fred Simon, "Scientific Exchanges and Technology Transfer to China: The Policy Issues," in Joyce K. Kallgren and Denis Fred Simon, eds., *Educational Exchanges: Essays on the Sino-American Experience* (Berkeley: University of California, Institute of East Asian Studies, 1987), 239.

34. Joyce K. Kallgren, "Development, Issues, and Prospects of Sino-American Cultural, Scientific, and Technological Exchanges," in John Bryan Starr, ed., *The Future of US-China Relations* (New York: New York University Press, 1981), 179–215.

Chapter Six

1. Randall E. Stross, *Bulls in the China Shop and Other Sino-American Business Encounters* (New York: Pantheon Books, 1990).

2. Jimmy Carter, *Keeping Faith: Memoirs of a President* (New York: Bantam Books, 1982), 186.

3. Wesley G. Pippert, ed., *The Spiritual Journey of Jimmy Carter* (New York: Macmillan, 1978), 21–22.

4. Carter, *Keeping Faith*, 207.

5. Ernst Troeltsch, *The Social Teachings of the Christian Churches*, trans. Olive Wyon (London: George Allen, 1931); see especially Vol. 1, 328–385, and Vol. 2, conclusion. See also Robert N. Bellah, Richard Madsen, William M. Sullivan, Ann Swidler, and Steven M. Tipton, *Habits of the Heart* (Berkeley: University of California Press, 1985), 243–248.

6. See Bellah et al., *Habits of the Heart*, 245–246; James Davison Hunter and John Steadman Rice, "Unlikely Alliances: The Changing Contours of American Religious Faith," in Alan Wolfe, ed., *America at Century's End* (Berkeley: University of California Press, 1991), 318–331; James Davison Hunter, *Culture Wars* (New York: Basic Books, 1991); and Robert N. Bellah, Richard Madsen, William M. Sullivan, Ann Swidler, and Steven M. Tipton, *The Good Society* (New York: Knopf, 1991), 197–206.

7. For a comprehensive history of the Christian colleges in China, see Jessie

Gregory Lutz, *China and the Christian Colleges, 1850–1950* (Ithaca, N.Y.: Cornell University Press, 1971).

8. Walter Guzzardi, Jr., *The Henry Luce Foundation: A History, 1936–1986* (Chapel Hill: University of North Carolina Press, 1988), 224–225.

9. United Board for Christian Higher Education in Asia, *Educational Programs Related to the People's Republic of China: General Statement* (1980). United Board archives.

10. Ibid.

11. Letter sent to American participants in the 1988 Nanjing colloquium. United Board archives.

12. See Philip L. Wickeri, *Seeking the Common Ground: Protestant Christianity, the Three-Self Movement, and China's United Front* (Maryknoll, N.Y.: Orbis Books, 1988), 154–195.

13. See, for example, the speech given by Ding Guangxun (K. H. Ting) in Toronto in November 1979: "Let me call the reader's attention to an alarming and dangerous matter: For thirty years now anti–New China groups abroad have never ceased in their efforts to foster separatism within Chinese Christianity. They talk ecumenism and oneness but do the work of undermining our unity. They send in money and secret messages and instructions and beam radio programs, all designed for nurturing opposition and carrying out smearing and splitting. . . ." See also Ding Guangxun's (K. H. Ting's) Opening Address before the Third Chinese National Christian Conference, October 6, 1980: "We are opposed to the anti-China plotting and the propaganda, infiltration and meddling on the part of anti-China elements in religious circles overseas." Documents translated and distributed by the Canada China Programme of the Canadian Council of Churches on the occasion of the conference "God's Call to a New Beginning," Montreal, Canada, October 2–7, 1981.

14. See Alan Hunter, "Continuities in Chinese Protestantism 1920–1990," *China Study Journal*, Vol. 6, No. 3 (December 1991): 5–12.

15. Michael H. Hunt, *The Making of a Special Relationship: The United States and China to 1914* (New York: Columbia University Press, 1983), 312.

16. Harry Harding, *A Fragile Relationship: The United States and China since 1972* (Washington, D.C.: The Brookings Institution, 1992), 149–150; Patrick G. Maddox and Anne F. Thurston, "Academic Exchanges: The Goals and Roles of U.S. Universities," in Joyce K. Kallgren and Denis Fred Simon, eds., *Educational Exchanges: Essays on the Sino-American Experience* (Berkeley: University of California, Institute of East Asian Studies, 1987), 58–79; Leo A. Orleans, *Chinese Students in America: Policies, Issues, and Numbers* (Washington, D.C.: National Academy Press, 1988).

17. For a discussion of popular complaints in China about the ability of high officials to get their children into American universities, see Ezra F. Vogel, *One Step Ahead in China: Guangdong under Reform* (Cambridge, Mass.: Harvard University Press, 1989), 411.

18. Richard Madsen, "Institutional Dynamics of Cross-Cultural Communication: U.S.-China Exchanges in the Humanities and Social Sciences," in Kallgren and Simon, *Educational Exchanges*, 199–202.

19. Steven Mosher, *Broken Earth: The Rural Chinese* (New York: Free

Press, 1983), and "Birth Control: A View from a Chinese Village," *Asian Survey,* Vol. 22, No. 4 (April 1982): 326–368.

20. See Madsen, "Institutional Dynamics," 202–206.

21. *Wall Street Journal,* July 25, 1983. See also *New York Times,* Editorial, March 19, 1983; Jeffrey Lincoln, "Steven Mosher and the Politics of Cultural Exchange," *The Nation,* Vol. 237, No. 176 (1983): 31. For academic accounts of the Mosher case, see Irving Louis Horowitz, "Struggling for the Soul of Social Science," *Society,* Vol. 20, No. 12 (1983): 3–15; and Marjorie Sun's series of articles in *Science:* May 13, 1983: 682; July 22, 1983: 348; August 26, 1983: 838; October 14, 1983: 147; May 18, 1984: 701; October 5, 1984: 28; and October 18, 1985: 298.

22. Fox Butterfield, *China: Alive in the Bitter Sea* (New York: Times Books, 1982).

23. Richard Bernstein, *From the Center of the Earth: The Search for the Truth about China* (Boston: Little, Brown and Company, 1982).

24. Richard Bernstein, "A Journey of Conscience," *New York Times Magazine,* April 16, 1989, 23ff. For an introduction to the case of Wei Jingsheng, see Geremie Barmé and John Minford, *Seeds of Fire* (New York: Farrar, Straus and Giroux, 1989), 277–289.

25. See the review of Mosher's *Broken Earth* by Norma Diamond, "Rural Collectivization and Decollectivization in China," *Journal of Asian Studies,* Vol. 44, No. 4 (1985): 785–792.

26. After the Tiananmen massacre, members of the China studies community and people who worked in foundations related to China began to reassess their approaches to China. As a result, the Ford Foundation changed its approach somewhat.

Chapter Seven

1. The Chinese government has called this a cultural imperialist plot for fostering "peaceful evolution" away from communism in the PRC. See Makesizhuyi Lilun Jiaoyu Cankao Ziliao Bianjibu (Editorial Department for Reference Materials on Marxist Theoretical Education), *Xifang Guojiade Heping Yanbian Zhanlue* ("Western Governments' Peaceful Evolution Strategy") (Beijing, 1990). There was no systematically organized plot—American relationships with China became too decentralized for that—but there was, as David Shambaugh puts it, "an unspoken consensus about the desired direction and end result of change in mainland China." He continues:

I think it is fair to say that all parties in the United States involved in making the government's China policy and facilitating exchange programs with the PRC share the view that American and Chinese national interests are best served by:

a more liberal political climate, leading ultimately to the demise of the CCP's political hegemony;

a market-led economy;

a more free social environment that tolerates and facilitates the freedoms of choice, religious belief, ethnic identity, and respect for fundamental human rights;

a peaceful and secure mainland China free from any external threat, and posing no military threat to the United States, its Asian allies, or other neighboring countries.

These are the goals and underlying premises that have guided the American approach to the PRC since 1979. This is largely an agenda for change. . . .

David Shambaugh, "Peking's Foreign Policy Conundrum since Tiananmen: Peaceful Coexistence vs. Peaceful Evolution," *Issues and Studies,* Vol. 28, No. 11 (November 1992): 80.

2. Erazim Kohak, "Ashes, Ashes . . . Central Europe after Forty Years," *Daedalus,* Vol. 21, No. 2 (Spring 1992): 209–210.

3. David Shambaugh, *Beautiful Imperialist: China Perceives America, 1972–1990* (Princeton, N.J.: Princeton University Press, 1991).

4. Quoted in ibid., 164.

5. Su Wei, *Xiyangjing Yu* [A Verbal Diorama] (Hangzhou: Zhejiang Wenyi Chubanshe, 1988), 1–7.

6. For good accounts of the reforms in Chinese journalism, see Shi Xiaoguang, *Communism and Communication: News Media and Political Communication in China* (Ph.D. Dissertation, University of California at San Diego, 1992), chap. 2; Judy Polumbaum, "The Tribulations of China's Journalists after a Decade of Reform," in Chin-chuan Lee, ed., *Voices of China: The Interplay of Politics and Journalism* (New York: Guilford Press, 1990), 33–68; and Chin-chuan Lee, "Mass Media: Of China, About China," in Lee, *Voices of China,* 3–28.

7. See Scott Simmie and Bob Nixon, *Tiananmen Square* (Seattle: University of Washington Press, 1989), 74.

8. Radio Beijing English Service, June 4, 1989. Transcribed in *China News Digest,* June 4, 1993.

9. The first few of these international-style luxury hotels were constructed through joint ventures with foreign investors. Toward the end of the 1980s, though, many of these buildings were being financed solely by Chinese enterprises, although they were built in modern Western architectural styles with modern Western construction techniques. The first hotels proved so profitable that there was a rush by government ministries throughout China to maximize their resources by investing surplus funds in one of these buildings, even ministries having nothing to do with housing construction. For example, in the late 1980s, the Ministry of Public Security financed the construction of a major new hotel in Beijing. As a result, by the end of the decade, the supply of luxury room space exceeded demand, and the ministries that had invested in them lost money. For an excellent account of the building of the first modern joint venture hotels in China, see Randall E. Stross, *Bulls in the China Shop and Other Sino-American Business Encounters* (New York: Pantheon Books, 1990), 196–219.

10. For an account of the context for the distress of intellectuals, see Andrew Nathan, *China's Crisis: Dilemmas of Reform and Prospects for Democracy* (New York: Columbia University Press, 1990), 95–115.

11. See Merle Goldman, "Culture," in Steven M. Goldstein, ed., *China Briefing, 1984* (Boulder, Colo.: Westview Press, 1985), 21–37.

12. In the early 1980s (according to an unconfirmed story I heard in Beijing in 1988), the Chinese leadership was embarrassed when, during an official motorcade for a visiting head of state, the visitor's Chinese-made Red Flag limousine broke down. Thereafter, a decision was made to import good Western-built limousines for high officials.

13. In 1988 I saw a motorcade for Rajiv Gandhi, then president of India, that vividly manifested the Chinese conception of hierarchy. At the front were about ten Mercedes Benzes; then followed five or six Chryslers; then several Nissans; finally, an old Chinese-manufactured police van.

14. For a concise summary of the Chinese government's ideology and practice toward the Third World from the 1950s through the Cultural Revolution era, see Thomas Robinson, "China Confronts the Soviet Union: Warfare and Diplomacy on China's Inner Asian Frontiers," in Roderick MacFarquhar and John K. Fairbank, eds., *The Cambridge History of Modern China, Volume 15* (Cambridge: Cambridge University Press, 1991), chap. 3, especially 220–254.

15. Alvin Toffler, *The Third Wave* (New York: Morrow, 1980).

16. Liu Binyan, *China's Crisis, China's Hope,* trans. Howard Goldblatt (Cambridge, Mass.: Harvard University Press, 1990), 103. "In 1979, China's GNP per capita ranked 108th in the world; by 1985, it had fallen to 126th. In 1971, China was on a par with Haiti and Pakistan, ahead of Sri Lanka and Sierra Leone; but now all four of these countries have moved ahead of China." (Actually, the revised estimates of China's per capita income cited in Chapter 1, footnote 35, present a more favorable view of China's ranking in the world economy. China now appears to be a "lower-middle-class" country, significantly richer than, say, Haiti but poorer than Mexico.)

17. These views are well represented in the papers by Kiang Wen-han, Zhao Fusan, Wang Zicheng, Tu Shihua, Han Wenzhao, and K. H. Ting, leaders of the Chinese three-self movement and the Catholic Patriotic Association, in Theresa Chu and Christopher Lind, eds., *A New Beginning: An International Dialogue with the Chinese Church* (Toronto: Canada China Programme of the Canadian Council of Churches, 1983), 88–120.

18. Shen Yi-fan, "Freedom as Viewed by a Chinese Christian," in Chu and Lind, *New Beginning,* 29–32.

19. See Ezra F. Vogel, *One Step Ahead in China: Guangdong under Reform* (Cambridge, Mass.: Harvard University Press, 1989), 313–337.

20. See Tom Gold, "Guerrilla Interviewing among the *Getihu,*" in Perry Link, Richard Madsen, and Paul Pickowicz, eds., *Unofficial China: Popular Culture and Thought in the People's Republic* (Boulder, Colo.: Westview Press, 1989), 175–192.

21. Patrick G. Maddox and Anne F. Thurston, "Academic Exchanges: The Goals and Roles of U.S. Universities," in Joyce K. Kallgren and Denis Fred Simon, eds., *Educational Exchanges: Essays on the Sino-American Experience* (Berkeley: University of California, Institute of East Asian Studies, 1987), 141; Stross, *Bulls in the China Shop,* 183–187; and Ruth Hayhoe and Sun Yilin,

"China's Scholars Returned from Abroad: A View from Shanghai," *China Exchange News,* Vol. 17, No. 3 (September 1989): 3–8, and Vol. 17, No. 4 (December 1989): 2–7.

22. The United States was their favored destination for study, not just because U.S. research universities were better than those of Europe or Japan but because the United States has been much more liberal than any other industrialized country about granting foreigners scholarship, work-study, and job opportunities.

23. Zhang Xinxin, "How Come You Aren't Divorced Yet?" in Link, Madsen, and Pickowicz, *Unofficial China,* 65.

24. Bei Dao, "The Answer," in Geremie Barmé and John Minford, *Seeds of Fire: Chinese Voices of Conscience* (New York: Noonday Press, 1989), 236. This anthology is an excellent introduction for English speakers of new currents of thought among Chinese intellectuals in the 1980s.

25. Theodore H. Von Laue, *The World Revolution of Westernization: The Twentieth Century in Global Perspective* (New York: Oxford University Press, 1987), 362.

Chapter Eight

1. The Chinese name of this series is *Heshang,* and there was considerable dispute within the western China studies community about how to translate it. The most common translation has been "River Elegy." But I am using here the translation published by Richard W. Bodman and Pin P. Wan, who think "elegy" too elegant to use for the Chinese *"shang,"* which is a rarely used term meaning "to die ahead of one's time" and incorporates an allusion to the famous poem *Guoshang* by the third century B.C. poet, statesman, and prophet of doom, Qu Yuan. "Deathsong," according to Bodman and Wan, best captures the connotations of senseless tragedy suggested by the term *"shang."* Su Xiaokang and Wang Luxiang, *Deathsong of the River: A Reader's Guide to the Chinese TV Series Heshang,* trans. and ed. Richard W. Bodman and Pin P. Wan (Ithaca, N.Y.: Cornell East Asia Series, 1991). This is the best introduction in English to *Heshang,* and I have relied on it heavily in writing this chapter. See also Stanley Rosen and Gary Zou, eds., "The Chinese Television Documentary 'River Elegy,'" *Chinese Sociology and Anthropology,* Vol. 24, Nos. 2–3 (Winter 1991–92 and Spring 1992).

2. There is by now a large body of literature on the "cultural fever" of the 1980s. For introductions to the themes in the cultural fever, see Perry Link, *Evening Chats in Beijing* (New York: W. W. Norton & Company, 1992); Zi Zhongyun, "The Relationship of Chinese Traditional Culture to the Modernization of China: An Introduction to the Current Discussion," *Asian Survey,* Vol. 27, No. 4 (April 1987): 442–458; and Richard Madsen, "The Spiritual Crisis of China's Intellectuals," in Deborah Davis and Ezra F. Vogel, eds., *Chi-*

nese Society on the Eve of Tiananmen (Cambridge, Mass.: Harvard Contemporary China Series, 1990), 243–260.

3. See Link, *Evening Chats,* chaps. 1 and 2; and Barry Naughton, *Growing out of the Plan: Chinese Economic Reform, 1978–1993* (New York: Cambridge University Press, 1994).

4. See Link, *Evening Chats.*

5. For typical examples of the advice purveyed by American economists in the late 1980s, see Lawrence J. Lau, "Economics Education and Economic Development," paper presented at the Nanjing Education Colloquium, "Education Toward Social Progress," Nanjing, China, 1988; and Gregory C. Chow, *The Chinese Economy* (New York: Harper and Row, 1985).

6. For a bibliography, see Bodman and Wan, *Deathsong,* 329–342.

7. Bodman and Wan, *Deathsong,* 104, 106.

8. Ibid., 116.

9. Ibid., 130.

10. Michael Schudson, *Advertising, the Uneasy Persuasion* (New York: Basic Books, 1984), 209–233.

11. The information in the above three paragraphs is summarized from Richard W. Bodman, "From History to Allegory to Art: A Personal Search for Interpretation," in Bodman and Wan, *Deathsong,* 19–22.

12. Among the participants at this meeting, held at the Beijing First Foreign Language Institute, was Frederic Wakeman, who reported this exchange in "All the Rage in China," *New York Review of Books,* March 2, 1989, 19–21. I was also one of the American participants at this seminar, along with Perry Link, David Keightley, Marshall Sahlins, and Benjamin Lee. My initial reaction was to criticize the series for making too harsh a criticism of Chinese culture. The position I take in this book was arrived at after several years of thinking about *Deathsong* and its cultural context.

13. The major works of Jin Guantao and Liu Qingfeng include Jin Guantao, *Zai Lishi Biaoxiangde Beihou* [Beyond the Phenomena of History] (Sichuan Renminchubanshe, 1983); Jin Guantao and Liu Qingfeng, *Zou Xiang Weilai Congshu* [Toward the Future Series] (Sichuan Renminchubanshe, 1983); Jin Guantao and Liu Qingfeng, *Wenti yu Fangfa Ji* [Problem and Method Collection] (Shanghai Renminchubanshe, 1986); and Jin Guantao and Liu Qingfeng, *Xingsheng yu Weiji* [Ascendancy and Crisis] (Hunan Renminchubanshe, 1984). See also Jin Guantao and Richard Madsen, "Heshang yu Dong Xi Fang Mianlinde Taozhan — Jin Guantao he Mai Disun de Duihua" [*Deathsong of the River* and the Challenge Faced by East and West — A Dialogue between Jin Guantao and Richard Madsen], in *Longnian de Beichuang* [The Distress of the Year of the Dragon] (Hong Kong: Sanlian Shudian, 1989), 147–167.

14. Wan, *Deathsong,* 74–76. Wan here is summarizing an article by Wang Luxiang, "Shiqu Jiayuan De Piaobozhe" [Drifters Who Have Lost Their Home], in *Longnian de Beichuang,* 178–182.

15. Su Xiaokang, "Shiminggan zhi wo jian" [My View of a "Sense of Mission"], *Qiushi,* No. 2 (1988): 47–48. Quoted in Bodman, "History to Allegory," 40.

16. Wang Luxiang, "Drifters," quoted in Wan, *Deathsong,* 76.

17. Fan Zhongyan, "Yueyang Lou Ji" [On the Tower at Yueyang], quoted in Wan, *Deathsong,* 78.

18. Su Xiaokang, "Sense of Mission," 40.

19. This discussion of "unofficial China" is based on Perry Link, Richard Madsen, and Paul G. Pickowicz, eds., *Unofficial China: Popular Culture and Thought in the People's Republic* (Boulder, Colo.: Westview Press, 1989), 2. The issues covered in this section are similar to those dealt with in discussions of "civil society" in China. I have preferred not to use the term "civil society" in this book; because the term is based on social theory aimed at explaining the rise of democracies in Europe and the United States, I do not think it captures the fluidity of relationship between state and society characteristic of contemporary China. The official/unofficial distinction comes from the language I heard used by Chinese intellectuals themselves.

20. See Merle Goldman, with Timothy Cheek and Carol Lee Hamrin, eds., *China's Intellectuals and the State: In Search of a New Relationship* (Cambridge, Mass.: Harvard Council on East Asian Studies, 1987); and Link, *Evening Chats.*

21. Zi Zhongyun's speech was published under the title "Convergence of Interests: Basis for Relations among Nations," in *Renmin Ribao,* December 21, 1988, trans. in *FBIS,* China, December 28, 1988, 5.

22. See Bodman, "History to Allegory," 19–22.

23. Ibid.

24. See Tu Wei-ming, "Cultural China: The Periphery as the Center," *Daedalus,* Vol. 120, No. 2 (Spring 1991), especially 15–16.

Conclusion

1. Harry Harding, *A Fragile Relationship: The United States and China since 1972* (Washington, D.C.: The Brookings Institution, 1992), 212.

2. See Judith B. Farquhar and James L. Hevia, "Culture and Postwar American Historiography of China," *positions,* Vol. 1, No. 2 (1993): 486–525.

3. Ibid., 507.

4. See Robert N. Bellah, Richard Madsen, William M. Sullivan, Ann Swidler, and Steven M. Tipton, *Habits of the Heart: Individualism and Commitment in American Life* (Berkeley: University of California Press, 1985), 27. "So long as it is vital, the cultural tradition of a people—its symbols, ideals, and ways of feeling—is always an argument about the meaning of the destiny its members share. Cultures are dramatic conversations about things that matter to their participants. . . ."

5. Charles Taylor, "Interpretation and the Sciences of Man," in Paul Rabinow and William M. Sullivan, eds., *Interpretive Social Science: A Reader* (Berkeley: University of California Press, 1979), 51–52.

6. Bennett M. Berger, *An Essay on Culture* (Berkeley: University of California Press, 1995).

7. John Courtney Murray, *We Hold These Truths: Catholic Reflections on the American Proposition* (New York: Sheed and Ward, 1960), 18–19.

8. The idea of a "horizon" is based on my reading of Hans-Georg Gadamer, *Truth and Method,* ed. Garrett Barden and John Cumming (New York: Seabury, 1975); and *Philosophical Hermeneutics,* trans. and ed. David E. Linge (Berkeley: University of California Press, 1976).

9. An earlier version of the ideas in this section was published in Richard Madsen, "Global Monoculture, Multiculture, and Polyculture," *Social Research* (Fall 1993): 493–511.

10. See Robert Heilbroner, "The Coming Meltdown of Traditional Capitalism," *Ethics and International Affairs,* Vol. 2 (1988): 63–77.

11. William M. Sullivan, *A Question of Integrity: The Crisis and Promise of Professionalism in America* (New York: Harper Collins, 1994).

12. See Bellah et al., *Habits of the Heart,* 44–48.

13. See Randall E. Stross, *Bulls in the China Shop and Other Sino-American Business Encounters* (New York: Pantheon Books, 1990), 248–274. The quote from the *People's Daily* is cited on 266. The original source is *Renmin Ribao,* June 20, 1982.

14. For accounts of the globalization of standards for managing organizations (these standards *seem* to make organizations efficient without necessarily doing so), see John W. Meyer and W. Richard Scott, *Organizational Environments: Ritual and Rationality* (Newbury Park, Calif.: Sage Publications, 1983); and George W. Thomas, John W. Meyer, Francisco O. Ramirez, and John Boli, *Institutional Structure: Constituting State, Society, and the Individual* (Newbury Park, Calif.: Sage Publications, 1987).

15. See Charles Taylor, *Hegel and Modern Society* (Cambridge: Cambridge University Press, 1979), 111–134.

16. Russell Jacoby, *The Last Intellectuals: American Culture in the Age of Academe* (New York: Basic Books, 1987).

17. For good analyses of the cultural forces that have sustained communities of opposition under state socialist regimes and sobering illustrations of how these forces can lead to civil chaos once these regimes fall, see Rubie Watson, ed., *Memory, History, and Opposition under State Socialism* (Santa Fe: School of American Research, 1994).

18. See Robert N. Bellah, Richard Madsen, William M. Sullivan, Ann Swidler, and Steven M. Tipton, *The Good Society* (New York: Knopf, 1991), 52–81.

19. See Daniel Bell, *The Cultural Contradictions of Capitalism* (New York: Basic Books, 1976).

20. Orville Schell, "China's Spring," *New York Review of Books,* June 29, 1989, 6.

21. Such is the problem discerned in Jürgen Habermas, *The Structural Transformation of the Public Sphere,* trans. Thomas Berger with the assistance of Frederick Lawrence (Cambridge, Mass.: MIT Press, 1989). (The original German edition of this book was published in 1962.) For a discussion of how Ha-

bermas's perspective might inform a research agenda for China studies, see Richard Madsen, "The Public Sphere, Civil Society, and Moral Community: A Research Agenda for China Studies," *Modern China* (Spring 1993).

22. Reinhold Niebuhr, *The Irony of American History* (New York: Charles Scribner's Sons, 1952), 149.

23. Vaclav Havel, "The End of the Modern Era," *New York Times,* March 1, 1992.

24. Quoted in Alasdair MacIntyre, address delivered at the inauguration of Paul Joseph Philibert, O.P., S.T.D., as president of the Dominican School of Philosophy and Theology, Berkeley, California, February 1987.

25. Tu Wei-ming, "Cultural China: The Periphery as the Center," *Daedalus,* Vol. 120, No. 2 (Spring 1991): 1–32.

Index

Academic exchanges, 151–58, 250n22; Chinese official policies, 98, 99, 100–101, 154, 157; and Chinese responses to American Dream, 166–67; Chinese student emigration, 152, 160, 183, 184–85; and intellectual loss of confidence, 183–84; journalistic vs. academic ethics, 156–58; Mosher case, 153–56, 157–58; and normalization, 133–35; and religious institutions, 142–46; and social development organizations, 160–61; and Tiananmen Square massacre media coverage, 6; and unofficial China, 204–5

Academic institutions: academic conferences, 33–39, 46; CCAS official China visits, 99–101; and *Deathsong of the River*, 198, 251n12; and drama, 5–6; Fairbank China visit, 103–4; and liberalism, 102–3; positive reports, 104–5; and Tiananmen Square massacre, 10–11; and U.S.-Chinese expanded contacts, 97–106. *See also* Academic exchanges

AIDS, 190–91

Alexander, Bill, 133

American Association of University Women, 41

American China myths: American Dream as primary reference point, 211–13; as drama, 4, 5, 232n15; and mythical facts, 59–60; and national unity, 58; and political struggle, 213; and real-ism assumption, 80–82; revolutionary redeemer myth, 29, 52–57, 202; and U.S. hegemony, 57–58. *See also* American Dream; Liberal China myth; Red Menace myth

American diversity: and Chinese cultural fragmentation, 186; institutional checks on, 189–90; and institutions, 91–92; and liberal myth creation, 36–37, 48, 49, 51, 237n50; and Tiananmen Square massacre, 24–25

American Dream, x–xi; competition, 179–80, 187–88, 219; and conformity, 91–92; elitist vs. populist, 127–28; as ideology, 16; and need for humility, 226–27; and Nixon initiative, 78–80, 84–85; and normalization, 126–31; and particularism, 218; as primary reference point, 211–13; and religious institutions, 138–39; and social development organizations, 161; and Tiananmen Square massacre, xvi; universalistic assumptions, 136–37; and U.S.-Chinese expanded contacts, 86, 87–90, 93–94; and Vietnam War, 87–88, 93. *See also* American China myths; Chinese responses to American Dream; Freedom; Institutional connections with China

American Friends Service Committee (AFSC), 32–33, 36, 46

American Institute in Taiwan, 122, 243n3

255

Printed in the United States
24772LVS00001B/300

9 780520 086135